Philosophy without Intuitions

The claim that contemporary analytic philosophers rely extensively on intuitions as evidence is almost universally accepted in current meta-philosophical debates and it figures prominently in our self-understanding as analytic philosophers. No matter what area you happen to work in and what views you happen to hold in those areas, you are likely to think that philosophizing requires constructing cases and making intuitive judgments about those cases. This assumption also underlines the entire experimental philosophy movement: only if philosophers rely on intuitions as evidence are data about non-philosophers' intuitions of any interest to us. Our alleged reliance on the intuitive makes many philosophers who don't work on meta-philosophy concerned about their own discipline: they are unsure what intuitions are and whether they can carry the evidential weight we allegedly assign to them. The goal of this book is to argue that this concern is unwarranted since the claim is false: it is not true that philosophers rely extensively (or even a little bit) on intuitions as evidence. At worst, analytic philosophers are guilty of engaging in somewhat irresponsible use of 'intuition'-vocabulary. While this irresponsibility has had little effect on first order philosophy, it has fundamentally misled meta-philosophers: it has encouraged meta-philosophical pseudo-problems and misleading pictures of what philosophy is.

Herman Cappelen is a professor of philosophy at the University of St Andrews, where he works at the Arché Philosophical Research Centre.

Philosophy without Intuitions

Herman Cappelen

OXFORD
UNIVERSITY PRESS

OXFORD
UNIVERSITY PRESS

Great Clarendon Street, Oxford, OX2 6DP,
United Kingdom

Oxford University Press is a department of the University of Oxford.
It furthers the University's objective of excellence in research, scholarship,
and education by publishing worldwide. Oxford is a registered trade mark of
Oxford University Press in the UK and in certain other countries

© Herman Cappelen 2012

The moral rights of the author have been asserted

First Edition published in 2012
First published in paperback 2014

All rights reserved. No part of this publication may be reproduced, stored in
a retrieval system, or transmitted, in any form or by any means, without the
prior permission in writing of Oxford University Press, or as expressly permitted
by law, by licence or under terms agreed with the appropriate reprographics
rights organization. Enquiries concerning reproduction outside the scope of the
above should be sent to the Rights Department, Oxford University Press, at the
address above

You must not circulate this work in any other form
and you must impose this same condition on any acquirer

Published in the United States of America by Oxford University Press
198 Madison Avenue, New York, NY 10016, United States of America

British Library Cataloguing in Publication Data

Data available

Library of Congress Cataloging in Publication Data
Library of Congress Control Number: 2012930985

ISBN 978–0–19–964486–5 (Hbk)
ISBN 978–0–19–870302–0 (Pbk)

For Rachel

Acknowledgements

I was, for a long time, convinced that philosophizing, at least as I had been trained to do it, relied essentially on intuitions and that the absence of a good account of their reliability revealed deep foundational flaws. I managed to partially repress those concerns until I started running a project on philosophical methodology with my colleague Jessica Brown at the Arché Centre at the University of St Andrews. Work on this project convinced me that my earlier concerns were unfounded and that this book was worth writing. I'm particularly grateful to Jessica Brown, Jonathan Ichikawa, Yuri Cath, and to the many PhD students and visitors who contributed to our work. I owe a great debt to my colleagues at the Centre for the Study of Mind in Nature at the University of Oslo, where the material was presented in seminars co-taught with Olav Gjelsvik. I also learned a great deal from him in a seminar we gave on Timothy Williamson's *The Philosophy of Philosophy*. Reflections on that book and conversations with Williamson have shaped my thinking about all issues having to do with philosophical methodology.

Along the way, I have profited from discussion with and comments from many people, including Derek Ball, John Bengson, Einar Bøhn, David Chalmers, Stew Cohen, Max Deutsch, Josh Dever, Tamar Gendler, Olav Gjelsvik, Carsten Hansen, John Hawthorne, Torfinn Huvenes, Henry Jackman, Kirk Ludwig, Anna-Sara Malmgren, Jennifer Nagel, Dilip Ninan, Bjørn Ramberg, François Recanati, Marco Ruffino, Jonathan Schaffer, Daniele Sgaravatti, David Sosa, Ernie Sosa, Rachel Sterken, Andreas Stokke, Brian Weatherson, Jonathan Weinberg, Timothy Williamson, and two anonymous referees for Oxford University Press.

Early drafts of chapters were presented at the Federal University of Rio de Janeiro, University of Texas, Austin and Rutgers University. I would like to thank audiences at these events. Those early drafts were significantly improved by detailed comments from Jennifer Nagel, Jonathan Weinberg, and Ernie Sosa.

Daniele Sgaravatti provided indispensable help as my research assistant over two years. He and Margot Strohminger also proofread the entire manuscript, correcting many, many errors both of typography and content.

This is my fourth book project with Peter Momtchiloff as my editor at OUP and I am grateful to him for help and support over these years.

My greatest debt is to Rachel, who made writing this book possible. The book is dedicated to her.

Contents

1. Intuitions in Philosophy: Overview and Taxonomy — 1

Part I. The Argument from 'Intuition'-Talk

Introduction to Part I — 25

2. 'Intuitive', 'Intuitively', 'Intuition', and 'Seem' in English — 29
3. Philosophers' Use of 'Intuitive' (I): A Defective Practice and the Verbal Virus Theory — 49
4. Philosophers' Use of 'Intuitive' (II): Some Strategies for Charitable Reinterpretation — 61
   Appendix to Chapter 4: Williamson on Intuition as Belief or Inclination to Believe — 83
5. Philosophers' Use of 'Intuitive' (III): Against the Explaining Away of Intuitions — 88

Part II. The Argument from Philosophical Practice

Introduction to Part II — 95

6. Centrality and Philosophical Practice — 98
7. Diagnostics for Intuitiveness — 111
8. Case Studies — 130
9. Lessons Learned, Replies to Objections, and Comparison to Williamson — 188
10. Conceptual Analysis and Intuitions — 205
11. A Big Mistake: Experimental Philosophy — 219

Concluding Remarks — 229

Bibliography — 231
Index — 239

Detailed Contents

1. Intuitions in Philosophy: Overview and Taxonomy   1
   1.1 The role of intuitions in the self-conception of contemporary analytic philosophers: Centrality   2
   1.2 Two arguments for Centrality: the Argument from 'Intuition'-Talk and the Argument from Philosophical Practice   4
   1.3 'Intuition' in Centrality   7
   1.4 More on how to interpret Centrality   12
   1.5 Burning questions for proponents of Centrality: the pessimists, the enthusiasts, and the concerned   17
   1.6 Rejection of Centrality: Philosophy without intuitions   18

Part I. The Argument from 'Intuition'-Talk
Introduction to Part I   25

2. 'Intuitive', 'Intuitively', 'Intuition', and 'Seem' in English   29
   2.1 The adjective 'intuitive' and the adverb 'intuitively'   30
   2.2 'Intuitive' as a hedge   36
   2.3 The noun phrase 'intuition'   39
   2.4 'Seem' and 'intuitive'   42
   2.5 Taking stock   47

3. Philosophers' Use of 'Intuitive' (I): A Defective Practice and the Verbal Virus Theory   49
   3.1 Constructive vs. defective theoretical terms   50
   3.2 Problems for 'intuition' in philosophy   52
   3.3 Disagreement over the theoretical role of intuitions   55
   3.4 Are unreflective uses of 'intuitive' meaningless?   57

4. Philosophers' Use of 'Intuitive' (II): Some Strategies for Charitable Reinterpretation   61
   4.1 First strategy: Simple Removal   63

	4.2 Second and third strategies: Snap and Pre-Theoretic	65
	4.3 The three strategies at work: Some complicated mixed cases	71
	4.4 Taking stock	77
	4.5 No appeal to special feelings, conceptual competence, or default justificatory status	77
	4.6 Back to Centrality and AIT: None of these interpretative strategies are Centrality-supporting	81
	Appendix to Chapter 4: Williamson on Intuition as Belief or Inclination to Believe	83
5.	Philosophers' Use of 'Intuitive' (III): Against the Explaining Away of Intuitions	88
	5.1 The argument against Explain	89
	5.2 Is there some intellectually useful activity that's mistakenly classified as 'explaining away intuitions'?	92

Part II. The Argument from Philosophical Practice

	Introduction to Part II	95
6.	Centrality and Philosophical Practice	98
	6.1 Methodological rationalism	99
	6.2 The influence of methodological rationalism	105
7.	Diagnostics for Intuitiveness	111
	7.1 Features of the intuitive	111
	7.2 Some initial qualifications	114
	7.3 More on the features of the intuitive	117
	7.4 Summary and additional reflections on how to operationalize appeals to intuitions	128
8.	Case Studies	130
	8.1 Perry on the problem of the essential indexical	132
	8.2 Burge on individualism and the mental	139
	8.3 Thomson's violinist in "A Defense of Abortion"	148
	8.4 Thomson and Foot on trolley cases	158
	8.5 Three epistemology cases: Lotteries, Truetemp, and fake barns	163
	8.6 Cappelen and Hawthorne on disagreement, predicates of personal taste, and relativism about truth	175

	8.7 Bernard Williams on personal identity and the fear of the prospect of torture	179
	8.8 Chalmers on zombies	182
	8.9 Conclusion	187
9.	Lessons Learned, Replies to Objections, and Comparison to Williamson	188
	9.1 What cases are: some generalizations	188
	9.2 Objections and replies	193
	9.3 Williamson on Evidence Neutrality, psychologizing the evidence, and analyticity	200
10.	Conceptual Analysis and Intuitions	205
	10.1 Hyperbole about intuitions leads to hyperbole about conceptual analysis	205
	10.2 Are there any conceptual truths, and, if so, are they philosophically significant?	210
	10.3 Conclusion: Centrality as a *sectarian* thesis	217
11.	A Big Mistake: Experimental Philosophy	219
	11.1 Experimental philosophy: Positive and negative	219
	11.2 The Big Objection to experimental philosophy: It attacks a practice that doesn't exist	221
	11.3 Experimental philosophy without intuitions?	224
	11.4 Experimental philosophy and the expertise defense of traditional philosophy	227
Concluding Remarks		229
Bibliography		231
Index		239

1

Intuitions in Philosophy:
Overview and Taxonomy

The claim that *contemporary analytic philosophers rely extensively on intuitions as evidence* is almost universally accepted in current metaphilosophical debates and it figures prominently in our self-conception as analytic philosophers. No matter what area you happen to work in and what views you happen to hold in those areas, you are likely to think that philosophizing requires constructing cases and making intuitive judgments about those cases. A theory of a topic *X* isn't adequate unless it correctly predicts intuitive responses to *X*-relevant cases. This assumption also underlies the entire experimental-philosophy movement: if philosophers don't rely on intuitions, why would anyone do experiments to check on intuitions? Our alleged reliance on the intuitive makes many philosophers who don't work in metaphilosophy concerned about their own discipline: they are unsure what intuitions are and whether they can carry the evidential weight we allegedly assign to them.

The goal of this book is to argue that this concern is unwarranted since the claim is false: it is not true that philosophers rely extensively (or even a little bit) on intuitions as evidence. At worst, analytic philosophers are guilty of engaging in somewhat irresponsible use of 'intuition'-vocabulary. While this irresponsibility has had little effect on first-order philosophy, it has fundamentally misled metaphilosophers. It has encouraged metaphilosophical pseudo-problems and misleading pictures of what philosophy is and how it is done.

This chapter provides a brief overview of the role this mistaken assumption about intuition plays in contemporary philosophy and an introduction to the not inconsiderable difficulties involved in a careful evaluation of it.

1.1 The role of intuitions in the self-conception of contemporary analytic philosophers: Centrality

Here is how Timothy Williamson introduces the assumption in his book, *The Philosophy of Philosophy* (2007):[1]

'Intuition' plays a major role in contemporary analytic philosophy's self-understanding. (p. 215)

When contemporary analytic philosophers run out of arguments, they appeal to intuitions. It can seem, and is sometimes said, that any philosophical dispute, when pushed back far enough, turns into a conflict of intuitions about ultimate premises: 'In the end, all we have to go on is our intuitions'. Thus intuitions are presented as our evidence in philosophy. (p. 214)

The assumption that we do rely on intuitions has given rise to a research project—that of understanding *how* we can rely on intuitions, *whether* we should rely on intuitions and *what* intuitions are. Again, here is Williamson:

Yet there is no agreed or even popular account of how intuition works, no accepted explanation of the hoped-for correlation between our having an intuition that P and its being true that P. Since analytic philosophy prides itself on its rigor, this blank space in its foundations looks like a methodological scandal. Why should intuitions have any authority over the philosophical domain? (2007, p. 215)

A spectacularly wide range of philosophers endorses the view that we as a matter of fact do rely on intuitions. Hilary Kornblith, an opponent of intuition-based philosophy, is one example:

George Bealer does it. Roderick Chisholm does it a lot. Most philosophers do it openly and unapologetically, and the rest arguably do it too, although some of them would deny it. What they all do is appeal to intuitions in constructing, shaping, and refining their philosophical views. (1998, p. 129)

Alvin Goldman, a proponent of intuition-based philosophy, is another:

One thing that distinguishes philosophical methodology from the methodology of the sciences is its extensive and avowed reliance on intuition. (2007, p. 1)

---

[1] Though Williamson is claiming that this assumption is endorsed by more or less all participants in contemporary meta-philosophical debates, it will become clear later in the discussion of Williamson's position that he does not himself endorse it.

A leading experimental philosopher, Jonathan Weinberg, agrees, describing the practice as essential to analytic philosophy:

> Intuitions are odd critters: intellectual happenings in which it seems to us that something is the case, without arising from our inferring it from any reasons that it is so, or our sensorily perceiving that it is so, or our having a sense of remembering that it is so. When they occur, they frequently stand out with great psychological salience, but they are not forthcoming about their own origins—envoys to our conscious deliberations from some unnamed nation of our unconscious cognition. But intuitions are also among the chief tools in the analytic philosopher's argumentative repertoire, in particular intuitions that a particular hypothetical case does or does not fall under some target concept. It can seem that analytic **philosophy without intuitions** just wouldn't be *analytic* philosophy. So there is a gulf between our understanding of intuitions and their importance to us, and as a result it is perhaps unsurprising that intuitions have become not just one of philosophy's tools but part of its subject matter as well. (2007, p. 318, my bolded emphasis)

Here is a first stab at an articulation of the assumption this diverse group of philosophers endorse—I'll call it 'Centrality':

Centrality (of Intuitions in Contemporary Philosophy): Contemporary analytic philosophers rely on intuitions as evidence (or as a source of evidence) for philosophical theories.

This book has two primary goals. The first is methodological (or meta-methodological): to figure out how to interpret Centrality. The second goal is to argue that Centrality is false: on no sensible construal of 'intuition', 'rely on', 'philosophy', 'evidence', and 'philosopher' is it true that philosophers in general rely on intuitions as evidence when they do philosophy.

As I see it, the majority of the participants in contemporary methodological debates have included Centrality in their common ground; this has generated their joint research program: some are in favor of intuition-based philosophy, some are against it, and others are simply deeply concerned and not sure what to think about what they take to be their own methodology. The rejection of Centrality makes most of these issues irrelevant and redirects philosophical methodology towards more productive issues.[2]

---

[2] This book is an attempt to refute Centrality in all its forms. I think I do that very conclusively. Sometimes, faced with this refutation, my audience will start doubting whether Centrality really is a widely accepted view. Further evidence of the overwhelming influence of Centrality on the self-understanding of contemporary philosophers can be found in Bealer (1992, 1996, 1998), BonJour (1998), DePaul and Ramsey (1998), Goldman and Pust (1998),

1.2 Two arguments for Centrality: the Argument from 'Intuition'-Talk and the Argument from Philosophical Practice

A difficulty in writing about Centrality is that *none* of those who rely on it in their theorizing ever present a systematic, detailed argument in its favor.[3] In George Bealer's work, for example, Centrality plays an essential role. But at no point does he present any evidence for the claim that philosophers as a matter of fact rely on intuitions as evidence. Bealer (1996) asserts that it is a "plain truth" (p. 3). Though he lists several arguments in which he says that intuitions are used as evidence, he doesn't tell us why he thinks those are cases in which philosophers rely on intuitions. Experimental philosophers, while on the other end of the theoretical spectrum, are equally cagey about why they think philosophers rely on intuitions. We find, for example, Weinberg (2007) telling us that "analytic philosophy without intuitions just wouldn't be *analytic* philosophy" (p. 318), but we are not told why. It is simply assumed in a great deal of literature that it is trivial and obvious that philosophers rely extensively on intuitions as evidence.

I take it two kinds of arguments are tacitly assumed. Part I of this book concerns the first kind of argument: I call it the *Argument from 'Intuition'-Talk* (AIT). Part II is about the second: the *Argument from Philosophical Practice*.

1.2.1 The Argument from 'Intuition'-Talk

Some philosophers are no doubt inclined towards Centrality in part because of the promiscuous way in which many contemporary philosophers use 'intuitive' and cognate terms. The reasoning is straightforward: If philosophers characterize key premises in their arguments as 'intuitive', we have reason to suspect they are, in some way or another, relying on intuitions as evidence.

Jackson (1998), Hintikka (1999), Pust (2000), Machery *et al.* (2004), Alexander and Weinberg (2007), Sosa (2007b), and Swain *et al.* (2008).

[3] This might seem like hyperbole, but I think it is literally true: the assumption is central to more or less all the current literature on metaphilosophy, but it is *always* just taken for granted; it is assumed to be obviously true or for some reason not in need of empirical justification. The normative version of the claim, that philosophers *should* rely on intuitions, is by contrast sometimes argued for (see, e.g., Bealer 1992, 1998).

It's not hard to find such usage among philosophers. Here are but a few examples, all from important work by prominent philosophers (emphases added):

Kaplan: "**Intuitively**, (6) ["I'm here now"] is deeply, and in some sense, which we will shortly make precise, universally, true." (1989, p. 509)

Hawthorne: "If, unbeknownst to me, a wealthy long-lost relative is planning to bequeath me a large amount of money in the very near future, though, by happenstance, it will turn out that the money is never bequeathed, then my self-ascription that I know I will not have enough money to go on an African safari is **intuitively** incorrect." (2004, p. 65)

Williamson: "**Intuitively**, what goes wrong is that the counterfactual supposition p can take one to worlds at which one believes p on too different a basis from that on which one actually believes." (2000, p. 310)

Burge: "I shall have little further to say in defense of the second and third steps of the thought experiment. Both rest on their **intuitive plausibility**, not on some particular theory." (1979, p. 88)

Such examples are not hard to find: open more or less any journal these days, and you're likely to find 'intuitive' or cognate terms after a quick browse. Such language encourages some proponents of Centrality. What better evidence can we have that philosophers rely extensively on intuitions?[4]

1.2.2 The Argument from Philosophical Practice

Here is how I think the second argument for Centrality should ideally be presented: a proponent of Centrality first specifies a set of features she thinks intuitive judgments have, say $F1, \ldots, Fn$, and then tries to show that the judgments philosophers rely on at central points in their arguments have $F1, \ldots, Fn$. This kind of argument need not rely on how philosophers use 'intuition'-terminology. The focus, instead, is on features of how we *do* philosophy—on the practice of arguing for philosophical views. Chapter 8 spells out the relevant features that we are asked to look for (summarized as $F1$–$F3$ in Section 8.1), and Chapter 9 goes through a number of case studies to see whether judgments with these features figure centrally in philosophical practice. For introductory purposes, here is a brief overview of the kinds of philosophical practices that can be cited in

---

[4] Other locutions are also appealed to by proponents of Centrality, e.g. 'what we would say', and 'it seems', as will become clear in Chapter 2.

support of Centrality (each of these will be explored further in later chapters):

1. *Intuition and the Method of Cases*: Proponents of Centrality typically assume that philosophers use something called 'the method of cases'. We can characterize it as follows:

   Method of Cases (Intuitive): Let X be some philosophically important topic. T is a good theory of X only if it correctly predicts our intuitions about X-relevant cases (whether actual or hypothetical).

   If intuitions figure centrally in the method of cases and the method of cases is the contemporary philosopher's chief tool, we have strong evidence for Centrality.

2. *Armchair Activity and Apriority*: Philosophy is often described as an 'armchair activity'. The claim is based on the widely held assumption that philosophers typically don't conduct experiments or do empirical research of any kind. If this is right, it raises the question of just how philosophical knowledge can be obtained 'from the armchair' (as it is often put). Intuitions are sometimes brought in as an answer: they provide the kind of a priori starting points for theorizing that allows us to stay in the armchair (see e.g. Bealer 1996 and BonJour 1998). It is worth noting that even some of those who reject the picture of philosophy as an a priori activity still think of philosophy as an armchair activity. Timothy Williamson so describes philosophy in his 2007.[5]

3. *Intuition and Conceptual Analysis*: Some of those who think philosophy is an armchair activity think it is so because philosophers are primarily engaged in so-called conceptual analysis, i.e. in the business of analyzing concepts such as *causation, reference,* and *justice*. Sometimes this view is accompanied by the assumption that the proper way to engage in conceptual analysis is by appeal to intuitions.[6]

4. *Rock-bottom Starting Points for Arguments*: Many philosophers think of intuitive judgments as having a kind of foundational epistemic status in philosophical theorizing, even without endorsing (2) or (3): intuitions provide evidence for other claims without themselves requiring

---

[5] See especially Chapter 6, §5, and Chapter 7, §3, of Williamson (2007).

[6] Goldman and Pust (1998) and Ludwig (2010) exemplify this approach. See Chapters 7 and 10 below.

evidence. All arguments must have foundational starting points, assumptions that are not subjected to further justification. It is not uncommon to find philosophers who think that philosophizing is characteristic in that its starting points are intuitions. Without intuitions, philosophizing could not get off the ground. Some of those who think this think it because they think philosophers are engaged in a priori conceptual analysis, but you don't need to have those commitments to think that intuitions have an important kind of privileged epistemic status.

For many of those who endorse Centrality, these four practices are closely connected: For some of those who endorse (2), the other three follow somewhat naturally. But not all proponents of Centrality endorse all of (1)–(4), and each element can be interpreted in different ways; these variations will be explored further in Part II.

Obviously, 'intuition'-talk is part of the practice of doing philosophy, so the distinction between the Argument from 'Intuition'-Talk and the Argument from Philosophical Practice is somewhat artificial. I suspect that in many cases the reason one or more of the practices are assumed to rely on intuitions is because those who engage in those activities use 'intuition'-talk extensively when they so engage. What this shows is that the failure of the Argument from 'Intuition'-Talk would have significant negative implications for the Argument from Philosophical Practice.

1.3 'Intuition' in Centrality

I am using 'Centrality' as a label for what is in effect a family of theses—you can spin out versions of Centrality by considering various interpretations of its key terms. This is an issue I'll return to over and over again in this book. Here I present a simple initial overview of some meanings some of the terms have been given by defenders of Centrality and I contrast these with some alternative interpretations that are more problematic for Centrality.

Those who endorse Centrality don't agree on what 'intuition' denotes—they don't even fully agree on what language Centrality is formulated in. While some think it is the 'intuitive' of English that occurs in that formulation, others think it is the 'intuitive' of a special idiolect, *Philosophers'-English*[7] (for more on this see Chapter 2). The taxonomy of

---

[7] Put another way, they take the 'intuition' in Centrality to be a technical philosophical term, which differs in meaning from 'intuition' in English.

intuition-theories can be done in different ways. Compared to, say, theories of knowledge, this is still a fairly unexplored territory, so even the large-scale categories are up for dispute. What follows is a classification that will be useful for the purposes of this work.

Many philosophers, including proponents of Centrality, take 'intuition' to denote a psychological (mental) state or event. Those who hold this view can be divided into two categories: those who think of intuitions as *sui generis* mental states and those who think of intuitions as a subset of some other kind of mental state.

Intuitions as sui generis *mental states*

According to, e.g., George Bealer intuitions are mental states that are *sui generis*, or not reducible to any other kind of mental state. He thinks that an agent A can have an intuition that p even if A doesn't believe that p and A can believe that p without having the intuition that p; moreover an intuition that p is also different from a guess that p, a snap judgment that p, and a (felt) inclination to believe that p (1998, pp. 208–10). Bealer provides a wealth of such negative characterizations. On the positive side, not much is said beyond claiming that intuitions are *sui generis*. The closest Bealer comes to a positive characterization that doesn't just re-use 'intuitive' is when he appeals to what he calls *intellectual seemings*:

At t, S [rationally] intuits that p if and only if at t, it intellectually seems to S that necessarily, p.[8]

But at no point are we told what intellectual seemings are.[9] Pust holds a view close to Bealer's, but doesn't think the seeming's content needs to involve necessity. Rather, according to Pust,

S has a rational intuition that p if and only if (a) S has a purely intellectual experience, when considering the question of whether p, that p, and (b) at t, if S were to consider whether p is necessarily true, then S would have a purely intellectual experience that necessarily, p. (2000, p. 39)

Again, we are not told what it is to have a purely intellectual experience; we are, perhaps, supposed to know them by acquaintance.

Intuitions as beliefs or inclinations to believe

---

[8] This is Pust's summary of Bealer's view (2000, p. 36).
[9] For a more detailed exposition of Bealer's view, see Chapter 6 in Part II.

Some of those who think intuitions are mental states or events are *reductionists about intuitions*. Some prominent philosophers, including van Inwagen, Lewis and Williamson (at least on one reading),[10] take 'intuition' to denote *any* belief or inclination to believe. This is the most liberal of all theories of what 'intuition' denotes. Other reductionists or eliminativists take 'intuition' to denote a particular subset of beliefs or inclinations to believe. This subset is generally taken to have one or more of the following four features:

  i. *Beliefs accompanied by special phenomenology*: Some intuition-theorists think intuitions are beliefs (or inclinations to believe) that come with a certain kind of phenomenology. Many intuition-theorists say that it is a necessary condition on an intuition that it comes with a certain phenomenology. Plantinga talks of "that peculiar form of phenomenology with which we are all well acquainted, but which I can't describe in any way other than as the phenomenology that goes with seeing that such a proposition is true" (1993, pp. 105–6).
 ii. *Beliefs with special kind of justification*: Some intuition-theorists think intuitions are beliefs (or inclinations to believe) that are justified a certain way. The way in which intuitions are justified is characterized both positively and negatively. On the negative side, it is often said that an intuition is a judgment that we can be justified in making even though it is not supported by experience, memory or inference. On the positive side, two kinds of views are common. Some think intuitive judgments must be based solely on conceptual competences (Goldman and Pust 1998, Bealer 1998, BonJour 1998, Sosa 2007a). Kirk Ludwig (2010) also advocates this strategy. He says that a judgment is an intuition only if it relies solely on conceptual competence:

> It is only if a judgment is *solely* an expression of one's competence in the contained concepts and their mode of combination that it counts as an apprehension of a conceptual or a priori truth. Insofar as we think of intuitions as insights into conceptual truths [*as Ludwig does*], they are to be conceived of as judgments or beliefs which are the product of our competence in the deployment of the concepts involved. (2010, p. 433)

---

[10] Although see Appendix to Chapter 4, note 25, for an alternative interpretation of these authors, particularly Williamson.

Others rely heavily on metaphors, invoking a special faculty whereby we can 'see' or become directly intellectually aware of certain truths. Plantinga (1993, pp. 105–6) and BonJour (1998) come close to this kind of formulation. Charles Parsons' groundbreaking work on Gödel's views on intuition provide the best introduction to this kind of view that I know of. Gödel says:

> The similarity between mathematical intuition and a physical sense is very striking. It is arbitrary to consider "this is red" an immediate datum, but not so to consider the proposition expressing modus ponens or complete induction (or perhaps some simpler propositions from which the latter follows). For the difference, as far as it is relevant here, consists solely in the fact that in the first case a relationship between a concept and a particular object is perceived, while in the second case it is a relationship between concepts. (quoted in Parsons 1995, p. 62)

Charles Parsons comments:

> In this passage and in many others, we find a formulation that is very characteristic of Gödel: In certain cases of rational evidence (of which we can easily grant modus ponens to be one), it is claimed that "perception" of concepts is involved. (1995, p. 62)

These brief descriptions do not exhaust the ways in which intuitions can be characterized in terms of their justification; alternatives will be explored later in the book.

iii. *Beliefs with a certain kind of content*: Some intuition-theorists exclude all judgments concerning contingent truths from the intuitive. Such philosophers follow Bealer and Pust in thinking that we can have an intuition that *p* only if *p* is a necessary truth.

iv. *Beliefs with a certain etiology*: Other intuition-theorists think intuitions are beliefs (or inclinations to believe) that are caused (or generated) in a certain way. There are many versions of this view. According to one version, often found in the psychological literature on intuitions, they are beliefs (or inclinations to believe) that are generated in a certain kind of 'spontaneous' or 'unreflective' way. Here is Jennifer Nagel's (forthcoming) initial description of the view:

> Mercier and Sperber describe intuitive judgments as generated by 'processes that take place inside individuals without being controlled by them' (Mercier and Sperber, 2009, 153). The spontaneous inferences produced by these processes modify or update what we believe 'without the individual's

attending to what justifies this modification' (ibid.).... When we read the emotions of others in their facial expressions—to take an example of an uncontroversial case of intuitive judgment—neurotypical adults are remarkably accurate at detecting and decoding the minute shifts in brow position and nostril contour that distinguish emotions such as surprise and fear (Ekman and Friesen, 1975). But judgments reflect these cues without *our* attending to the cues: the cross-culturally robust ability to recognize basic emotions does not depend on any personal-level attention to the facial configurations and movements that justify these swift intuitive classifications (Ekman, 1989; Ekman and Friesen, 1975).

Putting aside the details of this characterization, it exemplifies a general strategy: restrict the extension of 'intuition' to those beliefs (or inclinations to believe) that have a certain kind of etiology.

Three Centrality-unfriendly construals of 'intuition'

I turn now to some ways in which 'intuitive' has been construed that are not Centrality-friendly. These are construals that would render Centrality too obviously false, and so are not ones proponents of Centrality should, or are likely to, endorse.

A view that I'll return to throughout this work is that intuitions are beliefs or inclinations to believe that have a certain dialectical role. Here is Parsons characterizing philosophers' use of 'intuitive':

When a philosopher talks of his or others' intuitions, that usually means what the person concerned takes to be true at the outset of an inquiry, or as a matter of common sense; intuitions in this sense are not knowledge, since they need not be true and can be very fallible guides to the truth. (1995, p. 59)

I take this to be an instance of a view according to which the intuitive is characterized by its dialectical role. On such a construal, Parsons is proposing that 'intuitive' serves to mark off claims we happen to find in common ground prior to careful research of some topic *T*. Such propositions can have any kind of content, can be generated in any kind of way, and can be justified by any kind of evidential source. So 'intuitive', on this construal, does not denote an epistemic or psychological kind. As I will point out repeatedly below, this is a construal of 'intuitive' that is not Centrality-friendly.

Looking ahead, there are two additional views of the function of 'intuition'-talk that are not covered by the categories above and that are not what proponents of Centrality have in mind. In Chapters 2 and 5 I suggest that for many uses of 'intuitively', the most charitable interpretation treats it as a device of *hedging*: a way of qualifying a speech act (much like 'I think' functions in some utterances of 'She's in Paris, I think'). So used it does not denote any kind of mental state or source of evidence. Finally, and anticipating a view that will be explored in Chapter 3 below, there is also the possibility that some uses of 'intuitively' are semantically defective—they fail to have a semantic anchor and so literally mean nothing. Put loosely, the view here is that some uses of 'intuitive' are such a mess that they fail to mean anything at all. Note that this would be a proposal unfriendly to Centrality, in particular if 'intuition' as it occurs in Centrality is defective in just this way.

'Intuitive' as a context-sensitive term

Cutting across the above distinctions is the question of whether 'intuitive' is a context-sensitive term. This issue is not much discussed in the current literature, but I will argue that 'intuition' is context sensitive both in English and as used by philosophers. This, I will argue, has implications for the Argument from 'Intuition'-Talk. It also has the consequence that different utterances of the sentences that are used to express Centrality will mean different things depending on the context they are uttered in.

'Intuition' as non-factive

Practically all intuition-theorists[11] agree that if 'intuition' denotes a mental state, it is non-factive: you can have an intuition that *p*, even if *p* is false. It is also typically assumed that an agent can have the intuition that *p* even if she does not believe that *p* (this is why I constantly use the cumbersome 'belief or inclination to believe'). An example often used to illustrate these alleged features of intuitions is the naïve comprehension axiom: *For every predicate, there is a set that consists of all and only those objects that satisfy that predicate.* Many intuition-theorists say they have the intuition that the axiom is true even though they do not believe it and indeed know it to be false.

1.4 More on how to interpret Centrality

'Intuition' isn't the only component of Centrality in need of further clarification. Various issues will come up throughout this book, but five issues are worth highlighting at the outset.

---

[11] Although see Ludwig (2007) for an exception.

1. *Centrality and the distinction between evidence and sources of evidence*: In stating Centrality I left open whether it claims that philosophers rely on intuitions as *evidence* or as *sources of evidence*. Proponents of Centrality differ on which version they endorse. We find Bealer, for example, present as one of his central observations about philosophical practice that intuitions are evidence for philosophical theories (see e.g. Bealer 1996, p. 2). However, in other passages he talks of intuitions as a *source* of evidence (see Bealer 1992, n. 7). On the first view it is *A has the intuition that p* that serves as evidence. On the second view, p is the evidence and the source of that evidence is *that A has an intuition that p*. The distinction will play an important role at certain points, but when the distinction is not important I will, for simplicity, talk only of 'intuitions as evidence', by which I will mean 'intuitions as evidence or sources of evidence'.
2. *Centrality and philosophical theories of evidence*: A central question in epistemology and philosophy of science is the nature of evidence. It is striking that those who defend Centrality as a descriptive claim about philosophical practice typically do so without committing to any general theory about the nature of evidence. It is a view that is supposed to be acceptable to, more or less, anyone, independently of the endorsement of any *particular* philosophical theory of the nature of evidence more generally. The occurrence of 'evidence' in Centrality itself isn't supposed to be read as committing the defender of Centrality to a particular philosophical account of evidence.

I will for the most part follow proponents of Centrality in trying to stay neutral about the general issue of what evidence is. Nonetheless, it is difficult to run the debate about Centrality in complete isolation from these more general issues. To see how hard it is to be neutral on these issues, consider the influential view due to Williamson (2000), according to which one's evidence consists of one's knowledge ($E = K$). As we have seen, practically all those defending Centrality take intuitions to be non-factive and so an endorsement of Williamson's view would immediately make the practice described in Centrality deeply defective. Does that mean we should take all those who endorse Centrality to be committed to denying Williamson's view? Not necessarily. The way I have formulated Centrality, it describes what a certain group of people *treat* as evidence. That could, of course, be very different from what their evidence *is*. So a proponent of Centrality could endorse Williamson's view of evidence. In what follows I will try to avoid imposing a particular theory of evidence onto the proponent of Centrality.[12]

3. *Centrality as normative claim vs. Centrality as descriptive claim*: It is worth continually keeping in mind the difference between Centrality as a *descriptive* claim and as a *normative* claim. The descriptive claim says something about how philosophers, as a matter of fact, go about doing philosophy. It describes a practice and can only be verified by careful study of that practice. This is how Centrality is interpreted in this work. The normative versions concerns how philosophy ought to be done—it's compatible with the truth of Centrality construed normatively that, as a matter of fact, we do not rely on intuitions and so the refutation of the descriptive version doesn't amount to a refutation of the normative version.

That said, the two questions are not independent. In several influential arguments for the normative claim, the truth of the descriptive claim serves as the central premise. George Bealer's work (1992, 1996) can serve as an illustration here. According to Bealer, assigning no evidential weight to intuitions leads to what he calls "epistemic self-defeat" (1996, p. 8). All of the versions of this argument found in Bealer's work start with the assumption that intuitions as a matter of fact play an important evidential role in what he calls our 'standard justificatory procedure'. For example Bealer writes that "according to our standard justificatory procedure, intuitions are used as evidence (or as reasons). The evidential use of intuitions is ubiquitous in philosophy" (1996, p. 4). As a result, he says, those who want to exclude intuitions from our evidential base are

---

[12] There are a number of other issues about the nature of evidence that proponents of Centrality typically try to stay neutral on. Here are two: can physical objects—say a dead body—be evidence or is that status reserved for propositions? Similarly, the issue of whether coherentism is true will have an impact on the evaluation of Centrality. Proponents of Centrality typically assume that the truth of Centrality doesn't depend on how these issues are settled.

... confronted by a hermeneutical problem produced by their departure from the standard justificatory procedure. They would have us circumscribe our evidence by just excluding intuition.... The question to consider, therefore, is this: when we implement the standard justificatory procedure's mechanism of self-criticism does intuition get excluded as a source of evidence? (Bealer 1996, p. 8)

Bealer goes on to argue that intuitions will have to play a role in adjudicating whether intuitions should be included or excluded in what counts as admissible evidence—i.e. they will have to play a role in the standard procedure's mechanism of self-criticism. This is the source of the alleged 'epistemic self-defeat' of those who deny intuitions evidential status.[13] There are, in my view, many weak points in this argument, but what I want to highlight here is that the descriptive claim is at the center of the argument for why we *ought* to rely on intuitions. More generally, most of the arguments I know of in favor of the normative claim that intuitions *ought* to play a role assume that as a matter of fact they do. As a result, a rejection of the descriptive version of Centrality will serve to undermine most of the normative versions.

4. *Centrality as a generic:* The various formulations of Centrality presented above talk about what philosophers do. Claims of the form '*F*s are *G*s' are called generics, and they are hard to interpret. '*F*s are *G*s' can be true even though not all *F*s are *G*s. The pattern of allowable exceptions is a disputed issue and one of the central topics in the theory of genericity. This generic element of Centrality makes it hard to evaluate and leaves an uncomfortable amount of wiggle room for its proponents. It would, obviously, be preferable if proponents of Centrality-like claims avoided genericity and instead opted for more precise claims. Absent such precisification, I will treat this generic

---

[13] Here is Bealer's description of the practice of his opponent: "in their actual practice empiricists typically make use of a wide range of intuitions. For example, what does and does not count as an observation or experience? Why count sense perception as observation? Why not count memory as observation? Or why not count certain high-level theoretical judgments as sense experiences? Indeed, why not count intuitions as sense experiences? Likewise for each of the key notions that plays a role in the empiricist principles (i) and (ii) [Bealer's formulation of Quinean radical empiricism]. What does and does not count as a theory, as justified (or acceptable), as an explanation, as simple? The fact is that empiricists arrive at answers to these questions by using as prima facie evidence their intuitions about what does and does not count as experience, observation, theory, justified, explanation, simple. In their actual practice, empiricists use such intuitions as evidence to support their theories and to persuade others of them" (Bealer 1992, p. 105).

element of Centrality as a claim about what is characteristic of philosophy. It allows for some exceptions, but is true only if it applies to a wide range of paradigms of contemporary philosophical practice.[14]

5. *Centrality and philosophical exceptionalism*: Since Centrality is a claim about what is characteristic of philosophers, it should not be construed as an instantiation of a universal claim about all intellectual activity or even a very wide domain of intellectual activity. Suppose that *all human cognition* (or a very wide domain of intellectual life) appeals to intuitions as evidence, from which we can derive as a special instance that philosophers appeal to intuitions as evidence. Such a view would not vindicate Centrality, since according to Centrality the appeal to intuitions as evidence is meant to differentiate philosophy—and, perhaps, a few other kindred disciplines—from inquiries into the migration patterns of salmon or inflation in Argentina, say. If it turns out that the alleged reliance on intuitions is universal or extends far beyond philosophy and other allegedly a priori disciplines, that would *undermine* Centrality as it is construed in this work. Timothy Williamson (2007) puts a related point in terms of "philosophical exceptionalism" (p. 3). The targets in this work are those philosophers who endorse Centrality and construe it as an instance of philosophical exceptionalism (or at least exceptionalism about disciplines traditionally thought to be a priori). As a result, it will turn out to be crucial when evaluating an argument for the significance of intuitions to keep track of its scope. An argument that shows that *all* intellectual activity relies on intuitions as evidence, and then derives Centrality as a corollary, will not be acceptable given how Centrality is presented by its proponents.[15]

---

[14] The question of what we should count as paradigms is addressed in Part II.

[15] Are all the proponents of Centrality that I have cited so far also committed to a version of philosophical exceptionalism? I think the answer is 'yes', with some qualification. If you look at the various places where Centrality is articulated, including those cited above, you also typically find the claim that reliance on intuitions as evidence makes philosophy different from most other intellectual disciplines. Centrality proponents don't start out with the view that *marine biologists, archaeologists, economists, engineers, philosophers, etc. rely on intuitions as evidence*, and then do conjunction elimination to get to Centrality. The claim is that this is a peculiar feature of contemporary analytic philosophy. This is often connected to the view sometimes expressed by saying that philosophy is an armchair activity. Some construe this as the claim that philosophy is an a priori activity. Centrality is then thought to be an answer to

1.5 Burning questions for proponents of Centrality: the pessimists, the enthusiasts, and the concerned

Endorsement of Centrality gives rise to the impression that two connected questions are extremely important:

- What are intuitions?
- Can intuitions serve as evidence for philosophical theories?

If Centrality is true, these are indeed the burning questions of the day. If we have no clear answers to these questions, and in particular, if there is suspicion that the answer to the second question might be 'no', then contemporary analytic philosophers might be no better off than crystal ball gazers. Centrality proponents divide, roughly, into three categories: *the pessimists, the enthusiasts* and *the concerned*. Enthusiasts think Centrality is a *good thing*. They think intuitions can provide *good* and *solid* foundation for philosophy; it is the kind of evidence (or source of evidence) that we *should* be relying on. Examples of enthusiasts are Bealer, Pust, Sosa, Goldman, Ludwig, and, in more restricted domains, Chomsky, Gödel, and Rawls.

The pessimists accept Centrality and conclude that this is *bad news for philosophy* because intuitions are not solid or reliable as evidence for philosophical claims. Pessimists who see the reliance on intuitions as central to contemporary philosophy are thus very pessimistic about the current state of the profession. Examples of such pessimists include Stich, Weinberg, and many other so-called experimental philosophers.[16]

The third group I call 'the concerned': they endorse Centrality and thus accept the view that intuitions play an important role in contemporary philosophy. They are concerned by what they see as reliance on intuitions, they don't quite know how to do philosophy without it, and so agree with the enthusiasts and the pessimists that the research project of properly understanding what intuitions are is of outmost importance.

---

the question: How can philosophical knowledge be obtained from the armchair? Since the study of migration patterns of salmon and inflation in Argentina are not done in the armchair, the proponents of Centrality don't see it as relevant to those disciplines.

[16] Not only experimental philosophers, however, are pessimists in this sense; e.g., Kornblith (1998) and Cummins (1998) both represent this strand of thought.

1.6 Rejection of Centrality: Philosophy without intuitions

In this book I argue that Centrality, on any reasonable interpretation, is false. If you share that view, the Burning Questions will no longer burn. There's no urgency in figuring out what intuitions are and what epistemic status they have. It might be of some interest as a local issue in philosophy of mind, epistemology or philosophy of psychology, but it doesn't take on the kind of urgency it has for proponents of Centrality. If you reject Centrality, you have no reason to be a pessimist, an enthusiast or even concerned.

Centrality has many components, all of them spectacularly vague. Nonetheless, I argue that Centrality is false on *all* reasonable precisifications of *all* its components. In Part I of this book I evaluate the Argument from 'Intuition'-Talk. I argue that proponents of Centrality exaggerate the extent and centrality of 'intuition'-talk in philosophical texts. That said, there is, undeniably, quite a bit of such talk. I gave some examples above and I will give more below. However, even when we are faced with argumentatively significant occurrences of 'intuitive', it will turn out that the most charitable interpretation of such talk provides no support for Centrality. The role of this term is not to denote any kind of mental state or event that plays the kind of role Centrality ascribes to intuitions. In Part II of the book I put aside the question of how to interpret 'intuition'-talk and focus instead on the second argument for Centrality: the Argument from Philosophical Practice. I look at whether we can find evidence for Centrality in the philosophical practice of appealing to cases or thought experiments. The question of whether the method of appealing to cases relies on intuitions is an empirical question. It can only be settled by looking carefully at what philosophers do when they appeal to cases. The central chapter of Part II consists of a careful study of various philosophical cases or thought experiments from different areas of philosophy. In none of them is there a reliance on judgments that have any of the features that are supposed to be hallmarks of intuitions. I conclude that it is not true that philosophers who employ cases appeal to anything intuition-like. In sum: both of the arguments for Centrality are complete failures. While contemporary philosophers might be reasonably accused of using 'intuition'-terminology too promiscuously, they should be excused from the charge of doing anything that's reasonably described as 'relying on intuitions'.

Even though Centrality is widely accepted in contemporary metaphilosophical debates, it is not universally so. Timothy Williamson's book *The Philosophy of Philosophy* is a sustained and forceful attack on what he calls 'philosophical exceptionalism'. My argumentative emphasis in this book is different from Williamson's and I'll highlight several points of disagreement along the way; still, the overall aim is closely aligned with Williamson's. While Williamson is the most salient recent ally, he is not the only one. A pair of recent papers by Max Deutsch (2009, 2010) complements (and in part inspired) the kind of case studies that constitute the core of Part II of this book.[17] In other words, Centrality is by no means a universally accepted metaphilosophical view, and if there is at least the beginning of a movement that opposes it, think of this book as a contribution to it.

I find the rejection of Centrality liberating for the field of metaphilosophy. The rejection has significant implications: it allows us to finally put behind us the elements of what I call 'methodological rationalism' (see Chapter 6). It also makes the kind of research that is pursued by experimental philosophers more or less completely irrelevant to philosophical practice. Methodological rationalists (such as Bealer, Pust, and BonJour) and experimental philosophers (such as Stich, Weinberg and others)[18] are, as I see it, joined at the hips by a commitment to Centrality. Once Centrality is rejected, both methodological rationalism and experimental philosophy can be left behind.

A Centrality-purged philosophy of philosophy will be a very different field. In the philosophy of biology, the key questions arise in connection with *specific subfields of biology*. The key issues are specific to molecular biology, evolutionary biology, developmental biology, etc. Similarly, in the philosophy of physics: there are issues specific to special and general relativity, to quantum theory, etc. In the same way, a Centrality-purged philosophy of philosophy will be focused on methodological issues that arise within specific subfields. Such questions will arise in connection with work done in philosophy of language, theory of induction, political philosophy, theory of causation, etc. We will find, I'll suggest, that the best practitioners of those fields are already deeply engaged in those very debates—it's one of the chief characteristics of much good philosophy that

---

[17] Another recent paper that provides complementary arguments is Earlenbaugh and Molyneux 2009.
[18] See Machery et al. (2004), Alexander and Weinberg (2007), Swain et al. (2008), Weinberg et al. (manuscript).

it is methodologically self-conscious. In this respect, good philosophers are different from good biologists, physicists and mathematicians. There is no correlation between the top practitioners of these subjects and those best at thinking about the methodology of biology, physics, and mathematics, but in philosophy the correlation between those best at doing first-order and second-order philosophy is strong.

Endorsement of Centrality has made it seem plausible to some methodologists that philosophical methodology can be done at a very abstract level, disconnected from deep argumentative engagement with specific philosophical subfields. The thought goes something like this: if we are all relying on intuitions and something called 'the method of cases', then we can discuss the nature of intuitions and the method of cases in the abstract, more or less independently of direct engagement with the questions that philosophers working in specific subfields grapple with on a daily basis. In this way, one might succeed in convincing oneself that there is an autonomous field of philosophical methodology. I think if Centrality were true, this line of argument would be somewhat promising. But Centrality is false. The falsity of Centrality undermines this picture and redirects methodology to the appropriate level—it should be done in direct engagement with the work done in specific subfields. The debate within philosophy of language and linguistics about how to detect context sensitivity of various kinds provides a good illustration. This is an issue philosophers of language and linguists have worked hard on over the last century. A plethora of tests and diagnostics have been proposed, criticized and refined.[19] We now know much more at least about the various options and their respective weaknesses. Those of us who have worked on those issues have in effect been engaged in philosophical methodology—and done so at the appropriate level. It is unlikely in the extreme that an 'intuition-expert' with minimal training in linguistics, semantics and philosophy of language can make a constructive contribution to these debates. Constructive methodological reflections typically arise from inside the field and require deep understanding of specific subject matters.

Don't aspire to a theory of philosophical evidence

Those who defend Centrality and the use of intuitions in philosophy tend to present their views as an account of what unifies philosophy as a whole.

---

[19] For an overview of the contemporary views, see e.g. Stanley and Szabó (2000), Recanati (2004), Cappelen and Lepore (2005), Martí (2006), Cappelen and Hawthorne (2007, 2009).

The various philosophical subdisciplines have at least this much in common: they are a kind of armchair activity that relies essentially on an appeal to intuitions about cases or thought experiments. I have no such unifying story to tell. But I also don't think it's a goal worth aspiring to. The various activities that get classified together as 'philosophy' today are so classified as the result of complex historical and institutional contingencies, not because philosophy has an essence that ties it all together as a natural kind. There are, of course, partially overlapping questions, methods, and interests, but there is no reason to think that a philosopher working on the semantics of quotation is more closely intellectually aligned with someone working on interpreting Plato's *Protagoras* or the ethics of eating meat, than to someone working in computer science or formal semantics. Of course, people who work in philosophy departments and have graduate degrees in philosophy will very often have overlapping interests because they went through similar training and spend time around each other. But this is not a reason to have as a goal to come up with a positive account of philosophical evidence, even granting that this could be 'pluralistically disjunctive' (as suggested by an anonymous referee for OUP). There is literally nothing interesting to be said *in general* about the common 'evidential sources' of applied ethics, formal semantics, theories of perception, philosophy of quantum mechanics, etc.[20]

Hintikka's question: why Centrality now?

Jaakko Hintikka asks:

Where does the current popularity of appeals to intuitions come from? ... Before the early 1960s, you could scarcely find any overt references, let alone appeals, to intuitions in the pages of philosophical journals and books in the analytic tradition. After the mid-1960s, you will find intuitions playing a major role in the philosophical argumentation of virtually every article or book. Why the contrast? (1999, p. 127)

For those who endorse Centrality, this is a good question. More generally, and without endorsing Centrality as Hintikka seems to do in

---

[20] This isn't to deny that one could come up with 'a highly disjunctive and pluralistic' story: one could just go through the kinds of arguments and evidence appealed to in thousands of different philosophy papers and list them. It should be obvious that doing this won't give you anything that's interestingly described as a 'positive theory of philosophical evidence'.

this passage, we can ask: what intellectual traditions and influences made Centrality into a form of received wisdom at the end of the twentieth and beginning of the twenty-first centuries? How did we end up in an intellectual environment in which Centrality was in the common ground among more or less all those analytic philosophers thinking about metaphilosophy and philosophical methodology?

I am inclined to put weight on what I think of as a verbal tick (or virus): philosophers started to use expressions such as 'Intuitively, BLAH' a lot. The fact that philosophers started using such locutions created the illusion that Centrality is true. A key point of Part I is that when properly interpreted, such usage provides no support for Centrality. However, I do think such usage misleads metaphilosophers (and others) into endorsing Centrality. It is worth emphasizing that according to this diagnosis, the usage itself is not motivated by (or anchored in) any substantive philosophical commitments or views about intuitions or philosophical methodology—it's simply a verbal tick without any interesting philosophical foundation. There might be an interesting question to be answered about where this verbal tick originated and what allowed it to spread. These questions will be briefly addressed below, but I have no answer that I find satisfactory.

I don't think this verbal virus is the *only* explanatory factor, and I'm open to more substantive diagnostics as complements. Hintikka answers his own question as follows:

> The answer is simple. Intuitions came into fashion in philosophy as a consequence of the popularity of Noam Chomsky's linguistics and its methodology. According to a widespread conception, generative linguists like Chomsky were accounting for competent speakers' intuitions of grammaticality by devising a grammar, that is, a set of generative rules that produces all and only such strings that are intuitively accepted by these speakers. This kind of methodology was made attractive by the tremendous perceived success of Chomsky's theories in the 1960s and 1970s. (1999, p. 127)

This I take to be an interesting suggestion, but no more than that. To make it substantive, one would need to show that Chomsky's theories and work done on transformational grammar actually had direct influence on philosophers in moral philosophy, metaphysics, philosophy of mind, epistemology, etc., and not just in philosophy of language and linguistics. Hintikka does not back up his hypothesis with a more detailed historical investigation. The only example he discusses at any length is Kripke's

Naming and Necessity, and even in that case, no direct evidence of Chomsky's influence is presented. Hintikka mentions a few sentences in which Kripke uses 'intuition'-terminology, but he does not show that in those sentences Kripke was using 'intuition' in the way Chomsky did (or that the use was inspired by Chomsky's). That said it does seem plausible that Chomsky's work in linguistics (and the success of that work) played a role in the widespread endorsement of Centrality. If so, we have two explanatory elements: the verbal tick-diagnosis and Chomsky's influence.

To these two influences a number of others should no doubt be added. First, ordinary language philosophy and various trends influenced by the later Wittgenstein tended to emphasize 'what we would say' about various topics (and treated that as some kind of evidence). Some philosophers tend to move smoothly from 'We would say that p' to 'Intuitively, p' and so those who put weight on 'what we would say' could be construed as putting weight on intuitions. A second and related influence can be traced back to G. E. Moore. As emphasized in Part I, 'intuitive' has one use that is close to 'pre-theoretic'. Moore's philosophy put a great deal of emphasis on the pre-theoretic, and so, on one construal, on the intuitive. More generally, the various anti-theory traditions in twentieth-century philosophy—including the ordinary language movement and other philosophers influenced by the later Wittgenstein—tend to emphasize the pre-theoretic, and hence (on at least one construal), the intuitive. Yet another influence can be traced to Rawls' *A Theory of Justice* (and Goodman 1955, pp. 65–8, which it relies on). At crucial points in that work (and later papers), Rawls assigns a central role to something he calls 'intuitions'. It is not unlikely that Rawls' way of speaking influenced people outside political philosophy in a way analogous to Chomsky's alleged influence beyond the sphere of philosophy of linguistics.

These are but some brief initial indications of how Hintikka's question might be answered. I mention it here simply to emphasize that this book is not an attempt at a serious historical investigation into the question of why Centrality is such a widespread assumption in contemporary philosophy. The main goal is to show that Centrality is false, not to explain why it became so widely accepted.

Brief remarks about how to read this book

The two parts of this book can be read more or less independently of each other. If you are already disposed to think that the Argument from

'Intuition'-Talk is a poor argument, but you are inclined to think the Argument from Philosophical Practice is important, it might make sense to read Part II first. That said, one of the underlying themes of the book is that understanding 'intuition' and its use among philosophers is an indispensable steppingstone for understanding intuitions and their role in philosophy. And there are crucial components of Part II that rely on claims about 'intuition' that I take myself to have established in Part I.

In Part I, the central chapter is Chapter 4. Chapter 2 is a somewhat detailed introduction to the use of 'intuitive' and 'seem' in English, and those impatient to get to what I think about philosophers' use of 'intuitive', can feel free to skip it. Chapters 3–5 all concern the interpretation of 'intuitive' and cognate terms as they occur in philosophical texts. In Chapter 4, I present the substance of my positive view of how to interpret such talk.

In Part II, the central chapters are 7 and 8, and the latter in particular. Chapter 6 provides a bit of background material, and Chapters 9–11 draw out some of the consequences of the arguments presented in 7 and 8.

PART I

The Argument from 'Intuition'-Talk

Introduction to Part I

Here is a natural thought: if philosophers characterize key premises in central philosophical arguments as 'intuitive' and refer to the evidence for their theories as 'intuitions', we have good reason to think they rely on intuitions as evidence—after all, we're just taking them at their word. I call this the *Argument from 'Intuition'-Talk* (AIT). The next few chapters evaluate different versions of AIT.

Someone who wants to use AIT will have to answer the following questions:

1. *Quantitative Question*: To what extent do philosophers engage in 'intuition'-talk?
2. *Centrality Question*: How central is such talk to their arguments? Is it at crucial points in the arguments or as in marginal, easily eliminable points?
3. *Interpretative Question*: When such language is invoked, is the correct interpretation of it Centrality-supportive? It could be that the word is used, but with a sense that doesn't support Centrality (i.e. it isn't used to denote a kind of judgment or mental state that serves as evidence or a source of evidence).

My focus in what follows is on the Interpretative Question. Questions (1) and (2) will not be explored here, though I think anyone who wants to rest Centrality (at least in part) on AIT is obliged to provide answers to those two questions as well. Before I turn to (3), I'll make what will amount to some very inconclusive and programmatic remarks about (1) and (2).

Adequately answering (1) and (2) would require careful study of philosophical texts over the relevant time period, say from the 1950s up to present. The challenge would be to find out to what extent 'intuition' and cognate terms occur in important passages in typical philosophy texts published during that period. One might find that the use of these terms took off at a certain time; maybe that it originated in certain subfields and then gradually spread. To do this in any kind of serious way would require an enormous amount of work. No proponent of Centrality has done that work, and to do it goes beyond the scope of this book. If I were to venture a guess about what the result of such a study would be, it would be the following. Even cursory reading of philosophical texts will reveal that some philosophers use 'intuitive' and cognate terms quite a bit and others hardly at all, even when they engage in debates about the same topics and the same arguments. (Right now I am leaving open whether the usages are significant and what they mean, an issue I will return to later.) I know of no counterexample to the following bold empirical hypothesis:

> Let Q be a central question in any philosophical subdiscipline. By doing a simple and quick scholarly search, you will both find philosophers who present key arguments in connection with Q in an entirely 'intuition'-free way and philosophers who present those same key arguments by using 'intuition'-talk.

If this is right, it leaves AIT inconclusive at best: while we could take those who use 'intuition'-talk to provide evidence that there is tacit reference to intuitions in the texts where there is no such *explicit* talk, this is not the only option. Indeed we could easily go the other way and use those who *don't* engage in 'intuition'-talk as evidence that doing so is superfluous. We could say, *look, it can't be essential because these other participants in the debate don't engage in such talk at all.* Alternatively, as I will suggest, we should in the end place minimal weight on this issue and instead redirect our attention to the other argument for Centrality, the Argument from Philosophical Practice. As things stand, we simply have too little data to say anything conclusive about how extensive significant occurrences of 'intuition'-talk are. This is bad news for proponents of AIT and hands them the significant challenge of backing up their claim by empirical research into the corpus of philosophical texts.

In light of these concerns, I will focus on the Interpretative Question: When 'intuition'-terminology is used, is the correct interpretation of it Centrality-supporting? To approach these issues, two questions must be distinguished:

Q1: What is the denotation of 'intuitive' (and cognate terms) in English?

Surprisingly, Q1 is not the question most theorists of intuition focus on. They assume that there's a special philosophical usage of the term 'intuition'. I'll call the alleged idiolect of those who use the word in this special philosophical way, 'English$_p$'.[1] The question they ask is Q2:

Q2: What is the denotation of 'intuitive' (and cognate terms) in English$_p$?

Q1 is the analogue of a question most theorists of knowledge focus on: they are interested in the denotation of 'know' in English. They don't treat 'know' as a theoretical term—they are interested in the phenomenon that ordinary speakers of English talk about when they say things like 'John knows that Samantha is in Paris.' They might not think that every English use of the term is relevant to what they are theorizing about, but they rule out certain usages as deviant based on what ordinary speakers consider the core usage. For example, when we find that some speakers will use 'she knows that p' in cases where that speaker knows that p is false, we show this to be a deviant usage by appeal to more data about the meaning of the English word. Epistemologists don't, typically, react by saying: 'Well, that might be what 'know' means in English, but I'm interested in a theoretical sense of the word'. This, however, is not how intuition-theorists typically proceed. Timothy Williamson, for example, says:

The application of "intuition" and cognate terms **in philosophical practice** is scarcely more restricted than Lewis and van Inwagen suggest. (2007, p. 220, my emphasis)

---

[1] I call it an 'idiolect', but I don't mean to rely on any substantive assumptions about how to individuate idiolects. If you prefer to think of this as an English word that is used as a theoretical term in a certain discipline, but prefer not to think the practitioners of that discipline as speaking a separate idiolect, that will have no bearing on the argument in this section.

Kirk Ludwig says:

> What is the status of my claim about intuitions, or about the word 'intuition'? Am I making a claim about **actual usage** or is it a suggestion for a **revision** or a **precisification** of our terminology? 'Intuition' is a term in colloquial use, and it is a term used in psychology. **I am not of course interested in just any use of the term.** I am interested specifically with **(a particular) philosophical usage** (for it is not as if there is just one). (2010, p. 435, my emphases)

Pust says:

> ...my aim is to give an account of the psychological states the content of which are used as evidence for *philosophical* theories.... I do not aim here to discover what is meant by more colloquial use of the term 'intuition' or what disciplines other than analytic philosophy mean by the term. I will not, for example, be concerned with the use of the term 'intuition' in empirical psychology or common sense lore, except to distinguish it from the topic of my concern. Whatever the independent interest and importance of non-philosophical usage, it is not the topic of the present discussion. Our target is philosophical intuition. (2000, p. 30, original italics)

The underlying assumption seems to be that philosophers have developed an idiolect in which 'intuitive' means something different from what it means in English. If the intuition-theorist could find out what philosophers talk about when they appeal to intuitions, she would have achieved her goal—she would not be all that worried if it turned out that the philosophical usage didn't fully capture the usage in ordinary English. In this respect, the typical theorist of intuition is significantly different from the typical theorist of knowledge.

Though (at least some) intuition-theorists insist on the irrelevance of the use of 'intuitive' in English, I think the attempt to quarantine philosophers' usage from other usage ultimately fails. In the first chapter of Part I (Chapter 2) I discuss the various uses of 'intuitive' and cognate terms (including 'seem') in English, and in the remainder of Part I (Chapters 3–5) I discuss the (allegedly distinctive) use of those terms by philosophers.

2

'Intuitive', 'Intuitively', 'Intuition', and 'Seem' in English

Why an entire chapter on 'intuition'-talk in English?

Theorists of intuitions claim to theorize only about the allegedly distinctive philosophers' usage, so why a chapter about the use of 'intuitive' in English? No doubt, some readers will be impatient with this chapter (and for those who are *very* impatient, I suggest moving on to the next three chapters and then referring back to this as needed), but approaching philosophers' use of 'intuitive' with an understanding of its use in English will prove useful for several reasons. First, I will argue in what follows that philosophers who use 'intuitively' often do use it with its ordinary English meaning. Given this, those who base Centrality on AIT should be interested in the question of whether the locution 'Intuitively, *p*', as used in English, indicates that the speaker is relying on a special kind of evidential source. I will argue that it doesn't, and so AIT is undermined. Second, one might be interested in the question of what the extension of 'intuitive' is in English for the same reason many epistemologists want to understand the extension of 'know'. In one very straightforward way, the answer will tell you what intuitions are. Surely, those defending Centrality should have an interest in getting clear on that question.

This chapter isn't just about how to interpret 'intuition' in English, it is also about the various uses of the word 'seem'. Some intuition-theorists appeal to sentences containing the word 'seem' when they explicate what they take 'intuition' to mean. They see some kind of close connection between 'It seems that *p*' and 'Intuitively, *p*'. It will therefore be useful to also take a close look at the word 'seem' in English.

2.1 The adjective 'intuitive' and the adverb 'intuitively'

In English we have the **noun**: 'intuition', the **adjective**: 'intuitive', the **adverb**: 'intuitively', and the **verb**: 'to intuit'. My focus in this section is on the adverb and the adjective, and the goal is modest: *to make some observations about their use that will throw some light on what goes on when philosophers and others use these terms with their regular English meaning*. I should emphasize that the goal is *not* to engage in conceptual analysis of the concept of *intuition* or to engage in the dubious activity of lexical semantics.[2]

I start with the adverb and the adjective because there is less noise involved with these expressions than with the noun. With a proper understanding of the adverb and the adjective, we will gain most of the resources we need to understand the relevant features of 'intuition' too. The observations in this section fall into four categories:

(i) Observations about what 'intuitively' and 'intuitive' can be applied to;
(ii) Observations about the *thinness* of these concepts;
(iii) Observations about 'intuitively'/'intuitive' as a speech-act modifier; and
(iv) Observations about 'intuitively'/'intuitive' as a context-sensitive term.

2.1.1 What 'intuitive' and 'intuitively' can be applied to

'Intuitive' and 'intuitively' are applied to a wide variety of states, events, and things. We philosophers are used to thinking of them as characterizing thoughts, propositions or contents, but that's not the typical usage. Consider the following:

> **Operating Systems** can be intuitive, as in: "When the Palm Pre was announced, many people immediately compared it to the iPhone, due to its fluid menus, intuitive operating system, and sleek design."[3]

---

[2] As in most other cases, I think the semantics is uninformative when it comes to anything of philosophical significance. Putting aside issues of context-sensitivity for the moment, disquotational axioms of this form will suffice: x satisfies Intuitive (x) iff x is intuitive. We should expect nothing more informative from a semantic theory (for further discussion, see Cappelen and Lepore 2004).

[3] http://toshibatouchscreenlaptop.com/429/intuitive-phone-interfaces-the-new-black/

Gadgets can be intuitive: "On the grounds that a gadget should be instinctive, intuitive, something you can start playing with straight away, this fails."[4]

Melodies can be intuitive: "The simplicity of Ms. Michaelson's words forces a focus on her melodies, which are intuitive and pretty."[5]

Singing can be done intuitively: "'I didn't do it intellectually', Ms. Streisand said. 'I did it intuitively, unconsciously. I kind of like that.'"[6]

Chess playing can be intuitive: "Kasparov plays aggressively and somewhat intuitively, while Karpov is a technician, cool and precise, often taking his opponents apart bit by bit."[7]

Basketball videogame passing: "The new freestyle passing system is intuitive, allowing players to hold the left trigger and point the right stick toward a particular player."[8]

Connections with people can be intuitive: "His parents, Walter Horsbrugh and Sheila Beckett, were both actors, so perhaps it is natural that Oliver always had such an intuitive connection with cast and crew of the productions on which he worked."[9]

Even *dance partnerships* can be: "There are few ballet partnerships as intimately and intuitively close as that of Agnes Oaks and Thomas Edur."[10]

Of course, sometimes we apply 'intuitive' and 'intuitively' to sentences, formulations, speech acts, propositions, ways of knowing, etc. Consider the following:

We all intuitively know that the recession must be having a terrible effect on people who were already living with great insecurity of employment, food and shelter in the poorest parts of the world.[11]

---

[4] "Wand remote control," Janine Gibson, *Guardian*, October 2, 2009.
[5] *NYT*, September 2, 2009.
[6] "Streisand's Fine Instrument and Classic Instinct," Anthony Tommasini, *NYT*, September 24, 2009.
[7] *NYT*, September 5 2009.
[8] *NYT*, October 7, 2009.
[9] "Oliver Horsbrugh obituary," *Guardian*, September 27, 2009.
[10] "Dance preview: Agnes Oaks and Thomas Edur: Celebration, London," Judith Mackrell, *Guardian* January 24, 2009.
[11] "Fighting for human rights," Kate Allen *Guardian*, May 28, 2009.

It is intuitive that government spending financed by taxes merely redistributes existing dollars.[12]

It is intuitive that the approximation improves as h becomes smaller.[13]

It is intuitive that breadth of expression should correlate positively with evolutionary constraint, as genes that are active in many tissues are more likely to participate in cellular processes that are critical for organismal survival and reproduction; indeed, this relationship has been reported previously in a variety of organisms.[14]

It is almost impossible to find non-philosophers describing claims or points as intuitive, but here are some such uses by philosophers:

Remarks can be intuitive: "I will argue for this claim later in this section. For now I will make a few intuitive remarks about it." (Burge 2009, p. 270)

Ways of stating arguments or points can be intuitive: "Sally s-believes to degree 1 that the hair situation on Tom's scalp is either H or else not-H. If she were certain that H obtained, she would s-believe to degree 1 that Tom was bald; that is, intuitively put, Hs obtaining would, she is certain, secure that Tom was determinately bald." (Schiffer 2003, p. 220)

Concepts can be intuitive, as in: "So disbelief, or doubt, is I think an intuitive concept, of which it is natural to think that we have some pre-theoretical grasp, and which we can put to some philosophical work." (Schroeder 2008, p. 103)

Claims can be intuitive, as in: "These claims are very rough. They are meant to be intuitive, not probative. Argument will follow." (Burge 2009, p. 272)

Sometimes, it is not quite clear what kind of thing is being characterized as intuitive:

Perhaps because it seems intuitively true, the notion persists that running, especially when done long-term and over long distances, is bad for the joints. Indeed it would be hard to think otherwise when, with each foot strike, a runner's knee withstands a force equal to eight times his body weight—for a 150-lb. person, that's about 1,200 lbs. of impact, step after step.[15]

---

[12] "The Fatal Flow of Keynesian Stimulus", Brian Riedl, *Washington Times*, August 31, 2010.

[13] Wikipedia, "The Fundamental Theorem of Calculus" http://en.wikipedia.org/wiki/Fundamental_theorem_of_calculus

[14] "Grasping human transcriptome evolution: what does it all mean?", MC Oldham and DH Geschwind, *Heredity* (2006) 96, 339–40. Published online March 22, 2006.

[15] http://www.time.com/time/health/article/0,8599,1948208,00.html

Here the author describes a notion as intuitively true, and the charitable interpretation of that use of 'notion' is that it denotes the proposition *that running, especially when done long-term and over long distances, is bad for the joints.*

2.1.2 What is intuitiveness?

Is there anything informative we can say about what intuitive melodies, operating systems, ways of stating arguments or points, chess playing, and claims have in common? In general, I'm pessimistic about the prospects of informative explications, but there is one feature that stands out when these cases are considered: *there is some kind of ease, effortlessness, or spontaneity involved.* Another way of putting this is that *the acts involved don't require a lot of reflection or effort.* These remarks should be qualified right away: the kind of ease, effortlessness, and spontaneity will vary depending on whether we talk of melodies, operating systems or claims. I doubt that there is much more to say *in general* about intuitiveness. Note, for example:

(i) We *should not* include as a necessary condition on *A* being intuitive (or done intuitively) that *A* (or the doing of *A*) doesn't rely on *immediate perception* (think of dancing intuitively).
(ii) We *should not* include as a necessary condition the absence of extensive chains of reasoning (Kasparov, though playing chess intuitively, is thinking hard, sometimes for long periods of time).
(iii) We *should not* include as a necessary condition that the relevant act does not rely on memory (the relevant acts of singing, dancing and chess playing cannot be performed without relying extensively on memory).

Looking ahead, I think careful reflection on the features of these cases will help understand philosophical judgments that are characterized as 'intuitive'. In particular, like the Kasparov example, such philosophical judgments often involve careful reflection, inference and in some cases perception. In light of this, one might even start to question whether it is too strong to require that *there is some kind of ease, effortlessness, or spontaneity involved.* In what sense is this true about Kasparov's chess playing? More generally, many of the events we characterize as 'intuitive' will include elements that are highly reflective and require significant effort—how is that compatible with the characterization of the intuitive as requiring minimal or no reflection, effort, etc.? I have no clear answer to this, but here is a suggestion: most of the events we classify and describe in natural language are complex; they are in effect sequences of smaller events. In many cases, some of these smaller events are properly characterized as 'intuitive', while others are not. The question then is how to evaluate the intuitiveness of the entire sequence of events. I suspect what goes on is a weighting of the relative significance of the intuitive and the non-intuitive elements. In some sense, the role of the intuitive mental event when Kasparov plays has more significance than when his opponent Karpov plays. This rough idea is at least the beginning of a strategy for thinking about how events can be more or less intuitive. Obviously a lot of work will go into thinking about just how the intuitive and non-intuitive elements of a complex event interact and the way these interactions affect the overall evaluation of the intuitiveness of the complex event.

Is there anything general to say about the kind of spontaneity, effortlessness, etc., that is involved in the events we classify as 'intuitive'? I won't pretend to have anything approximating a complete answer to this—I take it to be largely a matter of empirical investigation. I will sketch two rough options:

- One option is that most of what there is to say about the relevant kind of spontaneity will be *domain-specific*. For example, there might be substantive things to say about spontaneity and effortlessness involved in operating systems or chess playing or melodies, but not much to say about all of these. On this view, there isn't much to say in full generality about intuitiveness.
- On the other hand, it might turn out that there is something unified to say about the kind of spontaneity involved in all cases. Here is one proposal (suggested to me by Jennifer Nagel): the kind of spontaneity and effortlessness involved is the result of System 1 processes, i.e. processes that are automatic, affective and heuristic-based—the kinds of processes that contrast with so-called System 2 processing. It is an open empirical question whether we will find that something like this is the case. It would be somewhat surprising if the ordinary term 'intuitive' perfectly matched what we will find about System 1 processing, but it wouldn't be all that surprising if it turned out to approximate and gravitate towards events generated by System 1 processing. If so, there might be a natural kind underlying those events we naturally characterize as 'intuitive'. It is obviously not a matter we philosophers can settle—it is a challenging task for psychology and cognitive science to find out how spontaneous,

unreflective judgments of this kind (or these kinds) are grounded, their evolutionary purpose, and how such judgments interact with reflection, inference, perception, memory and other cognitive activities.[16]

Note that there are ways of combining some of the domain-specific view of intuitiveness with the view that treats it more as a natural kind. Most of the events we characterize as intuitive are complex events—they consist of sequences of events. Suppose, for simplicity, that intuitive mental events are System 1-based, and that the non-intuitive are System 2-based. It could be that what varies between domains is relative weight of System 1 and System 2 processing. The 'amount' (insofar as that makes sense) of System 1 processing that is required for characterizing a complex event as 'intuitive' will vary between domains—it need not be the same in basketball, acting, philosophy, singing, and chess playing.

2.1.3 Context sensitivity of 'intuitive' and 'intuitively'

The context sensitivity of 'intuitive' and cognate terms shows up along at least three dimensions:

- 'Intuitive' is a gradable adjective: something can be more or less intuitive. It is commonly assumed that the content of a claim containing a gradable adjective is determined in part by a comparison class, a cut-off point in a scale or some combination of these. The comparison class and cut-off are determined in context, so it is should be fairly uncontroversial that for this reason alone 'intuitive' is a context-sensitive term.
- Sometimes the subject of 'intuitive' is left out, as when we say 'It is intuitive that p.' This is a form of context sensitivity. A comparison might help to bring this point out. Many philosophers of language think that weather reports like 'It is raining' contain an unpronounced location variable in the logical form and that it is context sensitive. These sentences have the form 'It is raining in x' where the value of x is a location that is determined in context. If 'It is intuitive that p' has

---

[16] Much of the psychological literature on intuitions is connected to the study of heuristics and biases. A good introduction to some of this literature can be found in Gilovich, Griffin, and Kahneman (2002). More representative work in this area includes Albrechtsen, Meissner, and Susa (2009), Evans (2007), Mercier and Sperber (2009), Plessner, Betsch, and Betsch (2008), Shah and Oppenheimer (2008), and Stanovich and West (2000, 2008).

the form 'It is intuitive that p to x' and the value of x is determined in context, this adds a second element of context sensitivity to 'It is intuitive that p.' It should be obvious that what is intuitive to Kasparov need not be to me, and that what is an intuitive development of the stock market for an experienced stockbroker need have no intuitive features for me.

- The vague paraphrase used above to characterize the common core of intuitive objects and events ("they are *easy* to grasp/understand/use, they don't require *a lot* of reflection or effort") involves expressions like 'easy' and 'a lot.' The content of these expressions will vary with context. What counts as 'easy' or 'a lot' of effort is fixed in some poorly understood way by factors such as context of utterance, the speaker's intentions and the topic of conversation.

As a result of these elements of context sensitivity, the set of intuitive judgments is no more fixed than the set of tall things. The set of the intuitive is fixed only relative to a complex and poorly understood set of contextual factors.

2.2 'Intuitive' as a hedge

Some terms can be used as *hedges*, and below I'll argue that 'intuitively' and 'intuitive' are extensively so used by philosophers. A hedge is an expression that functions, at least in part, to weaken the speaker's commitment to the embedded sentence. Mandy Simons (2007) has an excellent discussion of this and related phenomena. She traces her discussion back to Urmson (1952), and the key notion in her description is that of *a content having a main point status*. Here is an illustration:

(1) A: Why didn't Louise come to the meeting yesterday?
    B: I heard that she's out of town.

According to Simons, whatever content in B's utterance constitutes an answer to the question is the main point content. In the exchange above, the main point is expressed by the embedded clause. Two contents can be found in B's utterance in (1):

1Ba: that B heard that Louise is out of town, and
1Bb: that Louise is out of town.

(1Bb) is the answer to the question and thus constitutes *the main point* of the utterance in some significant sense. The reason for the 'main point' terminology is that we don't want to say that (1Bb) is *asserted*. According to Simons, 'I heard' (and other parentheticals) can be used to indicate a weakening of the speaker's commitment to the truth of the complement. An assertion on the other hand, is, according to Simons, "an act which commits the speaker completely to the truth of what is asserted" (p. 1041). This weakening does not prevent the content of the embedded clause from constituting the main point of the utterance.

What Simons says about the function of 'I heard' in (1B) can be extended to the use of many other expressions. Consider the following dialogues:

(2) A: Why didn't Louise come to the meeting yesterday?
    B: Apparently, she's out of town.

(3) A: Why didn't Louise come to the meeting yesterday?
    B: She's out of town, it seems.

No matter what else you want to say about the semantics of 'apparently' and 'seems', they can be used, in these kinds of sentences, to comment on the speaker's commitment to the embedded clause, which then constitutes the main point of the utterance. In both cases the speaker indicates a weakened commitment to the answer.[17]

I'm suggesting we understand many uses of 'intuitively' and cognate terms in light of such hedge uses. The pattern is this:

A: Why/how *p*?
B: Intuitively, *q*.

For example:

(4) A: Why does the dollar get stronger even though the US stock market has collapsed?
    B: Intuitively, it is because investors expect stock markets around the world to follow the US market.

---

[17] I should point out that Simons does not use the terminology of 'hedging'. She talks instead about "parenthetical uses" (p. 1034). She notes that these uses do not correspond to syntactic parentheticals. There are a number of issues raised in Simons' paper that I don't address here, e.g., the connection between parentheticals and evidentials and the parenthetical uses of factive and semi-factive verbs, since they will not have direct bearing on the issues under discussion here.

(5) A: How should White play in this situation?
    B: Intuitively, she should protect her queen.

The main point of B's utterance in (4) is that investors expect stock markets around the world to follow the US market in reply to A's question, and 'intuitively' serves to qualify this reply. B's utterance in (5) is similar except that the main point is that White should protect her queen.

What exactly is the qualification we can use 'intuitively' to indicate? To answer this is just as tricky as it is for (1)–(3) above; as for those cases I suspect the nature of the qualification will vary between contexts. Here are two paraphrases that indicate what's going on in at least some cases (in the next chapter I propose we often find these in philosophical texts):

Easy (audience-focused): In (4) the qualification indicates that the main point is an incomplete answer meant for easy consumption rather than the full theoretical answer which is more complicated, more difficult to understand, and takes more effort to process. I'll call this kind of qualification '*Easy*'.

Snap (speaker-focused): In (5) the qualification is used to indicate that the reply is given after brief, limited reflection. The qualification leaves open the possibility that a different answer would be given after careful analysis of the situation. I call this kind of qualification '*Snap*'. While *Easy* is focused on the audience, *Snap* is focused on the speaker: it indicates that the answer is the result of some kind of quick, spontaneous, and relatively unreflective judgment.

I should emphasize that the view proposed above is not that the semantic value of 'intuitively' is given by its hedging function. Attitude verbs like 'believe' and 'think' have interesting and complicated semantics, much studied by philosophers and linguists. I don't take the observations about their hedge use to be a contribution to the semantics of attitude verbs. It is a non-semantic, communicative function that such terms serve in part because of their semantics. Consider 'think' in 'I think she is out of town' given as an answer to 'Why didn't Louise come to the meeting yesterday?' Here 'think' denotes the psychological state people are in when they think. On one simple story, the semantic content is the proposition that the speaker stands in the thinking relation to the proposition *that Louise is out of town*. In a hedged use of 'I think she is out of town', the semantic content is *not* the main point of the utterance. The answer to the question is the content of the embedded clause, i.e. *that Louise is out of town*, which constitutes the main point of the utterance. This is an instance of a familiar phenomenon: the semantics of the uttered sentences isn't the main communicative point of the utterance.[18]

2.3 The noun phrase 'intuition'

These observations about the adverbial and adjectival forms can help clarify how the noun 'intuition' is used. Ignoring context sensitivity for now, here are some plausible connecting principles, first between 'intuitive' and 'intuition':

C: '*A* has the intuition that *p* (at *t*)' is true just in case *p* is intuitive to *A* (at *t*).

How are the adverbial and adjectival constructions related? I'll restrict my attention to cases where the object of intuition is something propositional and truth-evaluable (since this is what philosophers typically take an interest in) and the act in question is a judgment. Here is one way in which one could articulate the connection between *p* being intuitive to an agent *A* and *A* judging that *p* intuitively:

CC: 'It is intuitive to *A* that *p* (at *t*)' is true just in case *A* judges that *p* intuitively (at *t*).

(C) and (CC) are rough principles for four reasons:

(i) They ignore all the various sources of context sensitivity mentioned in Section 2.1.3. Were we to take these into account, several layers of complexity would have to be added.

(ii) In some cases we are willing to say that *A* finds *p* intuitive at *t*, even though we don't naturally say that *A* judges that *p* at *t* (just as we are willing to say that *A* has the belief that *p* at *t* even though *A* doesn't judge that *p* at *t*). We are willing to treat 'finding intuitive' as a state and we are treating judging as an event. To account for these cases we would need more machinery, perhaps including a dispositional

---

[18] See e.g. Cappelen and Lepore (2004) for more general discussion of this phenomenon. There are interesting questions to be explored here about just how the hedging function occurs. Simons mentions, but doesn't explore, a Gricean idea: the speaker expects the audience to realize that it would be obviously false that what explains Alice's absence from the meeting is *that the speaker thinks she is out of town*, and then the embedding of the answer within a propositional attitude verb is taken to be a hedge.

or modal element concerning what the judgment would be like at *t* had it taken place.
(iii) They don't generalize in any easy way to cases where the event or object characterized is not proposition-like (e.g. where acts of singing and dancing are described as intuitive).
(iv) Finally, note that I don't focus on claims like '*p* is an intuition' where there is no explicit talk of a subject finding *p* intuitive. I am assuming that such claims either implicate or directly express claims about what agents (at a particular time) find intuitive.

More complicated bridging principles could be constructed that would aim to overcome these limitations, but for the purposes of this work, the simpler versions will do. The goal is to show how an understanding of the adjectival and adverbial constructions can help illuminate the nominal construction. The simple story about the noun is that it refers to mental states or acts that are intuitive, where 'intuitive' is spelled out in the very thin way as in Sections 2.1 and 2.2 above.

2.3.1 Digression: intuitions and the 'sixth sense'

So far this is pretty straightforward. What generates some noise is that 'intuition' is often used to denote a kind of strange faculty that underlies judgments made intuitively. In a great deal of non-philosophical and non-scientific literature this faculty is described as the 'faculty of intuition' or the 'sixth sense'. A Google search for 'intuition' turns up an apparently infinite number of bizarre passages like these:

> Who hasn't been there: stuck between two choices, wishing for psychic guidance. Well, experts say everyone does have an innate superpower—it's called *intuition*.[19]

> That is what we call your sixth sense. Besides the 5 well-known senses like vision, hearing, smell, taste and touch there is a 6th sense, named intuition.[20]

There are many fascinating theories about the nature of this faculty. Most philosophers and non-philosophers think it is a myth, that there is no such special faculty. That's what I will assume in what follows and so will

---

[19] *Women's Health*, June 2009, p. 68.
[20] http://library.thinkquest.org/05aug/00386/6thsence/index.htm

entirely ignore this extensive usage of the term. This is not, I should emphasize, to deny that there can be an interesting empirical study of the nature of snap judgments, how these are developed, and how they depend on skills and training. What I will assume, without further argument, is that such judgments don't rely on a special faculty of the kind sometimes assumed in more mysterious literature—the mechanisms that generate snap judgments of the kind we sometimes call 'intuitions' are familiar ones: memory, training, background knowledge, etc.[21]

2.3.2 Taking stock: 'intuitively' and Centrality

When a speaker of English says 'Intuitively, BLAH', that does not show that she is relying on intuitions as evidence. First, what she says is highly context sensitive and there is no *one* content that is expressed by such utterances (and so no *one* version of Centrality can be supported). Second, 'intuitively' is typically *not* used to modify propositions or contents. Typically it characterizes things like operating systems, dance partnerships, and chess playing. In none of those cases is a thesis about evidence (or source of evidence) an appropriate summary of what is going on. In the occasional cases where 'intuitively' does modify a content, it is often used as a hedge, indicating the speaker's weakened commitment to that content. In some cases it is not used simply as a hedge, but also to make explicit that the speaker has not thought carefully about that content—that it is not the result of careful reasoning and that relatively little effort went into the process of reaching that conclusion. Again, no interesting and relevant version of Centrality is supported. This might be why intuition-theorists and Centrality supporters claim to take an interest only in a special technical use of 'intuitively'. The option of taking 'intuitively' to have a technical use is addressed in the next three chapters. But before turning to this option, I'll make some brief remarks about 'seem' in English and its connection to 'intuitively'.

---

[21] I also don't mean here to rule out the view that there is such a thing as 'rational insight' and that it works in ways analogous to perception (see e.g. Parsons 1995 and references therein). What I will assume is that this is not what the authors of the *Women's Health* article meant to refer to (in part because 'rational insight' as construed by philosophers such as Gödel doesn't give the kind of lifestyle and relationship advice that 'intuition' can according to *Women's Health*).

2.4 'Seem' and 'intuitive'

Those who think Centrality is supported, at least in part, by AIT, will no doubt insist that the support comes not just from use of 'intuitive' in its various grammatical forms, but also from use of terms such as 'seem'. One line of thought goes something like this: when philosophers talk about how things seem to them, and they rest their arguments on such seemings, then they are in effect relying on intuitions. George Bealer is an example of a Centrality proponent who explicitly connects 'seem' and 'intuitive' in this way. Bealer thinks intuitions are *sui generis* states and so in some sense irreducible to any other kind of state, but he does, nonetheless use 'seem'-terminology to explain what he thinks intuitions are. He says, for example:

> For you to have an intuition that A is just for it to seem to you that A. Here 'seems' is understood, **not as a cautionary or "hedging" term**, but in its use as a term for **a genuine kind of conscious episode**. For example, when you first consider one of de Morgan's laws, often it neither seems to be true nor seems to be false; after a moment's reflection, however, something happens: it now seems true; **you suddenly "just see" that it is true.** Of course, this kind of seeming is intellectual, not sensory or introspective (or imaginative). (Bealer 1996, p. 5, my emphases)

What follows are some brief observations about the meaning of 'seem' in English.[22] I conclude that the use of this term provides no support whatsoever for Centrality. I make four central points:

- The central use of 'seem' is as a kind of *generic evidential*—and so used it is often a hedge-term.
- 'Intuitive' and 'seem' are interchangeable in many contexts and this is explained by their respective, and closely related, hedging functions.
- They are not universally interchangeable—'seem' can't always be replaced by 'intuitive' and vice versa.
- 'Seem' is not ambiguous in the way Bealer says it is: 'seem' is not used to denote a genuine kind of conscious episode and it doesn't have a separate hedge meaning/function.

Reminders: some typical uses of 'seems to me' and 'seeming'

---

[22] Again, it would be possible for AIT supporters to claim that 'seem' as used by philosophers is a technical term, introduced with an extension significantly different from what it has in English. That claim fails for the same reasons as the analogous claim about 'intuitive', which is discussed in the next three chapters.

I start by reminding the reader of some typical uses of 'seem' in English.

Recession seems to put people in the mood for condoms.[23]

Danger Mouse seems to want fans to pirate his blocked release.[24]

Christine Brennan of USA Today wrote that she wants to believe he's changed, but isn't there yet, and Bill Plaschke of The Los Angeles Times said Woods veered between seeming honest and still holding back.[25]

It seems to me that Fred and others are nuts and totally out of touch with reality.

The sun seems to be dimming.[26]

Many developers have long complained about the strict, sometimes arbitrary-seeming standards it keeps over what apps it offers through its store.[27]

Yet if you ask Ms. Hastreiter—a woman so unconcerned with seeming cool or ironic that she actually talks about taking life's lemons and making lemonade—whether all that is great and thrilling about New York City actually came to an end, as some fogies insist, around 1985, she snorts.[28]

Assuming that the street-theater guerrilla troupe *Improve Everywhere's* latest joint, the instructively titled "No Underwear Subway Ride" is not an April Fool's hoax—and Charlie Todd, the group's leader and a seeming straight-shooter promises us it's not—you'd think it would have attracted some kind of law-enforcement attention the day it took place.[29]

Mr. Gao acknowledged that his seeming turnabout was sure to dishearten his backers, and he asked for their understanding.[30]

The economic freefall seems to have stopped.[31]

---

[23] *USA Today*, 2/12/2009
[24] http://www.theregister.co.uk/2009/05/19/danger_mouse_muzzled/
[25] Lynn Zinser, *NYT*, 6/04/2010.
[26] http://news.bbc.co.uk/2/hi/science/nature/4171591.stm
[27] Joshua Brustein, *NYT*, 02/04/2010.
[28] Guy Tribay, 07/04/2010.
[29] http://cityroom.blogs.nytimes.com/tag/street-theater/
[30] *NYT*, 07/04/2010.
[31] http://online.wsj.com/article/SB124256967243827608.html

It seems to me that most professional authors have a blog—should I make one too?

It seems to me that the world is too hard on teens.

It seems to me that with Robben on the left and another quick player on the right we will be very complete.

First observation: 'seem' as a generic evidential

'Seem' is standardly assumed to be an evidential in English, but there is minimal literature on its role as an evidential. It is particularly unclear what kind of evidence 'It seems that p' and 'the seeming that p' indicate that the speaker has for p. Even brief reflection on the cases above shows that 'seem' doesn't indicate possession of a *specific kind* of evidence. It is not *one* of testimony, hearing, vision or inference (or non-inference), *specifically*. The evidence that supports "Recession seems to put people in the mood for condoms" can be various kinds of statistics about sales patterns of contraceptives during recessions. The support for describing Tiger Woods as "seeming honest" can be observation of his body language, tone of voice, and the content of what he says. The evidential bases for the claims, "It seems to me that Fred and others are nuts and totally out of touch with reality" and "The sun seems to be dimming", are equally varied.

In the light of this, it is helpful to think of 'seem' as a kind of *generic evidential*: it doesn't indicate any specific kind of evidence, but it does say something about the evidence for the claim (without being specific about its source). The challenge is to specify *what* it says about the evidence.

Consider the following proposal about the nature of the evidential base, which I'll call 'Weak-Seem': 'It seems that p' requires only that there is *some* (maybe contextually salient) evidence (of some kind) that supports p. Note that such a view leaves room for a lot of pragmatic maneuvering. First, saying that there is 'some evidence *for p*' will typically implicate that *not all* the evidence *supports p* (either because there is contrary evidence or because you don't have access to all of it). Second, insofar as a proponent of Weak-Seem allows the domain of 'some' (in 'some evidence') to vary between contexts, we can think of 'seem' as picking out some evidence in a contextually specified subset of the total evidential base.

Here are some nice features of this simple proposal:

- On this construal, it is easy to get 'seem'-claims to come out true (at least as long as the domain of 'some' isn't too restricted); in particular, it is easy to see how the passages quoted above can be true.
- This proposal also helps make sense of claims like 'It seems red, but I know it is blue' when someone looks at a patch of paper knowing that it visually gives the impression of being red when it is really blue. In such a case, there is *some* evidence (the visual input) for redness, but overriding considerations tell in favor of it being blue.
- It might also explain why 'It seems to me that 2 + 2 = 4' is inappropriate when *all* the speaker's evidence indicates that 2 + 2 = 4.
- Finally, it explains the hedge function of 'seem'. The implicature, *not all evidence supports* p, is a way to hedge the assertion of *p*—you shouldn't assert *p* if the evidential base goes beyond the restricted evidence you have for *p* (more on which below).

However, Weak-Seem has some troubling consequences: the view predicts that it is very easy for 'seem'-claims to come out true and correspondingly hard for a negated 'seem'-claim to come out true. Of course properly restricting the domain of 'some' can help with both problems. For those who find Weak-Seem unacceptable, alternative strategies will treat 'seems that *p*' as communicating something of the form, 'Evidence of kind *K* indicates that *p*'. The challenge is to figure out how to properly specify *K*. One option[32] is to treat 'seem' as indicating the presence of specifically *indirect* evidence, where this is understood as testimony or inferential evidence. This might have some advantages, but would for example make 'It seems blue, but is red' come out false in a case where the direct perceptual evidence is of something blue, while the conclusion that it is red is reached indirectly (e.g. by inference).

Since these variations will not affect the points I make in connection with Bealer-like attempts to use 'seem'-talk to illuminate 'intuition'-talk, I won't explore them further here and will instead use the Weak-Seem proposal as a toy theory—one that clearly will need further refinement, but will do for making the points in the next few sections.

---

[32] This is an option that is often assumed in the literature on evidentials.

'Seem', 'intuitive' and hedging

It should already be clear that the use of 'seem' is importantly different from the standard use of 'intuitive': we saw that 'intuitive' typically indicates a kind of spontaneous, immediate reaction not based on extensive reflection. The generic evidential use of 'seem' does not have that function. It is compatible with careful reflection on the *available* evidence. The detective can say, after carefully looking at and reflecting on the crime scene, 'It seems he was killed on the bedroom and then moved to the bathroom'. There is no indication here of a lack of reflection or of a spontaneous judgment having been made.

The generic evidential use of 'seem' gives rise to hedge-uses that are not available for 'intuitive'. If the question under discussion is 'Why is the body in such a strange position on the bathroom floor?' and the answer given is 'It seems he was killed in the bedroom and then moved to the bathroom', we can treat the embedded clause of the latter as an answer to the question and so the main point of the utterance. The function of 'seem' is to hedge that answer, but not by indicating that no careful reflection or empirical research has been relied on. As I suggested above, the hedge indicates rather that the conclusion is reached after careful reflection on some *restricted* set of evidence, and the hedge comes in through the implication that more evidence can be forthcoming (i.e. the implication being that this isn't *all* the evidence). As we have seen, this is not how 'intuitively' is used.

Corollary: 'seem' does not denote 'a genuine kind of conscious episode'

Recall Bealer's claim that 'seem' is used "... as a term for a genuine kind of conscious episode" (1996, p. 5). I have to admit I am not quite sure what 'a genuine kind of conscious episode' is, but there is no clear sense in which whenever an agent has some evidence for something, she is enjoying a *certain kind* of conscious episode. We can easily make sense of sentences like "It seems to me that Fred and others are nuts and totally out of touch with reality", "It seems red, but I know it is blue" and "It seems to me that Woods was honest", without postulating a 'genuine kind of conscious episode'. No doubt, conscious events take place when it seems to someone that such-and-such is the case, but there is no unique kind of state such that if the speaker of "It seems to me that Fred and others are nuts and totally out of touch with reality" fails to be in it, he has said something false. This follows I think quite naturally from its use as a generic evidential. If an agent has considered the available evidence and concluded that it supports *p*, that agent need not undergo any specific kind of conscious episode. So the Bealer picture is mistaken on two fronts: first, 'seem' doesn't denote a kind of conscious episode, and second, 'seem' doesn't have a separate hedge use. The hedge function of 'seem' follows from it being a generic evidential.[33]

2.5 Taking stock

There is no neat summary of the various remarks in this chapter, and that is an important point in this context. It should be clear that there is no well-disciplined or well-understood unique function or meaning we can assign the terms 'intuitively', 'intuitive', 'seem', etc., as they are used in ordinary English. This is important for an understanding of Centrality. First, if 'intuition' as it is used in the formulation of Centrality is the ordinary English term, then Centrality has a false presupposition. There is no kind of mental state or event that is picked out by the relevant set of English terms and those terms are not used to denote a kind of evidential source. Second, AIT claims that philosophers' use of 'intuition'-terminology provides support for Centrality. If philosophers use the term as it is used in English, the argument fails:

- If in 'Intuitively, *p*' the term is used as a hedge, it is not used to denote a mental state or event that is an evidential source, and so Centrality gets no support.
- The same goes if the term 'intuitive' is used to describe a conclusion that is reached without careful reflection, to describe a point that is

---

[33] One could try to single out and investigate the properties of a subset of 'seemings', and maybe that subset could help us understand 'intuition'. Bealer tries to do this by talking about "intellectual" or "rational" seemings. Such talk is supposed to pick out a subset of seemings. This strategy can work only if we have an independent grasp of the relevant senses of 'rational' and 'intellectual'. But we don't. Consider again, "The recession seems to put people in the mood for condoms", or "The economic freefall seems to have stopped." There is nothing 'non-intellectual' or 'non-rational' about these, if those terms are taken in their regular English sense. Keep in mind I'm not here meaning to rule out that someone could introduce (or has introduced) a technical term, 'seem', that could be used to pick out something other than the English word 'seem'. This chapter, recall, is about the relevant terms in English, and I turn in later chapters to their use as theoretical terms.

presented as easy to grasp for the audience, or to denote a conclusion or a view that's reached quickly. In such cases the term is not used to denote an evidential source and so no evidence for Centrality is forthcoming.
- Finally, appeal to the alleged connections between 'seem' and 'intuitive' is misleading and does not strengthen AIT.

As I pointed out at the beginning of this chapter, many intuition-theorists seem to be aware of this fact, and so claim that they are investigating a special usage of 'intuitively' by philosophers. Maybe the thought is that those who articulate Centrality use 'intuition'-terminology in that special way and that it is this special use we should pay attention to when evaluating AIT. This is the view I turn to next.

3

Philosophers' Use of 'Intuitive' (I):
A Defective Practice and the Verbal Virus Theory

Many intuition theorists claim to theorize about a specialized use of 'intuition' among analytic philosophers, not about what ordinary speakers of English denote by their use of that term. As Pust puts it:

> I do not aim here to discover what is meant by more colloquial use of the term 'intuition' or what disciplines other than analytic philosophy mean by the term. (2000, p. 30)

This presupposes that there is such a thing as analytic philosophers' use of 'intuition'—that analytic philosophers have succeeded in introducing 'intuition' as a theoretical term with a meaning distinct from what it has in English. This chapter explores that view and concludes:

- The idea that analytic philosophers learn a new meaning for the word 'intuitive' simply by taking some philosophy classes, reading some books and talking to colleagues, is implausible in the extreme.
- That said, there are some philosophers who use 'intuitive' in ways different from how it is used in ordinary English. It is used as a theoretical term in a variety of philosophical traditions. But there is no unique or even dominant theoretical use of these terms among analytic philosophers.
- It might be that those philosophers who unreflectively use 'intuitive' (i.e. use it without having a particular philosophical theory of the intuitive in mind) are engaged in a kind of defective linguistic

practice—a practice where there's no semantic anchor point and the term fails to have a semantic value.

Speaking loosely, here is how I think of the situation we philosophers are in with respect to the word 'intuitive'. I call this 'the verbal virus theory of "intuition" proliferation.' Philosophers' use of 'intuition' is a kind of intellectual/verbal virus (or tick) that started spreading about thirty to forty years ago. It is a bad habit and we should abandon it. However, and this is important, the virus didn't have much effect on first-order philosophy. Though there are some important exceptions, in most cases there are ways to eliminate or reinterpret 'intuition'-talk so that the relevant arguments remain intact. The most damage caused by the 'intuition'-virus was on philosophical methodology. The virus helped convince those doing methodology that things called 'intuitions' play an important part in philosophical arguments. Hence the widespread acceptance of Centrality and the resulting misguided research projects that sprang out of endorsement of Centrality.

3.1 Constructive vs. defective theoretical terms

There are many ways in which terms that are not in ordinary, day-to-day English can be introduced into a discipline or a theory. Such introductions can succeed and serve a constructive role in the discipline, or not. There are success and failure conditions on the introduction of technical terms. Not every attempt to introduce a theoretical term will succeed—in some cases it is done poorly and the result is some kind of defective terminology. We have at present no effective procedure for distinguishing between constructive and defective introductions—we have few good theories of the different mechanisms through which such terms can be introduced (stipulation, appeal to paradigms, Ramseyfication, or, more vaguely, a pattern of use over time).

I suspect that if we treat 'intuition' as a theoretical term in philosophy, then it will fall into the category of defective introductions—introductions where the usage of the term is doing more harm than good. To argue this point in full would require a theory of the success and failure conditions on the introduction of theoretical terms, and that would take us beyond the scope of this work. The goal of this and the next section is simply to make a *prima facie* case that philosophers' use of 'intuitive' and cognate terms is very different from clear cases of successful introduction of theoretical terms, say in economics, and that according to some rough but plausible diagnostics for defectiveness, philosophers' use of these terms is defective.

Here are two terms from economics that I take to be *prima facie* cases of successful introductions of theoretical terms into a discipline:

> A consumer's **indirect utility function,** denoted by $v(p, w)$, gives the consumer's maximal utility when faced with a price level p and an amount of income w. The indirect utility function gives as output the value of the maximum utility that can be achieved by spending the budget w on the consumption of goods with price p.
>
> **The Pigou effect** is the wealth effect on consumption as prices fall. A lower price level leads to a greater existing private wealth of nominal value, leading to a rise in consumption.

There are some noteworthy features of these cases:

- There is no disagreement among economists about how to properly define 'indirect utility function' or 'Pigou effect.' Any competent member of the profession can give you these definitions. They are taught at introductory level.
- The terms serve an important and useful role in economic texts. They are used to articulate theories and points of disagreement—they are not themselves sources of disagreement and dispute.[1]
- There is more or less universal agreement on what cases constitute paradigmatic examples.

None of these are necessary or sufficient conditions, but they are at least rough diagnostics for when things are going well. It also gives us an idea of when a theoretical term is not doing well. I take the following to be diagnostics of when we have reason to believe the introduction of a theoretical term T is defective (or has negative consequences):

---

[1] This isn't to say that there are no substantive disagreements about e.g. indirect utility functions. It is only to say that those disagreements are not, typically, the result of differing definitions and confusions about metalinguistic issues. The disagreements are made possible by a shared initial understanding.

- *T* has no agreed upon definition among practitioners of the discipline.
- There is no agreement among participants in the discipline about what cases constitute core paradigms of the extension of *T*.
- There is no agreed upon theoretical role that *T* (or *T*'s extension) plays in the discipline.
- There is considerable disagreement and dispute within the discipline about *T* itself.

Again, these are not meant to be necessary or sufficient conditions for a defective introduction of a theoretical term, but they are reliable indicators that something has gone wrong.

3.2 Problems for 'intuition' in philosophy

With these diagnostics in hand, philosophers' use of 'intuition' seems problematic: There is no agreed upon definition of 'intuition'. There are no agreed upon paradigms. There is minimal unity in usage between different schools and subdisciplines and there is no group of experts within the discipline who agree on how the term should be used.

For those who doubt that 'intuition'-talk is correctly characterized in these ways, consider the following:

- For some philosophers the intuitive must by definition be based solely on conceptual competence (see e.g. Goldman and Pust 1998, Bealer 1998, Ludwig 2010). For others it's not a necessary condition (e.g. Lewis 1983, van Inwagen 1997, Kornblith 1998, Weinberg 2007, Sinnott-Armstrong 2008).
- For some philosophers, what is intuited must be a necessary truth (Bealer 1996, BonJour 1998, Pust 2000, Sosa 2007b), for others not (again see Lewis 1983, van Inwagen 1997, Kornblith 1998, Weinberg 2007, Sinnott-Armstrong 2008).
- For some philosophers, the intuitive must come with a special feeling or phenomenology (Bealer 1996), for others not (Goldman and Pust 1998, Ludwig 2010).

- For some the intuitive has to be true, for others we can sometimes have false intuitions. The latter is a clear majority view in this case; Descartes, Kirk Ludwig (2007) and, on Parsons' (1995) interpretation, Gödel, take intuitions to be factive.
- In an important philosophical tradition going back to Kant, Husserl and Gödel, 'intuition' is used to denote objects of perception. As Parsons writes:

> In the philosophical tradition, intuition is spoken of both in relation to objects and in relation to propositions, one might say as a propositional attitude. I have used the terms intuition *of* and intuition *that* to mark this distinction. The philosophy of Kant, and the Kantian paradigm generally, gives the basic place to intuition of, but certainly allows for intuitive knowledge or evidence that would be a species of intuition that. (1995, pp. 58–9)

This tradition is still alive among those working in the philosophy of mathematics, and also among those who write on the historical figures who use the term in this way. This is obviously very different from how the term is used e.g. by experimental philosophers.

- For some philosophers, the intuitive judgments are by definition reflective (Rawls 1971), for others they have to come with a kind of immediacy that rules out the kind of reflection required by Rawls.
- For some philosophers, the content of intuitive judgments must concern particular cases, for others the content can also be of general principles.

You might think that while these are reasons for concern, they are counterbalanced by widespread agreement on what to count as paradigms of intuitive judgments. Anna-Sara Malmgren, for example, considers a number of ways of characterizing intuitions, and settles on doing so "by reference to examples" (2011, p. 268). She says this option is

> ... vastly preferable, given the desire for a neutral starting point—all the others are bound to be controversial, and to limit the theoretical possibilities too much in advance. For our purposes, then, an intuitive judgement is any judgement relevantly similar to certain paradigms or examples (where it is left open what exactly makes for relevance). (2011, p. 268)

While I think Malmgren is correct that there is not even a rough characterization in terms of necessary or sufficient conditions that will capture the variety of uses of 'intuitive' among philosophers, I don't agree that appeal to so-called paradigms will do the job of unifying (and giving coherence to) the practice. The strategy fails for two reasons: first, there isn't agreement on a set of paradigmatic cases. Second, even if there were agreement, it wouldn't suffice to make it into a coherent practice. I consider these points in turn.

If asked to come up with a list of paradigms of the intuitive, I suspect there might be some overlap in labels that many (but not all) philosophers would use. They might mention Putnam's Twin-Earth case, Burge's 'arthritis' case, Perry's cases, Cohen's airport cases, the Gettier case, and a few others. However, there's no agreement on what those labels denote. The labels typically refer us to papers or complex arguments, but there are just too many judgments/claims in each of those papers for the label to be helpful. The paradigms can't each be a vaguely identified set of judgments/claims. For the strategy to work, the set of paradigms should be a set of particular claims/judgments. The problem is that as soon as we try to specify which particular propositions (or arguments) in those papers that are the intuitive ones, we immediately reencounter widespread disagreement. This is because disagreement about general characterizations trickles down to characterization about the particular case. The so-called Gettier case illustrates this point. In addition to all the papers trying to respond to Gettier, there is now a flourishing literature on what the content of the intuitive judgment about the Gettier case is.[2] Here are some suggestions as to what the 'real' intuition is (helpfully summarized, in part, by Chudnoff 2011, p. 330):

1. If an agent were related to p as Smith is according to Gettier's text, he/she would have a justified true belief that p, but not know that p. (Williamson 2007)
2. Necessarily: if every element in the Gettier story is true, then someone has a justified true belief that p, but does not know that p. (Ichikawa and Jarvis 2009)
3. Possibly: someone stands to p as in the Gettier case (as described), has a justified true belief that p, and does not know that p. (Malmgren 2011)[3]

---

[2] See Williamson (2007), Ichikawa and Jarvis (2009), Chudnoff (2011), and Malmgren (2011).

[3] Initially, Malmgren just tells us what the various intuitive judgments are, *loosely put* (2011, p. 264). I suspect the reason she doesn't actually specify the relevant judgments is that as soon as we say anything more precise (as she goes on to do), the consensus will shatter. Consider

4. In the story: Smith has a justified true belief that *p*, but does not know that *p*. (Chudnoff 2011)[4]

Since the Gettier case is often considered the paradigm of an intuition-based case, the fact that there's no agreement even in this case is good reason to think that the problem will generalize. And in fact it does. One lesson from the case studies in the next part of this book is that it is exceedingly hard (I argue impossible) to find a particular judgment (or set of judgments) in any of the alleged paradigmatic cases that there is agreement on classifying as intuitive.

My second concern with the strategy of relying on agreement on so-called paradigms is that even if some group of philosophers managed to sit down and agree on a few judgments they all would describe as 'intuitive', this is exceedingly unhelpful when there's no agreement on what counts as being relevantly similar to those cases. If members of the group project out from the paradigms in widely differing ways—and we know that's true about philosophers' use of 'intuitive'—then the initial consensus will not help unify or make coherent a defective practice. Disagreement about general characterization will trickle down to the level of particular cases and the accidental agreement on a few cases won't generalize in any helpful manner.

I conclude: there's disagreement at more or less every level and this disagreement is also reflected among those who write directly on intuitions. The 'intuition experts' are just as much in disagreement as philosophers who don't work on the topic. There is thus a striking contrast with how economists use e.g. 'utility function'.

3.3 Disagreement over the theoretical role of intuitions

It is also worth noting that the theoretical role and purpose of appeals to intuitions in philosophical discourse vary a lot (and so a Ramseyfication-strategy is unlikely to help). Consider, first, philosophy of mathematics, an

---

Malmgren's loose characterization of the Gettier judgment, "loosely put: the judgement that Smith has a justified true belief without knowledge" (p. 264). This is *not* the particular judgment that any participant in the current debate thinks of as the intuitive one (again, see references above).

[4] Chudnoff thinks many of these candidates are intuitive, but only (4) is what he calls "*basically* intuitively apparent" (pp. 330–1).

area where appeals to intuitions play an important theoretical role. It is also an area other philosophical disciplines often appeal to as a justification for appeal to the intuitive. However, in philosophy of mathematics the role of intuitions has traditionally been to support a form of Platonism, the kind of view associated with, for example, Gödel. Gödel thought of intuition as a form of perception that gave us access to mathematical truths and concepts. In a famous passage, he says:

> But, despite their remoteness from sense experience, we do have something like a perception also of the objects of set theory, as is seen from the fact that the axioms force themselves on us as being true. I don't see any reason why we should have less confidence in this kind of perception, i.e., in mathematical intuition, than in sense perception, which induces us to build up physical theories and to expect that future sense perceptions will agree with them, and, moreover, to believe that a question not decidable now has meaning and may be decided in the future.[5] (quoted in Parsons 1995, p. 65)

A related defense of non-naturalism about moral properties underlies much of G. E. Moore's appeal to intuitions in *Principia Ethica*. The point in this context is that both Gödel and Moore were enormously influential, but, nonetheless, the theoretical work they used intuitions for—a defense of non-naturalism—is not central to most of the contemporary appeals to the intuitive.

According to Jaakko Hintikka, much of contemporary 'intuition'-talk can be traced back to Chomsky's appeal to intuitions as evidence in linguistics. As Hintikka emphasizes, Chomsky's talk of intuition was a result of his commitment to Cartesianism, not a view that others who indulge in 'intuition'-talk typically take themselves to be in the business of defending. As Hintikka points out:

> Unlike his contemporaries, Chomsky could have a good intellectual conscience in appealing to grammatical intuitions, for he is a self-acknowledged Cartesian. He believes in innate ideas, at least in the form of an innate universal grammar. Thus, apart from details, Chomsky had, and presumably has, up his sleeves the same justification for appeals to intuition as someone like Descartes. (1999, p. 132)

The earlier Chomsky, in *The Logical Structure of Linguistic Theory*, advised against appeals to intuitions:

---

[5] See Parsons (1995) for an excellent critical introduction to Gödel's Platonism and the role intuitions play in Gödel's philosophy. That paper also gives an excellent account of how Gödel's use of 'intuitive' is related to Kant's.

It should be clear, then, why the linguist interested in constructing a general theory of linguistic structure, in justifying given grammars or (to put the matter in its more usual form) in constructing procedures of analysis should try to avoid such notions as "intuition." (1975 [1955], pp. 86–7)

This is about as far from an attempt to support Platonism in mathematics as we can get—yet another reason to suspect that the term is used in significantly different ways in the two contexts.

Consider next John Rawls, indisputably one of the most influential political philosophers of the twentieth century and someone who uses the word 'intuition' extensively. For him, appeals to 'intuition' are not attempts to defend Cartesianism or Platonism but rather an attempt to construct a political theory that accords with what he calls "considered judgments" (e.g. 1971, p. 42), where there is no requirement that such judgments are of Platonic objects or have any kind of Cartesian status. In general, Rawls' "considered judgments" are of all kinds and have no distinctive epistemic basis whatsoever.

Finally, consider an influential contemporary trend in metaphilosophy, according to which the intuitive delimits *judgments that are based solely on conceptual competence*. This is the kind of view that is found prominently in the metaphilosophical writings of Bealer and BonJour.[6] The theoretical goals are not those of Gödel, Moore, Chomsky or Rawls. The goals in this tradition are more distinctly metaphilosophical: to show how philosophy as an a priori enterprise is possible.

In sum, the discipline of philosophy seems to use the word 'intuitive' in a very wide range of ways and those uses are put to radically different theoretical purposes.

3.4 Are unreflective uses of 'intuitive' meaningless?

Nothing said so far amounts to anything like a proof that 'intuitive' as used by philosophers is a defective term. Someone wanting to defend the practice might try to show that there are clearly distinct subcommunities

---

[6] BonJour is actually sensitive to the risk of confusion inherent to the different meanings with which 'intuition' is used in the literature, and therefore he prefers the expression 'rational insight' to 'rational intuition', for which in any case he stipulates a semi-technical meaning. See BonJour 1998, p. 102, esp. n. 7.

within the discipline of philosophy that each use 'intuitive' in a distinct and clear way. If so, it could be that within each of these subcommunities, 'intuition' is a well-functioning term that contributes constructively to theory building. While I can't rule out that a case for this can be made, I think it would be exceedingly hard to defend this for those who use 'intuition'-vocabulary in unreflective ways. By 'unreflective' I mean speakers that satisfy at least these conditions: the speaker, at the time of speaking, didn't have a particular theoretical, stipulated definition in mind and didn't intend for her use to be anchored to a particular canonical text or tradition. I am a typical example of a contemporary analytic philosopher who has used 'intuitive' extensively in such an unreflective way. Looking over my previous written work I'm stunned by how much I have used 'intuition'-vocabulary. Here are some typical examples (both from Cappelen and Lepore 2004):

> One way that philosophers of language do so is to think about (or imagine) various utterances of sentences containing *e*. If they have intuitions that a *semantically relevant feature* of those utterances varies from context to context, then that, it is assumed, is evidence *e* is context sensitive. (p. 17)

> So far we have been assuming that contextualism in its various forms is limited to a small class of words that provoke contextualist intuitions of various sorts, e.g., about the uses of quantifiers, counterfactual conditionals, comparative adjectives, psychological, epistemic, and moral attributions. Some authors, however, set no such limits on intuitions about context shifting. (p. 31)

Brief autobiographical remark: when using 'intuition' in these cases, I had nothing particular in mind. Had I been asked what exactly I had in mind by an 'intuitive' judgment or proposition I would have had a hard time giving an articulate or precise answer. It was just a way of speaking that I picked up. I'm not sure exactly from where but it was just how people spoke when I went to school in the late 1980s and early 1990s, first at Oxford and then at Berkeley. People around me used to say things like 'Intuitively, BLAH', and I picked up that habit without thinking carefully about it. I suspect my own history in this respect isn't atypical of philosophers of my generation.

My focus in the next chapters will primarily be on the kind of unreflective speaker that I instantiate.[7] Our use of 'intuitive' is importantly

---

[7] Maybe the past tense 'instantiated' would be more appropriate since in the last couple of years I have become a bit more reflective.

different from those who use say 'brisket' without knowing what brisket is – without being able to distinguish briskets from other cuts of meat. There are familiar theories about how reference can be secured under conditions of ignorance and misinformation. On some views it suffices that speakers stand in an appropriate causal connection to the denotation or that they defer in the appropriate way to an expert group in their linguistic community. However, stories like these cannot be invoked to explain my and other unreflective speakers' use of 'intuitive'. The standard 'brisket' stories require that the speaker *defer* to the usage in their linguistic community.[8] If the speaker has no unified linguistic practice to be parasitic on and, moreover, isn't disposed to defer to anyone, it is much less clear what goes on. If I am right so far in this chapter, (1)–(6) characterize the typical unreflective philosophers' usage of 'intuition'-terminology:

1. *Distancing from English*: The speaker doesn't want to use the term with the meaning it has in English.
2. *Unclear Intentions*: The speaker is unable to articulate what the term means—if asked what intuitions are, she cannot give a clear answer.
3. *There is no unified subcommunity of experts to defer to*: There is no unified and generally recognized set of experts that the speaker defers to.[9]
4. *The speaker is simultaneously a member of several subcommunities in which the term is used in different ways*: Putting aside the issue of expert communities and focusing instead on the 'community of usage', the typical unreflective speaker is a member of a number of distinct such communities (I, for example, talked to Rawls scholars a lot, to linguists, and to historians—arguably they all make up distinct subcommunities).
5. *No agreed upon definition* (see above).
6. *No agreed upon set of paradigms* (see above).

If (1)–(6) correctly characterize many philosophers who indulge in 'intuition'-talk, there is reason for concern. One option at this point is to conclude that such uses are defective: they fail to secure a semantic content for 'intuition'-vocabulary. If so, the right thing to say about such uses is that they are, strictly speaking, meaningless. From a semantic point

---

[8] For the classic presentation of this, see Burge (1979).
[9] The speaker might recognize that some people have thought and written about intuitions, but also recognizes that members of that group vary widely in their views, and she herself has no favorite view.

of view, they utter sentences that don't express propositions (this, however, doesn't prevent them from saying something that's not gibberish, since there is often a significant gap between semantic content and what speakers say by sentences that express those semantic contents). However, while I think this view is exceedingly plausible, it is not a conclusion I want to build on in what follows.[10] The lesson I want to draw from this depressing state of affairs is rather that it is unclear in the extreme how to interpret unreflective uses of 'intuition'-talk by philosophers. Under such conditions we are free, maybe even required, to extensively rely on charity when engaging in interpretation. If we encounter a domain of discourse that's borderline defective, but where we have no reason to suspect fundamental irrationality on behalf of the participants, we should try to engage in what I will loosely call 'charitable reinterpretation'. Our challenge, taken up in the next chapter, will be to figure out how to best make sense of this usage, somewhat unconstrained by the (borderline) defective semantics of these terms. I will suggest that we have a variety of interpretative strategies open to us; the best interpretation will vary with context and in many cases it is massively indeterminate how best to construe 'intuition'-talk. However, in all the cases I consider, none of the charitable reinterpretations support Centrality.

---

[10] It is what I believe, but a full defense of the view will be deferred to future work where I defend this conclusion based on more general views of how terms can become defective. One issue that will arise is how far this kind of semantic defectiveness extends beyond 'intuition'-talk. Maybe a much wider range of philosophical terms, and certainly also terms in other disciplines, exhibit characteristics (1)–(6). My own view, not defended in this book, is that it is a very wide-ranging phenomenon, and that in philosophy terms like 'semantics' (likewise 'pragmatics'), 'a priori' ('a posteriori'), 'justification', 'belief', 'causation', 'evidence', 'person', and many, many other terms fall into this category.

Since it would take us too far afield to discuss this phenomenon in its full generality, the arguments in this book will not significantly rely on the idea that 'intuition'-talk is semantically defective.

4

Philosophers' Use of 'Intuitive' (II):
Some Strategies for Charitable Reinterpretation

Chapter 2 argued that the use of the expression 'Intuitively, BLAH' in ordinary, non-technical English provides no support for AIT or Centrality. Chapter 3 argued that the distinctly philosophical use of 'intuitive' is semantically defective—a linguistic practice bordering on gibberish. The charitable thing to do in such situations is to engage in charitable reinterpretation of the defective discourse and that's the goal of this chapter. The strategies for reinterpretation I suggest are not pretty, neat, or easy to summarize. The reinterpretations will be sensitive to the argumentative context, the question under discussion, and the thesis the author is trying to defend. This results in a lot of variability. The best I can do as an overview is the following division of reinterpretations into three main categories.

> **Strategy 1: Simple Removal.** In many cases, the best thing to do is just remove 'intuitive' and cognate terms. It will have no effect on the substance of the argument, but clarity and argumentative rigor will be improved.

The next two categories draw in part on the meaning of 'intuition' in English (see Chapter 2), and in part on the following passage from Charles Parsons (quoted earlier on p. 11):

When a philosopher talks of his or others' intuitions, that usually means what the person concerned takes to be true at the outset of an inquiry, or as a matter of common sense . . . (1995, p. 59)[1]

---

[1] He adds, "intuitions in this sense are not knowledge, since they need not be true and can be very fallible guides to the truth" (p. 59). This is related to BonJour's description of one of the ways in which philosophers use the term 'intuition': "the vague but useful sense of

I summarize the categories as Snap and Pre-Theoretic:

Strategy 2: Snap. So used, 'Intuitively, *p*' describes judgments or understandings that are (or can be) reached with relatively little reflection or reasoning. It can be used in this way both descriptively and as a hedge.

Strategy 3: Pre-Theoretic. So used, 'Intuitively, *p*' describes *p* as a conclusion reached prior to or independently of an investigation of the question under discussion. The speaker is often suggesting that *p* is in the common ground prior to theorizing. It can be used in this way both descriptively and as a hedge.

These three strategies (and variations on them) help us understand the vast majority of unreflective uses by philosophers. In many cases it will be indeterminate which strategy to pursue—the speaker's intentions don't settle it, the meanings of the words don't settle it, nor does the context settle it. This chapter provides a wealth of examples for the reader to explore. I conclude in Section 4.5 that if these are the right interpretative strategies, 'intuition'-talk by philosophers provides no support for Centrality.

Two preliminary points before moving on to the interpretative project. First, my strategy in this chapter differs significantly from what is found in most metaphilosophical discussions of intuitions and 'intuition'. Most intuition-theorists spend hardly any time trying to show how their accounts of 'intuitive', 'intuitively' etc., help make sense of actual use of this term in philosophical texts. This might have many reasons—I suspect the most important one is that these theorists take themselves to be engaged in at least partly a normative project where they can either stipulate what 'intuition' means or make a proposal for how it *should* be used. If that's the goal, the investigation of how the expression is actually used by philosophers might seem less important.[2] My goal is to evaluate AIT. In that context, careful attention to usage is essential—the goal is to find out how philosophers as a matter of fact use 'intuition' and related terminology.

'intuition' that is philosophically current, that which pertains to judgments and convictions that, though considered and reflective, are not arrived at via an explicit discursive process and thus are (hopefully) uncontaminated by theoretical or dialectical considerations" (1998, p. 102, n. 7).

[2] Though even for the normative project careful investigation of usage is important: how we do use the term has impact on how it ought to be used.

My second preliminary point is simply to encourage the reader to keep in mind that if I am right and not a single use of 'intuitive' has a clear and uncontroversial interpretation, that tends to undermine AIT. Centrality contains the word 'intuition' and proponents of Centrality must think it has a determinate meaning as it occurs in Centrality. Call this meaning M. AIT purports to support Centrality by appeal to how philosophers use 'intuition' and cognate terms. But if the relevant uses of 'intuition' differ widely in meaning, they can't in general have the same content as it has in that particular articulation of Centrality, i.e. M. So in general, use of 'intuitive' doesn't support Centrality.[3, 4]

4.1 First strategy: Simple Removal

The simplest strategy is this: remove the word 'intuitive' and keep what remains. Paradigmatically, go from 'It is intuitive that p' or 'I have the intuition that p' to 'p'. In many cases, this can be done with minimal revision and no loss of argumentative force. All we've done is surgically remove a little word that created confusion and probably shouldn't have been used in the first place. This passage from Jaegwon Kim serves as an initial illustration:

So a moral kind, which, by definition, is morally homogeneous–can be causally/ explanatorily heterogeneous in virtue of comprising radically different natural kinds. This seems intuitively right: just think of all the diverse actions that instantiate moral rightness—it would be "hopelessly off-base," to use Sayre-McCord's term, to expect them to exhibit causal homogeneity to any significant degree. The situation here seems essentially the same as the case of tables. (1997, p. 297)

---

[3] Compare here to the kinds of moves contextualists about 'know' will have to make in order to formulate general principles about the role of knowledge in, say, assertion or practical reasoning. In articulating such principles, contextualists should not *use* 'knowledge' since then the claim would be about what that word happens to mean in the context of the articulation of the principle and so not capture the relevant context sensitivity. One solution here is to go metalinguistic and that I suspect is what proponents of Centrality who endorse context sensitivity of 'intuition' as well as AIT would have to do.

[4] An additional reason to think that proponents of Centrality are committed to the non-context sensitivity of 'intuition' is that when they tell us what they think the word means, they never say that it is context sensitive (see for example Bealer 1992, 1996).

The word 'intuitively' doesn't serve any argumentative function in this text; deletion improves the passage by removing an obscure term from a point that otherwise is clear.[5]

The same strategy works well in the following passage from Williamson:

> In the lottery case, it is ~~intuitively~~ clear, given the nature of my evidence, that I did not know that your ticket did not win. (2000, p. 249)

Clarity, it seems to me, is improved by deleting "intuitively". What Williamson means to say is *that it is clear, given the nature of his evidence, that he did not know that the ticket did not win*. The move from 'It is intuitively clear' to 'It is clear' doesn't leave out anything of argumentative significance, but improves clarity.

For a third illustration, consider this passage from Kathrin Koslicki:

> [I]f, contrary to my remarks in the last two sections, Lewis' defense of Unrestricted Composition were successful, then it would follow that the material world is far more densely populated than we ordinarily assume it to be, with all manner of gerrymandered and intuitively bizarre mereological sums (such as the notorious "trout-turkey," whose parts are the, still undetached, upper half of a trout along with the, still undetached, lower half of a turkey). Most of these counterintuitive sums of course never turn out to be of any interest to us, outside of philosophical disputes over ontology, and thus, as Lewis allows, they never make it into the ordinarily restricted (and frequently fuzzy) range of our everyday quantifiers. (2008, p. 40)

Note first that Koslicki doesn't use 'intuitively' to modify 'gerrymandered', just 'bizarre'. Insofar as she's committed to the gerrymanderedness of these objects (not just their intuitive gerrymanderedness), it's hard to see that she is not also committed to their bizarreness. At no point in this article does anything depend on the intuitive bizarreness of these objects rather than their bizarreness. So elimination, it seems to me, will improve clarity here.

The Removal Strategy will work, I suspect, in a very wide range of cases. Careful study of uses of 'intuitive' will reveal that it often plays no significant argumentative role and that removal will improve overall argumentative transparency.

---

[5] The remaining 'seem' is used as a hedge, more on that below.

4.2 Second and third strategies: Snap and Pre-Theoretic

Removal doesn't always work. In what follows I sketch two alternative interpretative strategies that can be usefully explored when encountering ineliminable occurrences of 'intuitive' in philosophical texts: *Snap* and *Pre-Theoretic*. Each of these has a primary descriptive use, but each also gives rise to distinctive forms of hedging (just as 'I think' has a primary descriptive use that gives rise to a distinctive kind of hedging). In many cases it is indeterminate whether 'intuitive' is used descriptively or as a hedge.

4.2.1 Snap

Unsurprisingly, unreflective philosophers can often be interpreted as using 'intuitively' more or less as it is used in English. So understood, it is used to describe claims, judgments and answers to questions that are (or can be) reached with relatively little reflection or reasoning by the person giving the answer:

- *Snap-Judgment*: So understood, 'Intuitively, p' says that the judgment that p can be reached with relatively little effort and reasoning.[6]

As we have seen, what counts as relatively little reasoning and effort is highly context sensitive.

Sometimes 'intuitively' characterizes acts of understanding along similar lines:

- *Snap-Understanding*: So understood, 'Intuitively, p' says that p can be understood with relatively little effort and reasoning.

Snap-Judgment and Snap-Understanding are connected. Typically *Snap-Judgment* requires *Snap-Understanding*: if p is not easy to grasp, p can't be easy to judge true.

These two kinds of Snap interpretations give rise to at least two kinds of hedging:

---

[6] This is obviously a simplistic gloss on the phenomenon I have in mind. Some would want to also include the speed with which the judgment is made, and more detailed descriptions of the psychological mechanisms through which the judgment is reached. While those issues are interesting for a study of Snap judgments, they will not prove to be relevant to the issues discussed in this chapter. (For some references to the psychological literature on what I call 'Snap judgments', see note 16 in Chapter 2.)

- *Snap-Judgment Hedge*: So used, 'Intuitively, *p*' provides *p* (not *Intuitively, p*), as the answer to the question under discussion and the function of 'intuitively' is to weaken the speaker's commitment to that answer by indicating that the answer has been or can be reached in a Snap way (i.e. without elaborate or extensive reasoning on behalf of the person giving the answer). That the speaker flags this can be a way to indicate that she thinks additional reflection might be needed: she is less than fully committed to *p* because of the relative lack of careful reasoning that has gone into the judgment.
- *Snap-Understanding Hedge:* So used, 'Intuitively, *p*' provides *p* as the answer to the question and the function of 'intuitively' is to weaken the speaker's commitment to that answer by indicating that *p* is an answer meant for easy consumption—it is not a full or precise answer.

To illustrate first consider a passage from a Bloggingheads.tv exchange between Sober and Fodor. At a crucial point in the conversation, Fodor says:

Now look, Central Park is a very small place, right? And nevertheless it provides a supporting ecology, as it were, for this vast number of different kinds of phenotypes. I just think it is wildly unlikely that somebody is going to find a phenotype and a property of the environment, or find a set of phenotypes and a set of environmental properties that pair off in the required kind of way. That's not an argument, it's just an intuition.[7]

The Snap-Judgment interpretation makes sense of this. The conclusion *that it is wildly unlikely that somebody is going to find a phenotype and a property of the environment, or find a set of phenotypes and a set of environmental properties, that pair off in the required kind of way* has been reached without careful reasoning or empirical investigation. He uses 'intuition' to flag this and also to hedge his commitment to the conclusion.

I find that the Snap-Understanding interpretation is the easiest one to find examples of. Here is a passage from Ted Sider's paper, "The Evil of Death: What Can Metaphysics Contribute?", that lends itself to such an interpretation:

The presentist describes the past and future using these and other tense operators. For example, he would describe the ordinary fact that there once existed dinosaurs by saying in his fundamental language:
 (D) P (there exists a dinosaur)

---

[7] http://bloggingheads.tv/diavlogs/26848, 19.35–45

Intuitively, this means that the embedded sentence, 'there exists a dinosaur', is true with respect to some time in the past. However, the presentist denies that this intuitive gloss is any kind of metaphysical reduction. Rather, the tense operators are metaphysically unanalyzeable. (forthcoming, p. 7)

It doesn't look like 'Intuitively' can be removed here. Its function seems to be primarily to indicate that the gloss given of (D) (i.e. *that the embedded sentence, 'there exists a dinosaur', is true with respect to some time in the past*) is not fully accurate. It is an easy way to interpret (D), but not exactly correct.

A related point can be made about this passage from Plantinga:

A *quantificational model structure* is then a model structure together with a function *f(W)* that assigns to each *W* in *K* a domain of individuals—intuitively, says Kripke, these are the individuals that exist in that world. (1979, p. 124)

What is characterized as 'intuitive' is the description of the set of domain of individuals as *the individuals that exist in that world*. This is an easy-to-grasp characterization of the domain—the full theory will replace that characterization with a more accurate characterization that is less easy to process. As a result, the modifier 'intuitively' serves in part as a hedge, cautioning the reader to not take this as a fully accurate account of the domain.

In the following passage Schiffer is using 'intuitively' in more or less this way:

Sally s-believes to degree 1 that the hair situation on Tom's scalp is either *H* or else not-*H*. If she were certain that *H* obtained, she would s-believe to degree 1 that Tom was bald; that is, intuitively put, *H*s obtaining would, she is certain, secure that Tom was determinately bald. (2003, p. 220)

To put a point intuitively is, in this context, to put it in a way that is easy to understand and grasp—that doesn't draw heavily on theoretical machinery. Schiffer is hedging insofar as he tells his readers that this way of putting the point can be improved upon.

Finally, here's a passage from Keith DeRose:

Well, what is a 'clarifying device'? Though there may be significantly different ways of specifying the details of the notion (and those who wish to use the notion to object to contextualism may try out different precisifications), the basic idea is quite intuitive and straightforward. (2009, p. 180)

Again, Snap-Understanding seems an obvious way to interpret this; after all, the notion of 'a clarifying device' isn't true or false, and so the

Snapness is here most naturally used to describe the process of grasping or understanding the notion (it is not a Snap judgment of truth or falsity).

4.2.2 Pre-theoretic

According to the Pre-theoretic interpretation, 'Intuitively, p' means something close to 'Pre-theoretically, p'. 'Pre-theoretically' does not mean the same as *prior to all theorizing*. To characterize a judgment as 'pre-theoretic' is to describe it as being independent of the answer to a certain set of contextually determined questions, Q. Typically Q are the questions under discussion in the speech context. This is a gloss on Parsons' "what the person concerned takes to be true at the outset of an inquiry, or as a matter of common sense" (1995, p. 59).

'Pre-theoretically, p' doesn't rule out that p is easy to understand or that the judgment that p comes with the relevant kind of ease. In such cases, Pre-theoretic and Snap go together. That said, Snap and Pre-theoretic can come apart. That p is a judgment made independently of the answer to some set of questions, Q, doesn't rule out that p is complex and that it requires extensive reasoning and expertise to understand and evaluate.

'Pre-theoretic' can be used as a hedge. So used, 'Intuitively, p' provides p (not *Intuitively, p*) as the answer to the question and the function of 'intuitively' is to weaken the speaker's commitment to that answer by indicating that it is given prior to (or independently of) an adequate investigation into the topic under discussion. If the judgment that p is reached prior to investigating a set of questions Q, then it is, in a significant way, *uninformed* since it is reached without the benefit of knowing the answers to Q.[8]

Before giving some examples of how 'intuitive' is used in this way, here is an example, from Jeff King, in which 'pretheoretically' is used in the way I claim 'intuitively' is often used:

> To begin with, pretheoretically it seems that sentences encode pieces of information and that distinct sentences may encode the same piece of information, as is perhaps the case with 'snow is white', and 'schnee ist weiss'.... Second, we think that some things are the possessors of modal features such as being impossible, possible and necessary. Our pretheoretical talk suggests that these are the same

---

[8] However, that p is settled independently of the answer to Q (i.e. is pre-theoretic in the relevant sense) *need not* indicate a weakening of the speaker's commitment to p. She might think p is established independently of Q but still remain fully committed to p.

things that are true and false, since we talk of things being necessarily true, possibly false and so on. (2007, pp. 1–2)

The idea explored in what follows is that some philosophers would have used 'intuitively' where King uses 'pretheoretically' and might have succeeded in communicating pretty much what King does.[9] However, this also makes clear how difficult it is to understand 'pretheoretic.' The exact function of 'pretheoretic' in the above passage is hard to paraphrase. The use of the expression seems to have a dual function: it indicates some kind of hedged assertion of the three claims and at the same time serves as a reminder that these are propositions we are already committed to. They are in some sense in the common ground. Note the transition from 'pretheoretically' in the first sentences to 'we think' in the second sentence. The use of 'we think' serves as a reminder to the reader that the claim *that some things are the possessors of modal features such as being impossible, possible and necessary* is in the common ground at this point of investigation.

The Bloggingheads.tv exchange between Sober and Fodor on natural selection transcribed above provides another illustration. Sober says:

...and the main thesis of this part of Jerry's argument is that although the distinction between selection for and free-riding is intuitive—I hope, I think it is intuitive [*Fodor nods*]—in fact the theory of natural selection cannot actually make good on this concept, it can't really use this intuitive concept, although it pretends to do so.[10]

Sober here first characterizes *a distinction* (between *selection for* and *free-riding*) as intuitive. He goes on to describe this distinction as *an intuitive concept*. Putting aside the switch from *distinction* to *concept*, it is clear that this isn't a passage that lends itself easily to a Snap-Understanding interpretation. The distinction between selection for and free-riding is (fairly) complicated and requires knowledge and reflection to get one's head around. A natural interpretation of this exchange is to treat Sober and Fodor as agreeing to put in the common ground the proposition *that there is such a distinction and that an adequate theory should account for it*. This is settled pre-theoretically in the following restricted sense: it can be taken as established prior to settling the question under discussion (which is,

---

[9] Of course, if you mean 'pre-theoretic' it is better to use that term than to use 'intuitive'—so King is an example of how being a reflective speaker is better than being an unreflective user of 'intuitive.'

[10] http://bloggingheads.tv/diavlogs/26848, 10.33–56

roughly, whether Darwin's notion of evolution treats 'select-for' as in some sense a transparent context).

Here is another illustration of Pre-theoretic from Tyler Burge:

> I shall have little further to say in defense of the second and third steps of the thought experiment. Both rest on their intuitive plausibility, not on some particular theory. The third step, for example, certainly does not depend on a view that contents are merely sentences the subject is disposed to utter, interpreted as his community interprets them. It is compatible with several philosophical accounts of mental contents, including those that appeal to more abstract entities such as Fregean thoughts or Russellian propositions, and those that seek to deny that content-clauses indicate any *thing* that might be called a content. (1979, p. 88)

I will have more to say about this passage in Chapter 8 below. For now I want only to point out that it lends itself to the Pre-Theoretic interpretation. Burge is talking about the second and third stage of his famous arthritis thought experiment in "Individualism and the Mental." He is explaining why he will not discuss the second and third steps of that thought experiment—why the entire focus of his discussion is on the first step. On the proposed interpretation, he claims it is because what he says about those steps is in the common ground between him and his opponents prior to inquiry. Note that there is no indication that the judgments about the second and third steps are reached in a Snap manner. They might be for some, but they need not be.[11]

Here is Sider arguing against Jonathan Schaffer's version of monism. Sider says:

> I take monism seriously enough to give arguments against it. All fundamental properties, for the monist, are properties of the entire world. (They must be, for there are no other objects in the monist's ontology to *have* fundamental properties.) My arguments turn on this fact.
>
> What is *intuitively* wrong with monism is that it takes the fundamental facts to be facts about the whole world. When an object has an intrinsic property, for instance a certain shape, that **seems** to be a fact just about that object, not about the rest of the world. When two things are separated by a certain distance, that is of course not a fact about either object individually, but it **seems** to be a fact just about the two;

---

[11] I often find audiences object to this characterization of Burge's paper, but I have never seen any arguments presented for why Burge must be read as requiring the judgments in question to exhibit Snap-like features. There simply isn't any evidence of that in the paper. For further discussion of Burge's example, see Chapter 8 below.

the fact doesn't bring in any other objects. Now, there may be some facts that are much more holistic than this, for instance facts about quantum-entangled systems. But monism goes too far; it makes every fundamental fact *maximally* holistic. Only if we are *pluralists* and posit a plurality of sub-world entities can we avoid this consequence. (2007, pp. 2–3, my bolded emphases)

The use of 'intuitively' and the following two uses of 'seems' can naturally be construed as claims about what we are pre-theoretically committed to. As such, they also serve a hedging function, indicating that Sider does not take himself, at this stage, to have established that it is wrong to take fundamental facts to be facts about the whole world (or that when an object has a shape, that is a fact about that object, not about the rest of the world).

4.3 The three strategies at work: Some complicated mixed cases

One point that should be emphasized throughout is the complexity and difficulty of interpreting philosophers' use of 'intuition'-vocabulary.[12] There is no simple translation manual that will capture the richness and messiness of this practice. What I have outlined above are some strategies that I suspect will be helpful guidelines in a wide range of cases, but I don't expect it to be an easy task to apply these to all specific passages in which philosophers indulge their weakness for 'intuition'-talk.

To further illustrate these points, I will consider a number of typical passages in which philosophers use 'intuitive' and cognate terms unreflectively (i.e. use it without making clear what they mean by the term). I will start by looking at a number of passages in one of the greatest works of twentieth-century philosophy, Kripke's *Naming and Necessity*. This book is both a useful and important case study. It is useful because it illustrates natural applications of some of the interpretative strategies outlined above. It is important because a plausible case can be made that Kripke's extensive use of 'intuition'-terminology in that book influenced a generation of philosophers. Not only was the substance of this book enormously

---

[12] More precisely, what is difficult is to give informative paraphrases—the correct content can always be specified disquotationally (putting aside context sensitivity).

influential, but so too was its more elusive style and tone.[13] Kripke is a paradigm of a unreflective user of 'intuition'-vocabulary. He uses these terms extensively, applies them to ideas, notions, arguments, and claims; he talks about intuitions that are "natural" (pp. 5, 15), or "direct" (p. 14), but he *never* tells us what he means by these terms. While this is an unfortunate feature of an otherwise great work, there are, I will suggest, very innocuous and obvious interpretations of this use: more or less all the occurrences of these terms in *Naming and Necessity* mean something in the neighborhood of 'pre-theoretic'. As a background, recall that an ongoing theme of *Naming and Necessity* is that philosophers of language and metaphysicians have been misled by mistaken theories (he sometimes calls them "pictures"—see e.g. p. 94) of how names and other singular terms refer to objects.[14] He does three things: remind the reader of the views we hold prior to being misled by these theories, argue against the theories, and in favor of a new picture that better accords with our pre-theoretic views.

I'll start with some passages in which Kripke talks about the view that terms are rigid designators (these are all taken from the Preface). I will insert in square brackets the alternative interpretation and the claim is that nothing substantive is lost by these substitutions (at least there is no evidence in the text that Kripke had anything else in mind):

Our intuitive [pre-theoretic] idea of naming suggests that names are rigid, but I suppose that at one time I vaguely supposed, influenced by prevailing presuppositions, that since obviously there are contingent identities between ordinary so-called names, such ordinary names must not be rigid. (p. 4)

Eventually I came to realize—this realization inaugurated the aforementioned work of 1963–4—that the received presuppositions against the necessity of

---

[13] Hintikka's 1999 paper, "The Emperor's New Intuitions", uses Kripke as the paradigm of someone who relies on intuitions and his evidence is exclusively based on Kripke's use of 'intuition'-vocabulary.

[14] More generally, there is a kind of anti-theoretical tendency that runs through all of *Naming and Necessity*. It is hard to read the book without getting the sense that Kripke continuously expresses a general skepticism about philosophical theories, culminating in statements like: "(It really is a nice theory. The only defect I think it has is probably common to all philosophical theories. It's wrong. You may suspect me of proposing another theory in its place; but I hope not, because I'm sure it's wrong too if it is a theory.)" (p. 64). He talks a lot about 'pictures' as opposed to theories. Just what he means by 'a picture' and the connection between pictures and theories is not obvious. His use of 'intuitive' should be understood in that light and 'pre-theoretic' more or less captures what he has in mind.

identities between ordinary names were incorrect, that the natural **intuition [pre-theoretic view]** that the names of ordinary language are rigid designators can in fact be upheld. (p. 5)

Although the idea is now a familiar one, I will give a brief restatement of the idea of rigid designation, and the **intuition [pre-theoretic view]** about names that underlies it. Consider:

(1) Aristotle was fond of dogs.

A proper understanding of this statement involves an understanding both of the (extensionally correct) conditions under which it is in fact true, *and* of the conditions under which a counterfactual course of history, resembling the actual course in some respects but not in others, would be correctly (partially) described by (1). Presumably everyone agrees that there is a certain man—the philosopher we call 'Aristotle'—such that, as a matter of fact, (1) is true if and only if *he* was fond of dogs. The thesis of rigid designation is simply—subtle points aside—that the same paradigm applies to the truth conditions of (1) as it describes *counterfactual* situations. (p. 6)

Why would Kripke keep reminding the reader that the views he argues for are endorsed by speakers who have not been misled by false theories? This question has no simple answer, but in part it is because he thinks the pre-theoretic views we hold are true and that the philosophical theories he tries to undermine are false. So it's a kind of rhetorical device used to 'shake' readers out of what he takes to be their misguided training and philosophical prejudice. On such a construal, his appeal to what's intuitive is doing no *substantive* argumentative work—that work is all done when he gives arguments for his favored picture and presents evidence against the theories he opposes.[15] This interpretation is supported by a passage in which he more or less explicitly tells us that he means 'pre-theoretic' by 'intuitive':[16]

It is even suggested in the literature, that though a notion of necessity may have some sort of intuition behind it (we do think some things could have been otherwise; other things we don't think could have been otherwise), this notion [of a distinction between necessary and contingent properties] is just a doctrine

---

[15] Note that there is no evidence that Kripke at any point treats 'being endorsed prior to a theory' as carrying evidential weight (or being a source of evidence), i.e. there is no evidence that he treats being intuitive as carrying evidential weight. That *p* is endorsed by many people prior to theorizing is of course not in general evidence in favor of *p*.

[16] Related interpretation of this passage can be found in Deutsch (2010, p. 451, n. 2).

made up by some bad philosopher, who (I guess) didn't realize that there are several ways of referring to the same thing. I don't know if some philosophers have not realized this; but at any rate it is very far from being true that this idea [that a property can meaningfully be held to be essential or accidental to an object independently of its description] **is a notion which has no intuitive content, which means nothing to the ordinary man**. (p. 41)

I take "which means nothing to the ordinary man" to spell out what he means by saying that a notion has "no intuitive content". To have intuitive content, for Kripke, is to have content to the non-theoretician, i.e., roughly speaking, pre-theoretically.[17]

This is not to say that all of Kripke's use of 'intuition'-vocabulary is easy to interpret. Consider this passage from his paper "Outline of a Theory of Truth":

> We wish to capture an intuition of somewhat the following kind. Suppose we are explaining the word 'true' to someone who does not yet understand it. We may say that we are entitled to assert (or deny) of any sentence that it is true precisely under the circumstances when we can assert (or deny) the sentence itself. Our interlocutor then can understand what it means, say, to attribute truth to (6) ('snow is white') but he will still be puzzled about attributions of truth to sentences containing the word 'true' itself. Since he did not understand these sentences initially, it will be equally nonexplanatory, initially, to explain to him that to call such a sentence 'true' ('false') is tantamount to asserting (denying) the sentence itself. (1975, p. 701)

This strikes me as an example of massive indeterminacy and the interpretative task is hard. It is, for starters, unclear what the 'kind' of intuition he has in mind is. Is it a kind of intuition about what will happen when explaining 'true' to someone who does not understand it, or is the intuitive idea what we are trying to convey to such a person? Kripke seems to be appealing to the non-theoretical nature of the first set of claims—so a kind of 'pre-theoretic' reading could be involved. On the other hand, it is hard to see what would be lost if we read the first sentence as 'We wish to capture the following.' I suspect nothing of significance is lost. This, however, is not an obvious case and illustrates how hard it is to decipher philosophers' 'intuition'-talk.

---

[17] Limitations of space prevent an even more careful study of the ways in which Kripke uses 'intuition'-vocabulary, but my own sense is that practically all the occurrences of those terms in *Naming and Necessity* can be understood as something in the neighborhood of 'pre-theoretic' and that this reflects underlying anti-theoretical, pro-common sense assumptions that play important roles in his work.

Moving on from Kripke, consider next John MacFarlane on utterance truth:

> If utterance truth is a technical notion, we had better make sure our intuitions about it are in line with our theories, not the other way around. Rejecting a theory because it makes predictions about utterance truth that "sound funny" is not sound methodology. (2009, p. 246)

This is a puzzling passage. Here is one construal of what is going on: MacFarlane is suggesting that we make sure "intuition about [utterance truth]" are in line with our theories, and that we don't adjust our theories about utterance truth to our intuitions. This rules out the pre-theoretic interpretation, but is, maybe, compatible with the Snap-Judgment strategy. He issues the advice that theorists should work on adjusting their Snap judgments to their theories, not the other way around.

Next consider Cappelen and Hawthorne on relativism about truth:

> Consider the following case.
> *Case One*: Suppose Sabrina hears a conversation in which Nicole says 'Bill Clinton is an enemy and Hillary Clinton is a friend'. Suppose, unbeknownst to Sabrina, Nicole is a reporter that is describing the friends and enemies of a particular politician. Sabrina naturally hears Nicole as describing Nicole. Sabrina goes on to say to someone else 'Nicole said that Bill Clinton is an enemy and Hillary Clinton is a friend'.
>
> Now Sabrina certainly *could* have made a guarded speech. She could have said:
>
> > Nicole was talking the other day about someone, maybe herself, maybe someone else. She said that Bill Clinton is an enemy and Hillary Clinton is a friend.
>
> The latter speech is intuitively true. But what of the speech that Sabrina made in an unguarded moment? Intuitions may be a bit wobbly here, but it is tempting to think that she actually expressed something false by 'Nicole said that Bill Clinton is an enemy and Hillary Clinton is a friend' in that context (namely that Nicole said that Bill is an enemy of hers and Hillary is a friend of hers). (2009, pp. 42–3)

First note that the authors are *not* saying that the latter speech is judged true after quick and careless reflection. Speaking as one of the authors, I can report that the authors thought very carefully about this and expected their readers to do the same. That said, it is unclear exactly what the authors had in mind: one option is to eliminate 'intuitively' and focus on what remains, i.e. "The latter speech is true", or they could be interpreted as using 'intuitive' to indicate a kind of hedged commitment to the truth of the modified content.

My last example is from "Epiphenomenal Qualia" in which Frank Jackson is providing important stage setting for the Knowledge argument. Jackson says:

> There are many qualia freaks, and some of them say that their rejection of Physicalism is an unargued intuition. I think that they are being unfair to themselves. They have the following argument. Nothing you could tell of a physical sort captures the smell of a rose, for instance. Therefore, Physicalism is false. By our lights this is a perfectly good argument. It is obviously not to the point to question its validity, and the premise is intuitively obviously true both to them and to me.
>
> I must, however, admit that it is weak from a polemical point of view. There are, unfortunately for us, many who do not find the premise intuitively obvious. The task then is to present an argument whose premises are obvious to all, or at least to as many as possible. This I try to do in §I with what I will call "the Knowledge argument." (1982, pp. 127–8)

Jackson has gone on to write a lot about philosophical methodology and he has written about what he thinks intuitions are and their role in philosophy (Jackson 1998). I will, however, not take those views to be authoritative for how to interpret this passage. It seems to me that the three occurrences of 'intuitively' and the one of 'intuition' should be interpreted using a mixture of Pre-theoretic and Snap as follows (the bracketed material can replace the original in strikethrough):

> There are many qualia freaks, and some of them say that their rejection of Physicalism is an unargued ~~intuition~~ [Snap judgment]. I think that they are being unfair to themselves. They have the following argument. Nothing you could tell of a physical sort captures the smell of a rose, for instance. Therefore, Physicalism is false. By our lights this is a perfectly good argument. It is obviously not to the point to question its validity, and the premise is ~~intuitively obviously true both to them and to me~~ [in the common ground between the qualia freaks and me].
>
> I must, however, admit that it is weak from a polemical point of view. There are, unfortunately for us, many who do not ~~find the premise intuitively obvious~~ [pre-theoretically judge that the premises are true]. The task then is to present an argument whose premises are obvious to all, or at least to as many as possible. This I try to do in §I with what I will call "the Knowledge argument."

So understood, the goal of the Knowledge argument is to find premises that Jackson and as many as possible of his opponents can agree on without making controversial philosophical assumptions. He wants the premises to be *obviously* true: there is no indication that this means anything other than that they are easy to recognize as true, or can be agreed on by assuming relatively few controversial philosophical assumptions.

4.4 Taking stock

These are just a few strategies for interpreting philosophers' use of 'intuitive' and cognate terms. There is, I think, a research project here that those interested in the role of intuitions in philosophy should engage in, but so far have not: Look *in careful detail* at a wide range of philosophical texts containing 'intuitive' and propose interpretations. What the examples above should make abundantly clear is that no *one* interpretation will account for *all* cases. Moreover, for each case we look at it is massively underdetermined what exactly is contributed by 'intuitively'. I suspect that even with complete access to the speaker's mental states at the time of utterance, we couldn't settle it conclusively in any one of these cases.

It should also be clear from the examples above that it is particularly difficult to tell whether 'intuitively' is used as a hedge, used descriptively or both. However, in some cases it will be clear that we need a descriptive reading. Consider for example an utterance of 'Intuitively, *p*, but I don't think *p* is correct'. In such utterances, *p* is explicitly not presented as an answer to the question, and the main point of the first conjunct is to describe *p* as 'intuitive'—for example, as the quick, unreflective answer (assuming the Snap interpretation is correct in this case). The second conjunct makes clear that the speaker thinks the quick answer should be rejected. As a rule of thumb, such embedded occurrences indicate a descriptive rather than a hedge use.[18]

4.5 No appeal to special feelings, conceptual competence, or default justificatory status

The interpretative strategies I've made use of above have made no appeal to three elements that are much discussed in the contemporary literature on intuitions:

---

[18] Descriptive uses can occur unembedded too, and in those cases it is typically harder to tell descriptive and hedge uses apart.

1. *Special Feelings (seems-true phenomenology)*: Many intuition-theorists think that the intuitive comes with a special phenomenology. The examples of 'intuition'-talk considered in this chapter provide evidence that no reference to a special phenomenology is required to interpret such talk. As an illustration, consider again this passage from Schiffer:

> Sally s-believes to degree 1 that the hair situation on Tom's scalp is either *H* or else not-*H*. If she were certain that *H* obtained, she would s-believe to degree 1 that Tom was bald; that is, **intuitively** put, *H*s obtaining would, she is certain, secure that Tom was determinately bald. (2003, p. 220)

There is no evidence that Schiffer thinks that he has said something true only if *Hs obtaining would, she is certain, secure that Tom was determinately bald* is accompanied by a distinctive phenomenology. This point generalizes to the other cases discussed.

2. *Conceptual Competence*: Many intuition-theorists think that intuitive judgments are those *based only on conceptual competence*. The examples of 'intuition'-talk considered in this chapter provide evidence that when interpreting such talk, appeal to conceptual competence is entirely irrelevant. This passage from Jaegwon Kim illustrates the point:

> So a moral kind, which, by definition, is morally homogeneous—can be causally/explanatorily heterogeneous in virtue of comprising radically different natural kinds. This seems intuitively right: just think of all the diverse actions that instantiate moral rightness—it would be "hopelessly off-base," to use Sayre-McCord's term, to expect them to exhibit causal homogeneity to any significant degree. (1997, p. 297)

It would be an extreme overinterpretation of this passage to assume that Kim is claiming that it is a conceptual truth *that it is off-base to expect that all the diverse actions that instantiate moral rightness exhibit causal homogeneity to any significant degree*. This point generalizes to the other cases discussed. It is not a necessary condition on the truth of (unreflective uses of) a sentence containing 'intuitive' that it denotes a conceptual truth (or something that appears to be a conceptual truth).[19]

---

[19] This of course does not rule out that some philosophers might think the proposition in question is a conceptual truth. The claim is only that this is not required for the truth of what Kim says. For more on my view of conceptual truth and justification, see Chapter 10 below.

3. *Default Justificatory Status*: Many intuition-theorists think that intuitive judgments have a special kind of default justificatory status. Again, the examples of 'intuition'-talk considered in this chapter provide evidence that when interpreting typical 'intuition'-talk no appeal to such a special status is needed. Consider again this passage from Sider:

> The presentist describes the past and future using these and other tense operators. For example, he would describe the ordinary fact that there once existed dinosaurs by saying in his fundamental language:
> (D) P (there exists a dinosaur)
> Intuitively, this means that the embedded sentence, 'there exists a dinosaur', is true with respect to some time in the past. However, the presentist denies that this intuitive gloss is any kind of metaphysical reduction. Rather, the tense operators are metaphysically unanalyzeable. (forthcoming, p. 7)

It's completely implausible to take Sider to use 'intuitively' here to indicate that *this means that the embedded sentence, 'there exists a dinosaur', is true with respect to some time in the past* has a special kind of default justificatory status. Again, this point generalizes to the other cases discussed.

A reader could reasonably wonder whether the points just made are compatible with my emphasis on the great variability in uses of 'intuitive'. If there are so many different uses, how can I rule out that in at least some cases that term is used to describe a judgment accompanied by a special feeling, derived solely from conceptual competence or possessing some kind of special justificatory status?

I'm somewhat open-minded on this issue. However, when theorizing about a field as messy as this, the goal is to find some helpful generalizations and strategies for interpreting unreflective uses of 'intuitive' by philosophers not engaged in metaphilosophy. For those purposes, I think cases that require appeal to special feelings, conceptual analysis or special epistemic status will be outliers and so not helpful to focus on. These features are relevant for the most part when 'intuitive' is used by a small group of metaphilosophers; it is not characteristic of how the term is used unreflectively by philosophers who don't have a methodological point to make (and have no general theory of intuitions in mind). A general point about interpretation worth emphasizing in this context is that if an interpretation of an occurrence of 'intuitive' commits the author of the interpreted text to controversial views for which there is no independent evidence in the text, then that counts against the interpretation. This applies to all three proposals considered above:

- The claim that there are conceptual truths is highly controversial and for any particular propositions, the claim that *it* is a conceptual truth is even more controversial than the general claim that there are *some* (especially if it is not totally trivial like 'If a is taller than *b* and *b* is taller than *c*, then *a* is taller than *c*). So to saddle an unreflective philosopher who just casually happens to say 'Intuitively, *p*' with a commitment to *p* being a conceptual truth is an over-committing interpretation and therefore uncharitable.
- The assumption that claims characterized as 'intuitive' come with a certain phenomenology might seem somewhat innocent, but it is nonetheless controversial and it is inappropriate to assume that an unreflective use of 'intuition' commits the author to the view that the claim comes with a certain phenomenology and that what she says *cannot* be true unless that phenomenology is present. This is particularly significant if you share Williamson's view that the alleged special phenomenology is a myth, as I do. Williamson, to take but one example, explicitly argues that there is no such special phenomenology when he reflects on claims typically characterized as 'intuitive' (2007, p. 217). It would be uncharitable in the extreme to take occurrences of 'intuitive' in his work as being false if there is no such feeling present.
- Finally, the idea that some propositions have a special, default justificatory status is controversial even among epistemologists. Those who think *some* propositions have such a status seldom agree on which particular propositions have that kind of status or what it is to have it. So, again, to take an unreflective utterance of 'Intuitively, *p*' to commit the speaker to the view that *p* has this special and controversial kind of epistemic status is an inappropriate over-interpretation.

What I see as a significant advantage for the interpretative strategies outlined in this chapter is that they are *light*. They keep the number of controversial commitments we attribute to the authors at a minimum.[20]

---

[20] This is not to deny that the proper interpretation of some sentences will require attributing somewhat controversial views to speakers. If, for example, Davidson (1967) is correct, then anyone who says 'Juliet kissed Romeo quickly at midnight' is committed (in some sense) to the

4.6 Back to Centrality and AIT: None of these interpretative strategies are Centrality-supporting

According to AIT, Centrality gets support from philosophers' use of 'intuitive' and cognate terms. Philosophers' use of such terms allegedly supports the view that they treat intuitions as evidence or as sources of evidence. That claim is undermined by the interpretative strategies proposed above. To see why, consider them in turn:

- The Removal-strategy is not supportive of Centrality. When the term is removed, AIT is undermined.
- It should be equally obvious that the three hedge-strategies provide no support for Centrality. Saying that *p*, with a hedge (i.e. not as a full-out assertion), is in no way to treat something called 'intuition' as evidence or a source of evidence.
- When 'intuitive' is used to mean roughly the same as 'pre-theoretic', the speaker is saying that *p* is a judgment that has been or can be justified without taking a stand on the question under discussion. This doesn't identify an evidential source for *p* or say anything about how *p* is justified. So again Centrality is not supported.[21]
- Finally, Snap interpretations provide no support for Centrality. If I tell you that *p* is a claim that's *easy to process* or *the answer you'd come to without thinking very carefully*, those are not features that in any relevant sense constitute a *source of evidence*. Not having thought very carefully about *p* isn't a source of evidence for *p*. Presenting *p* in a simple way isn't a source of evidence. If *p* can serve as evidence it is not because *p* has these

existence of events—even those philosophers who are theoretically committed to there being no events. The claim here is that uses of 'intuitive' are not like that—the process of charitable reinterpretation doesn't require imposing such commitments on speakers.

[21] This is not to deny that there might be philosophical theories of evidence according to which what is agreed on in a context can, by virtue of being agreed on (or being in the common ground), serve as evidence in that context. That, as we have seen, is not what proponents of Centrality have in mind when they use 'evidence'. Note also that if the claim that philosophers rely on intuitions as evidence came down to the claim that when they engage in inquiry, they rely on what is in the common ground, then the reliance on intuitions has nothing specifically to do with philosophy. Anyone who investigates any question will have a starting point and rely on a common ground with their interlocutors. Note also that a critique of intuition (e.g. experimental philosophers') would, on this construal, involve a critique of allowing a common ground in a conversation—surely an absurd form of skepticism.

features—they are incidental to its potential status as evidence. Even though some methodologists include Snapness as an element in the intuitive, no proponent of Centrality that I know of wants to attribute to philosophers the view that Snapness has some kind of special evidential status. That view would be deeply uncharitable. Why would anyone, philosopher or not, think that *in general*, spontaneous unjustified judgments should have special evidential import? It is, literally, an absurd position to hold in its full generality. Charity doesn't involve attributing absurd views to people. Surely everyone, be they philosophers, dancers, sushi chefs, or dog walkers, think that, *in general*, it is a bad idea to rely on spontaneous judgments you're not in a position to provide arguments for when you engage in theorizing (as opposed to practical reasoning). We philosophers, in particular, pride ourselves of being able to argue for views, to think carefully and systematically about everything. It is bizarre to attribute to us, as a group, the view that beliefs arrived at without careful reasoning should be of particular theoretical (as opposed to practical)[22] value.[23]

So Centrality gets no support from these interpretations of 'intuition'-talk. If these interpretative strategies work broadly it undermines the idea that 'intuition'-talk provides support for Centrality.

No doubt some will grant my claims about the various interpretations of 'intuitive' not being Centrality-supporting, but claim that Centrality was never motivated by such talk. They will claim that the reliance on intuitions is revealed not in the way philosophers speak but in what they *do*—their reliance on intuitions is revealed by a close study of the kinds of arguments and procedures they rely on. An evaluation of such claims is the topic of Part II of this book.

---

[22] It should be obvious that certain kinds of unreflective and quick judgments are important for practical reasoning and reasoning when one has little time to make decisions. But philosophy is not like that—we have endless time and our conclusions have hardly any practical implication (and in the few cases when they do have practical consequences, we *really* want to think carefully).

[23] If you need any further reasons to see why this view in its full generality—I look at restrictions of various kinds later—should be rejected, consider answers to why-questions. According to this version of Centrality, Snap judgments constitute a source of evidence. If E is my evidence for p, then at least in some contexts it would be appropriate to give E as a reply when asked 'Why p?' However consider the following answer to 'Why p?': 'Because I judge that p without thinking about it and can give no reasons for it'. What a dreadful reply that would be! If we are looking for charitable interpretations, that's just not on the table.

After I had submitted this manuscript to OUP, Cian Dorr (2010) published a review of Ladyman and Ross' book, *Everything Must Go*, in which he succinctly and elegantly captures much of what I have tried to argue for in this chapter. Dorr says:

> Often, saying 'Intuitively, P' is no more than a device for committing oneself to P while signalling that one is not going to provide any further arguments for this claim. In this use, 'Intuitively...' is more or less interchangeable with 'it seems to me that...'. There is a pure and chilly way of writing philosophy in which premises and conclusions are baldly asserted. But it's hard to write like this without seeming to bully one's readers: one can make things a bit gentler and more human by occasionally inserting qualifiers like 'it seems that...'. It would be absurd to accuse someone who frequently gave into this stylistic temptation of following a bankrupt methodology that presupposes the erroneous claim that things generally are as they seem. But the sprinkling of 'intuitively's and 'counter-intuitive's around a typical paper in metaphysics is in most cases not significantly different from this. It may be bad style, but it is not bad methodology, or any methodology at all, unless arguing from premises to conclusions counts as a methodology.

I wish I had been able to include a more extensive discussion of the implications of my views for the issues discussed by Dorr in that review. Hopefully many of the connections are fairly obvious.

Appendix to Chapter 4: Williamson on Intuition as Belief or Inclination to Believe

Williamson (2007) considers the kinds of uses that I surveyed in Chapter 4. He doesn't conclude that there is a variety of uses and extensive variability between contexts. Instead he concludes that philosophers as a group use 'intuition' in an invariant way to denote any belief or inclination to believe. The line of reasoning goes like this. He considers various proposals for how to restrict the extension of 'intuition' to some subset of beliefs or inclinations to believe, and for each such proposed limitation he finds a paradigmatic example of a contemporary philosopher using the term to denote some belief outside that extension. In effect, there is no kind of belief or inclination to believe that is not called an 'intuition' by some contemporary philosopher in some context or other. In the light of such data, Williamson seems to endorse the kind of view expressed by Lewis and van Inwagen in the following passages:

Our "intuitions" are simply opinions; our philosophical theories are the same. Some are commonsensical, some are sophisticated; some are particular, some general; some are more firmly held, some less. But they are all opinions, and a reasonable goal for a philosopher is to bring them into equilibrium. (Lewis 1983, p. x)

Our intuitions simply are our beliefs—or perhaps, in some cases, the tendencies that make certain beliefs attractive to us, that "move" us in the direction of accepting certain propositions without taking us all the way to acceptance (philosophers call their philosophical beliefs intuitions because 'intuition' sounds more authoritative than 'belief'). (van Inwagen 1997, p. 309)

Commenting on these passages from Lewis and van Inwagen, Williamson says:

The application of 'intuition' and cognate terms in philosophical practice is scarcely more restricted than Lewis and van Inwagen suggest. (2007, p. 220)

Consider the view:

BEL: In philosophical usage, 'A has the intuition that p' is true just in case A believes or is (consciously) inclined to believe p.

Lewis, van Inwagen and Williamson seem to be endorsing BEL in the passages quoted above.[24]

Overgeneration

In the previous chapters, I took the wide range of cases to which philosophers applied 'intuition' to be evidence of a variety of uses, not of a very broad stable (i.e. context insensitive) extension. One reason for

---

[24] I should emphasize that in personal communication Williamson has stressed that the view I say he considers and tentatively endorses is not one he fully endorses. Williamson (p. c.) says the following about the relevant passage from *The Philosophy of Philosophy*: "I expressed myself so cagily on p. 220 because it is very unclear to me what the denotation of 'intuition' as used by philosophers is. I agree that the paragraph suggests something like BEL, but philosophers' use of the word is so much all over the place that its denotation in their mouths is pretty unclear, at least to me. In suitable circumstances (e.g. when a relevant form of judgment scepticism is salient), philosophers will call just about any belief or inclination to believe an 'intuition', but that doesn't mean they're right. But I don't think that there is some more specific psychological kind for their use to latch onto. The ordinary use of 'intuition' is somewhat more specific, but also unclear. That's why I'm against using the word in philosophy. So I'm not committed to BEL, and have no desire to describe the way the word 'intuition' is used in detail—why describe a mess in detail?" (Thanks to Williamson for letting me quote this passage from an informal email message.) I should also point out it might be uncharitable to attribute BEL to Lewis and van Inwagen based just on the quoted passages. My interest in this appendix is in BEL and I'm not going to dwell on the interpretative complications.

thinking that BEL isn't the right conclusion to draw is that it seems to overgenerate. It predicts that we can *always*, in *all (relevant) philosophical contexts*, use 'intuition' and 'intuitive' about any belief or inclination to believe.[25] Consider (a)–(c):

(a) My mother lives in Oslo.
(b) Right now I see a computer in front of me.
(c) In mixed quotation the semantic value of an expression is active even though the expression is quoted and so in some significant sense referred to.

If BEL were true, then in *all* contexts, *any* 'contemporary analytic philosopher' should be happy to describe these as intuitions I have. That, however, is simply not true. Lots of philosophers of the relevant kind would find it bizarre in the extreme to classify these as intuitions. What you can find, I think, are *some* philosophers who in *some* contexts would classify (a)–(c) as 'intuitions'—in particular if the sentences are uttered in contexts where skeptical doubts are salient. As Williamson points out, in response to a philosopher who argues that there are no mountains, it wouldn't be strange to reply, 'Well, intuitively, that's a mountain' (pointing at a mountain) (p. 219). Similarly, if a philosopher claimed that it's false that humans live in cities or that no human ever has seen a physical object, that would be characterized as in tension with the intuitions that my mother lives in Oslo and that I can see a computer in front of me. Similarly, I can think of contexts in which theoretical claims such as (c) can be characterized as 'intuitive'. Just what characterizes such contexts will be made clearer in the next chapter, but roughly it is the kind of context in which (c) is in the common ground of the discussion or (c) is taken for granted pre-theoretically (i.e. prior to the particular theoretical question under discussion). (c) is chosen with care: I am an example of a philosophers who has characterized it as 'intuitive' in earlier writing in just this kind of context.[26]

In sum, I think the conclusion we should draw from the spectacular variability in usage is not that the extension of 'intuition' includes all beliefs and inclinations to believe, but rather that there is some kind of

---

[25] I take the relevant contexts to be something like those of 'contemporary philosophical debate'.
[26] See Cappelen and Lepore 1998, 2008.

undisciplined variability in use, which is not yet fully understood. The goal of this chapter was to try to find some patterns in that mess.

Undergeneration

BEL is about the noun 'intuition'. It is hard to see how the proposal extends to the more common adverbial ('intuitively') and adjectival ('intuitive') uses. Consider first the following passage from Schiffer:

Sally s-believes to degree 1 that the hair situation on Tom's scalp is either *H* or else not-*H*. If she were certain that *H* obtained, she would s-believe to degree 1 that Tom was bald; that is, intuitively put, *H*s obtaining would, she is certain, secure that Tom was determinately bald. (2003, p. 220)

Here the adverb modifies *the way a point is put or stated*. Schiffer's use is not peculiar or unusual; 'intuitively' doesn't just modify the act of believing or judging, it is used to modify all kinds of things and events (see Chapter 2 above). BEL cannot accommodate these uses because such cases involve no belief relation to a proposition. So BEL lacks the required kind of generality.

BEL is not Centrality-friendly

Finally, note that if we use BEL to interpret Centrality, then it turns into a thesis with no *specific* relevance to philosophy. As I said in Chapter 1, for Centrality to be true, the reliance on intuitions has to be something characteristic of philosophy (and a few kindred disciplines). Centrality interpreted by BEL says that philosophers use beliefs (and inclinations to believe) as evidence. The Burning Question, interpreted by BEL, asks whether philosophers can and should rely on beliefs as evidence. But it is unmotivated to ask that question *specifically* about philosophy. It is a question that can be asked about any human cognitive activity. There are interesting questions to ask, in complete generality, about the relation between evidence and belief, and about the reliability of human beliefs. The latter question is one we discuss when we encounter the skeptic, and the former one we discuss when evaluating e.g. coherentism. However, neither coherentism nor skepticism is about philosophy *specifically*. They are views about all human intellectual activity. Coherentists think that all beliefs are justified by other beliefs and there is no way out of the web of beliefs. For a coherentist, Centrality combined with BEL is a trivial instantiation of a completely general principle about human cognition and the nature of evidence. An evaluation of coherentism goes beyond the scope of this book. Likewise, skepticism is a general view about *all* human beliefs not a thesis specifically about the beliefs of philosophers. Just as this book is not an attempt to evaluate coherentism, it is not a book about skepticism and a discussion of skepticism about intuitions construed as skepticism about the reliability of human beliefs *in complete generality* is beyond the scope of this work.[27]

[27] Note also that if coherentism is what motivates Centrality (interpreted using BEL), we are owed an explanation of why 'intuition'-talk is so prevalent among philosophers compared to say among economists or physicists. Coherentism is a general claim about evidence, and so there is no explanation for why philosophers would go around using 'intuitive' more than others.

5

Philosophers' Use of 'Intuitive' (III):
Against the Explaining Away of Intuitions

This chapter is about a particular kind of 'intuition'-talk that is not easy to charitably account for using the strategies outlined in the previous chapter. Many philosophers engage in an activity they describe as 'explaining away intuitions'. An underlying assumption can be articulated roughly as Explain:

> **Explain**: Suppose A has shown (or at least provided good arguments in favor of) not-p. If many of A's interlocutors (and maybe A herself) are inclined to sincerely utter (and so commit to) 'Intuitively, p', then A is under an intellectual obligation to explain why this is the case (i.e. why there was or is this inclination to utter and commit to 'Intuitively, p').[1,2] She should not full-out endorse not-p before she has discharged this obligation.

In this chapter I argue that Explain is false. I think endorsement of it often goes hand in hand with the mistaken endorsement of Centrality. Once Centrality is rejected, Explain should be as well. In the first chapter of this book I said that the widespread endorsement of Centrality has not had widespread negative consequences for first-order philosophy (its

---

[1] This metalinguistic formulation might seem unnecessarily confusing, but it is needed in case 'intuitive' has a context-sensitive meaning (as I think it does). Talk of 'sincerely uttering' replaces 'believing what's expressed by' in order to accommodate the cases where 'intuitive' is used as a hedge, and so there is no full-out belief expressed.

[2] To make things simple, I assume that we have settled that not-p (or at least made it sufficiently plausible for us to endorse it) and that all that remains as a *potential* obstacle is the commitment to 'Intuitively, p'.

negative effects are primarily restricted to metaphilosophy). That claim should be qualified: one negative effect is the widespread endorsement of Explain (and the negative effect of Explain on a great deal of first-order philosophy). That said, philosophers who attempt to 'explain away intuitions' are not always engaged in a completely pointless exercise, and at the end of this chapter I say a bit about what kinds of constructive activities are sometimes mistakenly classified in this way.

Since the claims in this chapter tend to sound more radical than they really are, I want to be very clear on just what claims I'm making. Suppose A (or a group of A's interlocutors) are disposed to commit to a statement of the form 'Intuitively, p' and then go on to show (or at least provide good arguments in favor of) not-p. Does that initial commitment (to what was expressed by the statement of 'Intuitively, p') mean that A ought to do something that's accurately characterized as 'explaining away the intuition that p' before endorsing not-p? The answer is: 'No. If you've established that not-p, you've done what you need to do with respect to the question, "Is p the case?" Explaining why some people endorse what's expressed by 'Intuitively, p' is completely irrelevant and does not at all help answer the question under discussion (i.e. "Is p the case?").'

That said, there are other, loosely related, tasks and questions that sometimes come up when discussing *whether* p *is the case*. One loosely related question is why person A believes p and person B believes not-p. If a group of interlocutors are trying to find out whether p is the case, and A has established not-p, then part of being a cooperative conversation partner is letting interlocutors know where they've gone wrong. That will involve letting them know if they have relied on an unsound or invalid argument in their reasoning towards p. That again will often require trying to find out *why* they think p. However, answering this and related questions does not contribute to answering the question, 'Is p true?', and it is not helpfully described as 'explaining away the intuition that p'.

5.1 The argument against Explain

The argument against Explain is simple. I consider the various meanings the previous chapter proposed that 'Intuitively, p' can have in a philosophical text and see whether any of those provide any support to Explain. I conclude they don't.

Consider first the various descriptive uses of Snap and Pre-Theoretic.[3] So understood, 'Intuitively, *p*' can be paraphrased along something like these lines:

- At the outset of inquiry we believed or were inclined to believe *p*.
- Without thinking carefully, we are inclined to believe *p*.
- *P* is an easy-to-grasp way of presenting the answer to the question, but not fully accurate.

When 'Intuitively, *p*' is so interpreted, it is hard to see any reason to accept Explain. Suppose a philosopher *A* has presented a good argument for not-*p*. The fact that some judge or are inclined to judge that *p* before thinking carefully about the topic isn't something that *in general* needs to be explained by *A*. The question under discussion is whether *p* is the case. The argument for not-*p* addressed and settled that question.[4]

Next consider hedge uses of 'Intuitively, *p*'. These are cases where *p* is presented as the answer to the question, and the function of 'intuitively' is to hedge the speaker's commitment. She is presenting *p* as something less than a full-out assertion. Now, recall our philosopher *A* who has a good argument for not-*p*. That someone (even if it were *A*) at some point made a hedged assertion that *p* is not something that *A* needs to explain, having established that not-*p*. Her argument for not-*p*, if successful, establishes why people shouldn't assert *p*, hedged or otherwise. There is no explanatory work remaining.

Consider finally a case where the appropriate interpretation of an occurrence of 'intuitive' in a sentence is total elimination—the paradigmatic case is where we go from 'Intuitively, *p*' to '*p*'. Now, suppose again that *A* has established not-*p*. She has a compelling argument for not-*p*. In that case, explaining why some are committed to 'Intuitively, *p*' amounts to explaining why some are committed to *p*. For the reasons given above, that's not something *A* needs to do in order to answer the question under discussion, 'Is *p* the case?'

---

[3] See Chapter 2 for the distinction between descriptive and hedge uses of these terms.

[4] I keep the account of Explain distinct from the question of how we react to disagreement with peers. There is an extensive literature on this topic and it has interesting implications for philosophical methodology, but not for the question of how to deal with Pre-theoretic or Snap judgments. Judgments that fall into those categories are marked as not being 'peer' judgments in the relevant way (since they are made prior to inquiry or without intellectual carefulness).

It should be clear why (at least some of) those who endorse Centrality also endorse Explain. Those who endorse Centrality and AIT think that philosophers' utterances of sentences like 'Intuitively, p' express endorsement of the claim that p is backed up by a special kind of evidential source. If you think that (and you think the source is generally reliable),[5] then there is something to be explained. On this view, the endorsement of 'Intuitively, p' expresses endorsement of something that constitutes evidence for p. This is obviously not something a proponent of not-p can legitimately ignore. However, the upshot of the previous chapter was that this is not a sustainable interpretation of philosophers' use of 'Intuitively, p'.

Abstracting from questions having to do with the content of 'Intuitively, p', there's a more general point: it is not a failure of an answer to the question whether p that the respondent doesn't also explain why a lot of people make mistakes when they try to answer this question. People who don't think carefully often make all kinds of mistakes. This is a well-known fact. Many people feel attracted to false beliefs. That too is a well-known fact. But, in general, those who figure out what the world is like are under no obligation to explain how the misguided go astray. Of course, if the question under discussion is the Big Question: 'What is the total correct theory of the entire universe?', then we should also explain why people have mistaken views of the universe since such mistakes are part of the universe. However, when the question is limited to whether p (where p isn't a total description of the universe) then a good argument for not-p typically suffices to discharge the relevant intellectual obligations.

It should be clear that these points about the unacceptability of Explain have nothing specifically to do with philosophy. Consider these cases:[6]

Case 1: We have some observational evidence that pencils bend when put in water, but we eventually adopt a theory (of, say, rigid bodies) saying they remain straight. We still want an explanation of the appearance of bending, and it's still within the ambit of physics to provide that explanation, but it comes from a separate component of physics—optics, rather than movement of rigid bodies.

---

[5] I take it those who are pessimists about intuitions, e.g. those in the negative experimental philosophy movement, should agree with me in rejecting Explain. If you think intuition is unreliable, then you should also think that someone's belief *that intuitively,* p has no relevance to whether p.

[6] Thanks to Josh Dever for these cases and more generally discussion of Explain.

Case 2: We have some observational evidence that the lines in the Müller-Lyer are of different lengths, but we eventually adopt a theory (of, say, measurement) saying they are the same. Again, we want an explanation of the original appearances, but now it doesn't come from physics at all—it comes from the study of human vision.

Case 3: At the far end of the spectrum, we might have a case in which I see someone in the distance and think he's Neale. When we get closer, I see that it's not Neale, it's Dever. There is, in a thin sense, something remaining to be explained (why I thought he was Neale). Someone constructing a total theory of the universe should, maybe, provide an explanation of why I made the mistake, but it is certainly not an obligation undertaken by someone who tries to answer the question, 'Who is that?'

One thing that these cases bring out is that what we take to be an 'intellectual obligation' in various contexts is highly dependent on contingent disciplinary boundaries and what we take the question under discussion to be. As a result, there's unlikely to be any simple and unified story about what a theorist at a particular point in inquiry is 'obliged' to explain.

5.2 Is there some intellectually useful activity that's mistakenly classified as 'explaining away intuitions'?

It is worth emphasizing and I hope it is clear from the above that when philosophers do what some of them describe as 'explaining away an intuition', there is sometimes something useful going on. Here are some intellectually constructive activities that are sometimes mistakenly labeled as 'explaining away an intuition':

Suppose you've presented a very good and convincing argument for not-p. Suppose also that your argument fails to convince your interlocutors. They stick with p. There are many things you can do at this point, two of which are salient:[7]

---

[7] For related points see Ichikawa 2009. I'm sympathetic to some of what Ichikawa says in that paper (in particular the last two sections where he cautions philosophers against putting much weight on the project of explaining away intuitions), but it is presented in terminology

1. One strategy is to point out false premises or invalid forms of reasoning on behalf of the interlocutors: if I have given excellent arguments for not-*p* but my interlocutor persists in her commitment to *p*, then if I can point out the mistake that leads her to hold on to *p* (e.g. that she is using an unsound or invalid argument), I might succeed in changing her mind.
2. A second strategy is this: suppose I've engaged in a bit of amateur psychology of my interlocutor and I suspect that there is some non-rational cognitive mechanism that prevents her from giving up her commitment to *p* (or makes her strongly inclined towards *p*). In some such situations, it might help to point this out to her. Getting one's interlocutor to see what is blocking endorsement of not-*p* can help remove the block (of course, the extent to which this is effective is an open empirical question).

There are obviously lots of other things I can do when encountering recalcitrant interlocutors, but what is important to note is that neither of these strategies has anything specifically to do with philosophy, philosophical argumentation or reliance on the intuitive. They are completely general strategies for dealing with recalcitrant interlocutors. So the fact that these two strategies are valuable provides no support for Explain.

As I have articulated it, Explain is a kind of metalinguistic thesis. It is a thesis about what to do when certain forms of sentences are committed to. This made it easy to base the criticism of Explain on the interpretative strategies outlined in previous chapters. However, this might not go down well with those who think Centrality is a thesis that has very little to do with how philosophers use 'intuitive' and primarily to do with important tacit features of philosophical practice. Such Centrality proponents might claim that Explain is supported, not by anything that has to do with what we commit to when uttering 'Intuitively, BLAH', but by the tacit reliance on intuitions that (allegedly) underpin much philosophical argumentation. I agree that I have not yet refuted this somewhat elusive version of Explain, but if the arguments of Part II are correct, the reply will fail. The goal of the next six chapters is to argue that it is false that philosophical practice tacitly relies on an appeal to intuitions.

---

that presupposes endorsement of both Centrality and Explain. I think it is important to emphasize that an upshot of the rejection of Centrality is the rejection of Explain.

PART II

The Argument from Philosophical Practice

Introduction to Part II

Centrality, as formulated in Chapter 1, doesn't require that philosophers ever talk about intuitions. It leaves open the possibility that the reliance on intuitions is implicit. So I often get this reply after presenting my view of what the word 'intuitive' means: it doesn't really matter how to interpret explicit 'intuition'-talk in philosophical texts. That's not the primary evidence for Centrality. The primary evidence for Centrality is the *implicit* reliance on intuitions in philosophical practice. In particular, when philosophers use the so-called *method of cases*, they rely on intuitions. That's why Centrality is true—not because of the content of 'intuition'-talk in philosophical texts.

The distinction between implicit and explicit reliance on intuitions can be brought out by an analogy with perceptual evidence. It is not the case that those who rely on perceptual evidence always or even typically make that reliance explicit. You claim: "Your keys are on the table over there." Your claim is based on perceptual evidence, but you don't (need to) make that explicit by saying "I see that your keys are on the table over there." The thought is that reliance on intuitions in philosophy is like that— in the relevant contexts, reliance on intuitions is so obvious, that it is not needed to make it explicit. In particular: it might be claimed that the method of cases so obviously relies on appeals to intuitions that it somehow makes the proper understanding of 'intuition'- talk irrelevant.

What is the method of cases? Here is one possible articulation:

MOC: A theory of some philosophical topic X, T, is an adequate theory only if it can account for (or explain or predict) intuitions about X in actual and possible cases.

The claim that Centrality is made true by this method can be articulated as Centrality$_{(M)}$:

Centrality$_{(M)}$: Philosophers rely (in some epistemically significant way) on intuitions when they make judgments about cases.[1]

The next few chapters are attempts to better understand Centrality$_{(M)}$ and then evaluate it. One point is crucial throughout: I treat Centrality$_{(M)}$ as a descriptive claim about the activity of some people who call themselves philosophers. As such, the way to evaluate Centrality$_{(M)}$ is to check on what these people are doing. It's a form of intellectual anthropology.

Here is an overview of what follows:

- Chapter 6 is focused on some of the key empirical claims that are often made about the method of cases by those who write on the philosophy of philosophy. I focus first on a tradition I call *methodological rationalism* and then show how a wide range of philosophers opposed to methodological rationalism buy into a number of the key descriptive claims made in that tradition.
- Chapter 7 is an attempt to 'operationalize' the characterizations outlined in Chapter 6: i.e. an attempt to articulate features to look for in a written text or verbal exchange that would be indicative of an appeal to the intuitive.
- Chapter 8 is devoted to an investigation of a number of paradigmatic cases/thought experiments from various subfields of contemporary philosophy.
- Chapter 9 draws lessons from the case studies: I conclude that on any precisification of 'intuition' (and other key terms) Centrality$_{(M)}$ is false. The overall conclusion is that there is no 'implicit' reliance on intuitions in philosophical practice and so the argument from philosophical practice provides no support for Centrality.

---

[1] This reliance can be implicit—it does not require any explicit use of 'intuition' vocabulary.

- Chapter 10 considers a more limited version of Centrality, one restricted only to cases where philosophers just engage in so-called 'conceptual analysis'. I argue that such a restriction has no real-world instantiation, and is unmotivated.
- Chapter 11 draws conclusions from all of this for the experimental-philosophy movement. Experimental philosophy is an attempt to empirically investigate the intuitions of non-philosophers. That research project makes sense only if philosophers rely on intuitions when they do philosophy. Since philosophers don't rely on intuitions, it is hard to see any motivation for doing experimental philosophy. This conclusion is, obviously, not to be confused with the claim that philosophers shouldn't rely on empirical data and experiments—what we don't need are experiments on intuitions.

A point I will come back to repeatedly over the next few chapters is that a lot of contemporary methodology fundamentally misdescribes what actual philosophical practice is like. There is a tendency to engage in an almost aprioristic approach to the question of what philosophers do and how they go about doing what they do. My working assumption in what follows is that any general claim about philosophy and philosophers is in need of empirical backing. We can only get that from studying philosophers and what they do.

6

Centrality and Philosophical Practice

The focus in this part of the book is on how those who endorse Centrality think the reliance on intuitions shows up in philosophical practice, not in how we talk about that practice. The next chapter provides a set of diagnostics for when someone relies on an intuition when evaluating a thought experiment. This chapter provides some background leading up to those diagnostics. I start with a tradition in philosophy that I call 'methodological rationalism'. I focus initially on this tradition because it is particularly explicit and clear in its description of a Centrality-based conception of philosophical practice. However, 'methodological rationalism' is a view endorsed by only a small minority of philosophers and most of those who endorse Centrality reject it (indeed, many prominent Centrality supporters have written extensively against methodological rationalism). The punch line of this chapter is that even philosophers deeply opposed to methodological rationalism (e.g. experimental philosophers such as Stich and Weinberg, Kornblith, Goldman, Pust, Ernest Sosa, and even Williamson) buy into important elements of its conception of how philosophy is being done.[2] Much of the debate between the methodological rationalists and their opponents *presupposes* the descriptive adequacy of important elements of the methodological rationalists' picture of philosophical activity.

[2] It is worth emphasizing (since readers of earlier drafts of this manuscript were misled on this point) that I don't see the methodological rationalists as the primary target of my criticism in this part of the book. They are but one target among all those who endorse the descriptive adequacy of their conception of philosophical practice. The point of this chapter is, in part, to show how widespread that endorsement is, even among those who abhor methodological rationalism.

6.1 Methodological rationalism

By 'methodological rationalism' (MR) I have in mind a view that has been endorsed by Bealer, BonJour, and Plantinga, among others. This kind of view is sometimes characterized as 'moderate' rationalism, but while it might be moderate compared with the views of, say, Descartes and Spinoza, the view is hardly moderate by any contemporary standards and so I will drop the modifier. I add the 'methodological' to indicate that I am interested in the kind of rationalism that connects views of a priori conceptual truth to philosophical methodology.[3]

In a series of papers George Bealer has developed a version of MR that will serve as an anchor point for my presentation. Others in this tradition incorporate only parts of Bealer's picture and interpret some of the elements differently from him. Some of these variations will be noted along the way. I break the presentation of this kind of view into four parts:

- MR on what philosophers seek;
- MR on philosophical method;
- MR on what intuitions are; and
- MR on what justifies the use of intuitions.

6.1.1 MR on what philosophers seek

According to Bealer,

> Nearly all philosophers seek answers to such questions as the nature of substance, mind, intelligence, consciousness, sensation, perception, knowledge, wisdom, truth, identity, infinity, divinity, time, explanation, causation, freedom, purpose, goodness, duty, the virtues, love, life, happiness and so forth. (1996, pp. 3–4, my emphases)

I take this to be an empirical claim about what certain people—philosophers—seek. One goal of this and the next few chapters is to alert the reader to these empirical claims and then test them against philosophical

---

[3] Many philosophers defend views of the a priori, conceptual justification, etc., but take up no significant commitment about philosophical methodology. In the introduction to Boghossian and Peacocke (2000), e.g., the authors write: "If we adopt the *most permissive* available reading of 'independent from experience', according to which a priori knowledge just is non-empirical knowledge, then, as noted above, we seem to have intuitively clear instances of a priori knowledge of the principles of logic, arithmetic, geometry, probability, of the principles of colour incompatibility and implication, of some definitions, *perhaps of some truths of philosophy itself*" (p. 8, my emphases).

practice. Bealer makes two further striking claims about what it is to seek 'the nature' of these phenomena:

(i) According to Bealer, we ask questions (and seek answers) that are *general* in this sense: the questions and their answers "do not pertain to this or that individual, species, or historical event." The questions philosophers ask are, according to Bealer, "phrased in quite general terms without mention of particular individuals, species, etc." (1996, p. 3). According to this view, we are not interested in, for example, what *reference* is for creatures with cognitive and social structures similar to ours. Such answers, according to Bealer, do not have the kind of generality we philosophers seek. A theory of reference should tell us how, say, an omniscient un-embodied god that exists in a universe that contains just one fox that is circulating slowly around a crystal ball, can refer to that fox and that crystal ball.

(ii) According to Bealer, philosophers also look for *necessary* answers: "In being interested in such things as the nature of mind, intelligence, the virtues, and life, philosophers do not want to know what those things just happen to be, but rather what those things must be, what they are in a strong sense" (1996, p. 3). If our theory of freedom, reference and belief just tells us what those things actually are (or what they are in worlds relevantly similar to this one) it fails to answer the question we philosophers pose.[4]

6.1.2 MR on philosophical method

Methodological rationalists have a view about *how* philosophers go about answering their questions. Bealer calls it our 'standard justificatory procedure' and so-called intuitions play a central role. According to Bealer, we philosophers typically proceed as follows. We first describe a real or possible situation. We canvas intuitions about this situation. Those intuitions then provide the basis for further theory building. An example from epistemology: we describe a situation in which someone has seen thousands of white

---

[4] Bealer notes that not all philosophical claims fit this characterization but adds that "In most if not all cases, noncentral philosophical propositions are immediate consequences of central philosophical propositions plus auxiliary empirical propositions that have little philosophical content in and of themselves" (1996, p. 3).

poodles that from a distance look exactly like sheep. She happens to glance upon the one real sheep among the poodles and forms the true belief that *that is a sheep*. About this case, Bealer says:

> We find it intuitively obvious that there could be such a situation like that described and in such a situation the person would not know that there is a sheep in the pasture despite having a justified true belief. This intuition—that there could be such a situation and in it the person would not know—and other intuitions like it are used as evidence that the traditional theory is mistaken. (1996, p. 4)

After the first step in the Standard Justificatory Procedure, we subject these initial intuitions to what Bealer calls 'dialectical critique'. We construct theories that systematize the surviving intuitions and then test those theories against further intuitions. The procedure is repeated until some kind of equilibrium is reached (p. 28, n. 3). According to Bealer, there are "countless" examples of this procedure in philosophy (p. 4). He mentions only five of these countless examples: "Chisholm's perceptual-relativity refutation of phenomenalism, Putnam's perfect-pretender refutation of behaviorism, all the various twin-earth examples, Burge's arthritis example, multiple-realizability, etc., etc." (p. 4).

6.1.3 MR on what intuitions are

What are these things Bealer calls 'intuitions' and that he thinks play such an important role in the practice of doing philosophy? The view can be summarized in four steps, all of which should be familiar from Part I:

1. *Seemings*: If S has an intuition that p, then it seems to S that p (where 'seems' is not used in its hedging sense according to Bealer).
2. *Distinctive Phenomenology*: Proponents of MR typically think that there is a distinctive phenomenology that a mental state must have in order to count as an intuition. Plantinga's description is as good as it gets:

    > ...that peculiar form of phenomenology with which we are all well acquainted, but which I can't describe in any way other than as the phenomenology that goes with seeing that such a proposition is true. (1993, pp. 105–6)

3. Sui Generis *Conscious Episodes*: As we saw in Chapter 1, Bealer doesn't think intuitions can be reduced to other propositional attitudes: "On my view, intuition is a *sui generis*, irreducible, natural, propositional

attitude which occurs episodically" (1996, pp. 28–9, n. 6). Intuitions are thus different from beliefs, inclinations to believe, guesses, hunches and other propositional attitudes we are familiar with.[5]

4. *Apriority and Necessity*: Bealer thinks we philosophers seek answers that are necessary truths of a certain kind and intuitions as he construes them are supposed to provide such answers a priori. Intuitions provide **a priori** justification of **necessary truths**. As a consequence, the kind of intuitions that we philosophers allegedly appeal to is, according to Bealer, importantly different from 'physical intuitions'. The intuition *that if I were to drop this computer it would fall to the floor*, is what Bealer calls a *physical* intuition. It is not a priori and it doesn't concern a necessary truth. The philosophically relevant set of intuitions he labels 'rational'. A rational intuition "presents itself as necessary: it seems that things could not have been otherwise" (2000, p. 3).[6]

6.1.4 MR on the source and justification of intuitions

Traditional rationalists sometimes rely on perceptual metaphors when they describe how intuitions give us insight: they like to talk of 'seeing that such-and-such' (we saw the expression used by Plantinga above and, in scare quotes, by Bealer). For some rationalists, this is not a metaphor. Gödel construed intuitions as a form of perception:

The similarity between mathematical intuition and a physical sense is very striking. It is arbitrary to consider "this is red" an immediate datum, but not so to consider the proposition expressing modus ponens or complete induction (or perhaps some simpler propositions from which the latter follows). For the difference, as far as it is relevant here, consists solely in the fact that in the first case a relationship between a

---

[5] Intuitions are, according to Bealer, different from beliefs, inclinations to believe and hunches in being less susceptible to external manipulation and influence (see e.g. Bealer 1996, p. 6).

[6] Others follow Bealer with some modification. Pust for example doesn't think the necessity component is part of the intuition itself, and so appeals to a *disposition to have an experience of necessity*:

S has a rational intuition that p if and only if (a) S has a purely intellectual experience, when considering the question of whether p, that p, and (b) at t, if S were to consider whether p is necessarily true, then S would have a purely intellectual experience that necessarily p. (2000, p. 39)

Ernest Sosa requires no awareness, actual or potential, of the modal status of the proposition involved, but he still excludes contingent propositions as objects of 'rational intuition' (see the discussion of Sosa 2007b in 6.2.3).

concept and a particular object is perceived, while in the second case it is a relationship between concepts. (quoted in Parsons 1995, p. 62)

Parsons comments on this passage:

In this passage and in many others, we find a formulation that is very characteristic of Gödel: In certain cases of rational evidence (of which we can easily grant modus ponens to be one), it is claimed that "perception" of concepts is involved. (1995, p. 62)

Contemporary, so-called moderate rationalists don't typically follow Gödel in taking the perceptual metaphors literally. Instead they talk of intuitions having their source in conceptual competence (see also Section 1.3). Bealer explicitly distances himself from Gödel's view. While he does think there's a tie between intuitions and truth, "the tie does not have a mysterious, or supernatural, source (as perhaps it does in Gödel's theory of mathematical intuition); rather, it is simply a consequence of what, by definition, it is to possess—to understand—the concepts involved in our intuitions" (Bealer 2000, p. 2). In other work he says that "it is constitutive of determinate concept possession that a person have a certain kind of capacity for intuitions regarding the behavior of the concept" (1996, p. 12).

Methodological rationalists differ in what they take concepts and concept possession to be and in the nature of the tie between truth and intuitions. As a result, this element of their view is particularly hard to pin down precisely and with any kind of generality. One helpful general characterization is found in Williamson, who characterizes the notion of *a purely conceptual justification* as "a privileged status in respect of knowledge or justification which a sentence or thought has in virtue of the conditions for understanding its constituent words or possessing its constituent concepts" (2007, p. 52). In general, methodological rationalists are committed to the idea that philosophical inquiry at its core relies on intuitive judgments that have this kind of privileged status.

6.1.5 *Brief digression: descriptive and normative elements of MR*

My interest is in the descriptive elements of MR. However, when reading the texts in which MR is articulated, it is sometimes hard to distinguish between normative and descriptive elements of MR. Bealer, for example, makes many claims that are descriptions of actual philosophical practice. As we have just seen, he talks about what philosophers seek, what kinds of questions they ask, what kinds of answers they are interested in, and how they go about answering their questions. It is a crucial element in many of his arguments that we actually engage in what he calls "the standard justificatory procedure" (1996, p. 3). That said, there are some passages in which Bealer realizes that he is describing an *ideal* but non-actual practice. According to Bealer, agents can have rational intuitions (the ones we rely on in philosophy) only when they are in certain cognitive conditions and in some passages Bealer says that it is unlikely that any of us, individually, will ever be in those conditions. He says:

> The strong modal tie between intuitions and the truth holds relative to theoretical systematizations arrived at in cognitive conditions that are of a relevantly high quality. Such conditions might be beyond what individual human beings can achieve in isolation. It is plausible that we approximate such cognitive conditions only in sustained cooperation with others, perhaps over generations. And even here, it is an open question whether we will ever approximate them sufficiently closely. (1996, p. 7)

Insofar as intuitions are mental states that have the relevant kind of modal tie to truth, Bealer in effect says that no *one* of us are likely to ever have intuitions. That again throws doubt on what he says about the standard justificatory procedure—how can we right now be engaged in a procedure that requires us to have mental states none of us are likely ever to be in?[7]

The normative element in BonJour is more direct. He claims:

> [T]he need for an account of genuine and non-tautological a priori justification seems to me especially urgent for philosophy itself. While it is not my purpose to argue the matter in detail here, my conviction is that philosophy is a priori if it is anything (at least if it is anything intellectually respectable); and that the practice of even those who most explicitly reject the idea of substantive a priori justification inevitably involves tacit appeal to insights and modes of reasoning that can be understood as a priori in character, if they are justified at all. (1998, p. xi)

Roughly speaking, according to BonJour, there might be many philosophers who don't do philosophy in the way he advocates, but they lack

---

[7] I won't try to answer this question here since extended Bealer exegesis would take us too far afield. Suffice it to say that this seems to me a significant problem. On the one hand the view requires the descriptive adequacy of what the calls the 'standard justificatory procedure', while on the other hand the passages just quoted say that we are not—and *cannot* be—engaged in the kind of activity described as 'the standard justificatory procedure'.

intellectual respectability. So rather than a description of what his colleagues are doing, this is an evaluation of it.

In sum, to be fair to the various proponents of MR, it is worth keeping in mind that not all their characterizations of philosophy are descriptive. My interest is primarily in the question of whether Centrality is a correct description of current philosophical practice. I conclude that it is not. However, there is an indirect normative element in what I do in the next four chapters: I show that papers that by wide consensus constitute some of the best philosophy of the twentieth century, do not meet the standards imposed by MR proponents. If that is correct, we have a choice: follow the methodological rationalists in treating these philosophers as not being intellectually respectable or rejecting MR's standards for respectability.

6.2 The influence of methodological rationalism

While full-blown methodological rationalism is a heavy theoretical package to take on—one most philosophers reject—most contemporary philosophers endorse many of the descriptive elements of MR. So while many philosophers reject the more theoretical commitments found in MR about the connections between concept possession, apriority and philosophy, they accept the *descriptive adequacy* of something like *P1–P4* (I'll call the conjunction of these 'Picture'):

P1: Intuitive judgments are mental states (or events) with a distinctive etiology or phenomenology or both.

P2: Intuitive judgments are at the center of philosophical argumentation—in particular they are essential to the method of cases.

P3: Intuitive judgments about cases are treated by philosophers as having a kind of epistemic status, which is different in kind from that of typical judgments based on perceptual input, memory, testimony, or those reached by inference from such judgments. The privileged status can be described as a kind of *default justification*.

P4: Philosophers assume that it is because intuitions have this privileged status that they can provide the foundation for the method of cases, and that this method can be at the core of philosophical inquiry.

I suggest that Picture, as a watered-down version of MR, is a common core of descriptive claims about philosophical practice that underlies the widespread commitment to Centrality (especially among those who base it on the Argument from Philosophical Practice).[8] *P1–P4* are intentionally vague. *P1* leaves room for different characterizations of the distinctiveness of the intuitive. It is also left open how to construe 'central role' (in *P2*), 'privileged', 'default' (both in *P3*), and 'foundation' (in *P4*).

The next subsections provide a brief overview of philosophers who are deeply opposed to MR but who still endorse Picture.

6.2.1 Experimental philosophers: endorsement of picture combined with pessimism

Experimental philosophers endorse Picture in its entirety, find it lacking and conclude that we should be critical of much contemporary philosophizing. Here is Jonathan Weinberg, a prominent experimental philosopher, outlining how he sees standard philosophical method. Weinberg's interest is in "the extant practice of appeal to intuitions as philosophical evidence, [in which] one cites one's application or withholding of a concept from a given case, usually a hypothetical one, in defense of (or in order to attack) a particular philosophical claim" (2007, p. 320). Weinberg characterizes the target judgments as follows:

Such citations thus are meant to carry argumentative, evidential weight, but one is not usually required to offer any further argumentation for the intuition itself. In particular, no empirical evidence is required, because one is presumed to have stipulated all the contingencies in the construction of the hypothetical, and one is applying only one's mastery of the concepts involved and not any empirical knowledge. Such citations are thus, in one sense, foundational: although they are used to provide evidence, one does not, and need not, provide further evidence for them. (p. 320)[9]

---

[8] Note that since *P1–P3* say nothing about how 'intuitive' is used, the description could be true even though those terms are never used by those who participate in the practice.

[9] However, as Weinberg points out, intuitions "are not generally taken to be incorrigible or indubitable" and "We may choose not to endorse an intuition, if the balance of evidence speaks against it; or if one comes to think that the intuition was not formed in a sufficiently truth conducive way, say, because one did not previously attend to a subtle relation between aspects of the case" (pp. 320–1). This, of course, is all compatible with *Picture*.

Note that Weinberg endorses not just Picture, but a description that includes also very significant elements of the more controversial parts of MR: according to Weinberg, our goal when we make intuitive judgments about cases is to rely solely on our conceptual competence. Empirical knowledge should play no role whatsoever when we make the relevant kind of judgments about cases. Intuitive judgments about cases are of necessary truths (or falsehoods). Of course, Weinberg describes this practice in order to go on to criticize it, while the proponents of MR do so in order to celebrate it. However, Weinberg's description has to be accurate for his criticism to have a target. It's hard to overemphasize the importance of this in the evaluation of experimental philosophy. If their target is misdescribed, then they are attacking a straw man, and in particular the attacks fail to have relevance to what is really going on in philosophical argumentation (Chapter 11 is devoted to an elaboration of this point).

6.2.2 Goldman and Pust: endorsement of Picture combined with conceptual analysis as empirical practice

Goldman (2007) and Goldman and Pust (1998) provide good examples of philosophers who are deeply opposed to methodological rationalism but nonetheless fully endorse Picture as descriptively adequate. Goldman starts his 2007 by stating Centrality as if it is a self-evident truth: "One thing that distinguishes philosophical methodology from the methodology of the sciences is its extensive and avowed reliance on intuition" (p. 1). He rejects the emphasis on apriority in MR but accepts that intuitions are generated by conceptual competence. Concepts, on this view, are real psychological entities that reliably generate our intuitive judgments and these judgments constitute basic sources of evidence in philosophy: they are, like perception, *generally* reliable. Goldman writes:

It's part of the nature of concepts (in the personal psychological sense) that possessing a concept tends to give rise to beliefs and intuitions that accord with the contents of the concept. If the content of someone's concept F implies that F does (doesn't) apply to example x, then that person is disposed to intuit that F applies (doesn't apply) to x when the issue is raised in his mind. . . . possessing a concept makes one disposed to have pro-intuitions toward correct applications and con-intuitions toward incorrect applications—correct, that is, relative to the contents of the concept as it exists in the subject's head. However, our description of these dispositions must be further qualified and constrained, to get matters right. (2007, p. 15)

Absent interference (e.g. from theoretical biases), our intuitions are reliable evidence in the study of concepts, according to Goldman. Conceptual analysis is, on this view, an empirical practice and intuitions play an important role: they reveal features of the psychological states that are concepts.

6.2.3 Sosa on intuitions and intellectual virtues

Ernest Sosa's body of work is in large part devoted to a defense and development of a version of virtue epistemology, where the notion of an epistemic competence plays a central role. This is also the perspective from which he describes the role of intuitions in philosophy. Sosa's characterization of intuitions within a virtue/competence theoretic framework follows Picture quite closely. In Sosa (2007b) he first tells us what it is for an intellectual seeming to be intuitive:

An intellectual seeming is *intuitive* when it is an attraction to assent triggered simply by considering a proposition consciously with understanding. (Of course, one may so much as understand the proposition only through a complex and prolonged process that includes perception, memory or inference). (pp. 60–1)

He then uses intuitive intellectual seemings to give an account of when an agent rationally intuits that p:

S *rationally* intuits that p if and only if S's intuitive attraction to assent to <p> is explained by a competence (an epistemic ability or virtue) on the part of S to discriminate, among contents that he understands well enough, the true from the false, in some subfield of the modally strong (the necessarily true or necessarily false), with no reliance on introspection, perception, memory, testimony, or inference (no further reliance, anyhow, than any required for so much as understanding the given proposition). (p. 61)

Like Weinberg's, this characterization buys into a version of Picture that is very close to what we find in MR: the relevant kind of intuitive judgments are based exclusively on considering their contents 'consciously with understanding'—no additional reliance on perception, memory of inference is needed. Sosa also follows MR in classifying only necessarily true (or false) propositions as intuitive. Where he diverges from MR is in the appeal to the subject's competence (where this is understood as an epistemic virtue). That is a significant difference, but it is still worth noting that there are important elements of agreement.

6.2.4 Kornblith: endorsement of Picture combined with revisionism

Hilary Kornblith is fundamentally opposed to MR. He rejects the view that philosophers should use intuitions with the goal of understanding our concepts. Philosophers should not study concepts, according to Kornblith, but instead non-conceptual features of the world. Epistemologists, for example, should study knowledge, not the concept of knowledge. However, he takes these to be normative claims about how philosophers *should* proceed—he does not think this is how they *actually* proceed. Kornblith takes Picture to be a correct description of how we actually proceed and says that if we were to endorse his view of what philosophers should do, philosophy would have to undergo a radical methodological shift. He concludes:

> If what I've said here is even roughly correct about some of the targets of philosophical interest, then the standard philosophical method will need to be revised. As I've argued here, however, whatever one's views about the targets of philosophical interest, the standard method will require substantial revision. The kind of conservative approach to philosophical methodology which Goldman and many others favor will not, I have argued, hold up to scrutiny. The only remaining possibilities, then, involve highly non-trivial changes in philosophical practice. (2007, p. 47)

6.2.5 Williamson (at least on one reading): endorsement of Picture combined with revisionism

Finally, maybe most surprisingly, Timothy Williamson endorses some important elements of Picture in work otherwise devoted to refuting methodological rationalism (and related views). Williamson rejects the traditional distinction between the a priori and the a posteriori. He does, however, still think that philosophical judgments about thought experiments belong to a special category: he describes them as a source of what he calls armchair knowledge. In the characteristic judgments about thought experiments, empirical evidence plays no clear evidential role. Williamson says:

> We may acknowledge an extensive category of *armchair knowledge*, in the sense of knowledge in which experience plays no strictly evidential role, while remembering that such knowledge may not fit the stereotype of the *a priori*, because the contribution of experience was far more than enabling. (2007, p. 169)

For example, according to Williamson the judgments we make about a Gettier case fall into this intermediate category of armchair knowledge. They are neither clearly a priori nor clearly a posteriori. He says that the "experiences through which we learned to distinguish in practice between belief and non-belief and between knowledge and ignorance play *no strictly evidential role in our knowledge*" (p. 169, my emphasis). However, it is still not experience that is *required* for concept possession because "subtle differences between two courses of experience, each of which sufficed for coming to understand 'know' and 'believe', [can] make for differences in how test cases are processed, just large enough to tip honest judgments" about a Gettier case:

Such individual differences in the skill with which concepts are applied depend constitutively, not just causally, on past experience, for the skillfulness of a performance depends constitutively on its causal origins. (p. 168)

There are interesting questions about just how to interpret Williamson's remarks about armchair knowledge, but no matter how the details are spelled out, it is clear that he thinks judgments about Gettier cases (and other paradigmatic thought experiments) are not like judgments where experience plays a clear evidential role. This contrasts sharply with the view I will defend in Chapters 8–10: if we are to make any generic claim about the kinds of judgments we make about philosophical thought experiments, they do not fall into this kind of intermediate category since experience plays a clear evidential role in our assessments of thought experiments. Williamson is right to move away from the aprioristic picture we are given by MR, but he doesn't move far enough (For further discussion of Williamson's view, see Section 9.3.).

7
Diagnostics for Intuitiveness

In the next chapter I consider a number of case studies to see whether they confirm the claims proponents of Centrality make about philosophical practice. This chapter lays the groundwork for those case studies.

7.1 Features of the intuitive

Anyone interested in Centrality as an empirical claim about philosophical practice should take an interest in *how* it can be refuted or supported. Can we find diagnostics for appeals to the intuitive?[1] Suppose you are reading a philosophy paper. The piece of paper you are looking at has some sentences on it. Those sentences express various propositions that (hopefully) stand in interesting logical relations to each other. We have now put behind us the idea that occurrences of 'intuition' in that text is a reliable indicator of reliance on the intuitive in the sense intended by Centrality proponents. So what do we look for? How can we find evidence of a reliance on the intuitive? Answering these questions is made difficult by the extensive disagreement among Centrality proponents about what intuitions are. It is difficult, maybe impossible, to find a set of diagnostics that fully capture all the phenomena different intuition-theorists appeal to. I focus on three complex features that, according to at least a fairly wide range of intuition-theorists, are characteristic of appeals to the intuitive.

---

[1] One reaction I've had to this question is that it presupposes some kind of unacceptable verificationism. It doesn't. I'm simply operating on the assumption that if someone makes an empirical claim about how a group of people go about doing something (e.g. arguing about philosophy), then they should be prepared to present evidence to back up that claim.

F1: Seem True/special phenomenology. According to most intuition-theorists, an intuitive judgment has a characteristic phenomenology. (See Section 6.1.3.)[2]

F2: Rock. According to most intuition-theorists, an intuitive judgment has a special epistemic status. Roughly characterized, and I will say more about this below, intuitive judgments serve as a kind of rock bottom justificatory point in philosophical argumentation. *Intuitive judgments justify, but they need no justification.* They have what I will call 'default justificatory status'.[3]

For those who believe that some propositions have this special status, it is never made very clear just how to identify them. How do we tell whether a claim made in a text has default justificatory status? Two diagnostics are helpful:

F2.1: Non-inferential and Non-experiential. If p is treated as justified even though appeals to experience (memory, perception) play no clear evidential role in the judgment that p and p is not inferred from other premises, that is evidence that p is treated as having the kind of special epistemic status that Rock attempts to capture.[4]

F2.2: Evidence Recalcitrance. Let's say that p is *evidence recalcitrant* for a subject S under the following conditions: (i) S is inclined to believe that p. (ii) S has some arguments A for p. (iii) If, however, it turns out that A are not good arguments for p, that does not remove S's inclination to endorse p. If p exhibits (i)–(iii), that's an indicator that p has Rock status for the subject in question.[5]

---

[2] Note that for some intuition-theorists this is a phenomenology that accompanies beliefs or inclinations to believe, but not all theorists think of it that way. Bealer, for example, says, "intuition is not an inclination to believe or an inclination-to-believe accompanied by a 'glow' or some other 'positive' quality" (1996, p. 28, n. 6). Rather, the phenomenology is what individuates the *sui generis* mental state of intuition.

[3] This is, maybe, a relative of the kind of thing e.g. Jim Pryor calls 'immediate justification': "When your justification to believe P comes in part from your having justification to believe other, supporting propositions, I'll say that those latter propositions **mediate** your justification to believe P.... When your justification to believe P does *not* come from your justification to believe other propositions, I'll call it **immediate**" (2005, p. 184).

[4] Of course, it is difficult to spell out 'no clear evidential role' and 'non-inferential' without entering into controversial territory, but at this stage we are simply looking for rough diagnostics and increased precision isn't yet needed for our purposes.

[5] Why think that this kind of recalcitrance should be counted as evidence in favor of a proposition having the kind of normative status Rock gestures towards? What does this kind

F3: Based solely on conceptual competence. As we have seen in the previous chapter, according to many intuition-theorists, a (correct) judgment that *p* counts as intuitive only if it is justified solely by the subjects' conceptual or linguistic competence (see Sections 1.3 and 6.1.4). Those who believe that some judgments are justified solely by conceptual competence disagree about what concepts are, what the relevant kind of competency is, and what 'solely' should be taken to mean. Hence there is no consensus on a set of criteria that effectively can be used to detect the presence of such judgments. This makes looking for them in philosophical texts very hard. That said, many of those who believe in conceptual justification will rely on something like F1 and F2 as diagnostics: if we find that F2 (including F2.1 and F2.2) and F1 are *missing*, that is, by most accounts, evidence that the judgment in question is not based solely on conceptual competence. Note also that most proponents of conceptual justification think only *necessary truths* can be so justified.[6] If so, a debate over a contingent claim is not a candidate for this kind of justification. If so, whenever we find philosophers making a claim that is not a necessary truth, we can assume that F3 is not a good explanation of how it obtains its justification.[7]

For many philosophers, F3 does all the work F2 does. Why distinguish them? Powerful and influential arguments have been presented over the last forty years to the effect that there are no conceptually justified claims (and that there is no analytic-synthetic distinction). In part for that reason, I don't want to tie the appeal to the intuitive too closely to that idea. In order to be charitable to Centrality proponents, I want to leave open the possibility that there are true interpretations of "Philosophers rely on

---

of psychological propensity have to do with the relevant kind of normative status? The answer I'll give to these questions below is, in effect, 'nothing, as far as I can see', but the initial thought is this: someone claims that it is possible for propositions to have a certain kind of normative status, *N*. If, like me, you are interested in whether a particular claim, say *c*, made in a philosophy paper, has *N*, you have to ask yourself, *How do I tell whether c has N?* The suggested reply is this: if the relevant set of agents is disposed to treat *c* as evidence recalcitrant, that's an indicator that *c* has *N*. After all, the idea is that we are *prima facie* justified in our belief that *p*—we take *p* to be justified independently of the arguments that could be given for it—and so the undermining of one of those arguments shouldn't remove our allegiance to *p*.

[6] See Section 6.1.3 above. Note that F1 and F2 do not assume that the content of intuitive judgments are necessary truths.

[7] Note that for some proponents of Centrality, necessity also figures in the phenomenology: see e.g. the quotes from Bealer and Pust in Section 6.1.3 above.

intuitions" despite there being no conceptually justified propositions. In particular, I want to leave open the possibility of an intuition theorist who thinks that intuitive judgments have a kind of Rock status even though that judgment isn't based solely on conceptual competence.

The remainder of this chapter is devoted to elaborations on F1–F3, but before getting to that, here are some initial qualifications.

7.2 Some initial qualifications

Absence of F1, F2 and F3 is evidence of absence of a reliance on the intuitive: The claim here is not that F1–F3 *suffice* for discovering appeals to the intuitive. What will be important in what follows is that the *absence* of all of F1–F3 in an argument is strong evidence that there is no reliance on the intuitive in that argument. Though proponents of Centrality disagree among themselves about just what the intuitive is, they agree that if all of F1–F3 are absent, that is evidence of an absence of the intuitive. In the case studies that I investigate in the next chapter, we will consistently find an absence of all of F1–F3 and that will on all views of intuitions be evidence of their absence.

F1, F2 and F3 are not helpful for discovering whether philosophers tend to psychologize evidence: We already saw (in particular in Chapter 4), Williamson (on one reading), Lewis, and van Inwagen take 'intuitions' to denote all beliefs and inclinations to believe. When 'intuition' in Centrality is so interpreted, it amounts to the claim that philosophers psychologize evidence. I'm separately interested in the question of whether it is characteristic of philosophers that they tend to psychologize evidence—i.e. whether it is characteristic of philosophical practice that philosophers tend to take their beliefs and inclinations to believe as evidence when talking about non-psychological subject matters. F1–F3 are not particularly helpful for checking on that hypothesis, so that is a question I will address separately (in Chapter 9).[8]

Speed of judgment left out: In some literature on intuitions, they are characterized in part by how *quickly* they are made. So construed, speed

---

[8] I should emphasize again that my goal is not to evaluate coherentism construed as a general theory of what constitutes evidence. My interest is only in whether there is some reason to think that philosophical practice is distinguished from other domains by a tendency to psychologize evidence.

of the judgment in part determines whether a judgment counts as an intuition. I have chosen not to include this as one of the diagnostics simply because it is too easy to refute. There is simply no evidence of an appeal to speed of judgments in any of the cases I consider in the next chapter and I think it is uncharitable to Centrality proponents to assume that they include this as an important indicator of the intuitive.

Actual and effective presence of F1–F3: Not normative or modal: The goal of this book is to argue that it is not a characteristic feature of philosophical practice that it relies on appeal to intuitions. That's compatible with it being *possible* for philosophers to rely on intuitions. It is also compatible with it being 'better', in some sense, to do philosophy while relying on intuitions. My view is that the normative and modal claims are false, but the arguments against Centrality don't rely on or presuppose that view.

Not only are modal and normative claims about the practice largely irrelevant to an evaluation of Centrality, it is also important to focus on *effective* and *non-idle* occurrences of the intuition features F1–F3. To see what I have in mind consider the following possibilities:

- Suppose some epistemologists in an isolated village in Scotland have found out that the judgment that *p* has Rock status. Obviously, this discovery could have absolutely no bearing on philosophical practice more generally. It leaves open the possibility that practicing philosophers around the world don't recognize *p*'s special status—that this status has no effect whatsoever on how *p* is treated in philosophical discourse. The imagined discovery in Scotland is compatible with philosophers in the rest of the world treating *p* as needing backing by experience or reasoning, and otherwise treating it as if it had no special status. Under such conditions, I will say that an intuition feature is present (assuming now that the Scottish epistemologists are right), but it is *idle* and *non-effective*. Idle and non-effective presences of intuition features do not constitute support for Centrality.
- On the other hand, suppose Williamson is right and there are no judgments that are justified by relying solely on conceptual competence. This doesn't rule out that philosophers spend much of their time seeking conceptual truths and that this goal guides actual philosophical practice. If Williamson is right, this kind of practice would be fundamentally defective—it would be like we were all seeking unicorns—but so much the worse for actual philosophy. It would still

be true that actual philosophy is guided by an attempt to find conceptual truths, as proponents of Centrality claim.

- Final example: suppose methodological rationalists are right and there is a special phenomenology accompanying intuitive judgment, which is indicative of something very significant about those judgments. Suppose p is a proposition the contemplation of which is accompanied by this special phenomenology. Suppose also that p plays an important role in philosophical argumentation. This is all compatible with the phenomenology having no effect on philosophical practice (philosophers treat it as a kind of weird unpleasant itch that occurs whenever they think about p—it has no influence on their philosophizing). If so, F1 could be present, but not *effectively* so, and its presence would not constitute support for Centrality.

In sum, to evaluate Centrality we should focus only on effective occurrences of F1, F2 and F3. If these features are present, but their presence has no recognizable effect on philosophical practice, it does not constitute support for Centrality. Centrality is a claim about how philosophers actually treat certain kinds of judgments, not about how they *could* or *should* treat them.

The Relevant Unit of Investigation: When looking for significant Intuition-Features we have to decide on what the relevant **unit of investigation** is. Do we look at particular passages in texts where, e.g., a thought experiment is presented? Do we look at the entire theory that the passage contributes to? Or do we look even further, at the philosophical debate that a particular argument contributes to? In what follows I will move back and forth between different units. Obviously, the first place to look is at a particular sequence of sentences in a larger text. However, often the correct interpretation of those sentences will depend on the larger theory the sentences contribute to. Sometimes I look more broadly at the way in which certain arguments and thought experiments are treated over time in a philosophical debate. Some thought experiments, e.g. those of Perry, Burge, and Thomson, are discussed over and over again by philosophers over many years and a diachronic perspective gives a better picture of how the thought experiment affects philosophical practice.

7.3 More on the features of the intuitive

7.3.1 Intuitions and distinctive phenomenology

Let me remind the reader of how phenomenology is supposed to help us individuate intuitions. Pollock writes:

> Logically intuiting something is a phenomenologically unique experience which, although it may not be analyzable into other more familiar kinds of experience, is nevertheless a kind of experience a person can be quickly taught to recognize and label. (1974, p. 321)

Here, again, is Plantinga's (non) description of an alleged feature of intuitive judgments:

> ... that peculiar form of phenomenology with which we are all well acquainted, but which I can't describe in any way other than as the phenomenology that goes with seeing that such a proposition is true. (1993, pp. 105–6)

Bealer, maybe getting at the same thing, gives us an example appealed to by many of those who believe in the existence of distinctive phenomenology:

> ... when you first consider one of de Morgan's laws, often it neither seems to be true nor seems to be false. After a moment's reflection, however, something happens: it now seems true; you suddenly "just see" that it is true. (1996, p. 5)

Two issues arise when trying to use this as a diagnostic: first, how do we determine whether a claim made in a philosophical text is accompanied by such a feeling in the relevant group of subjects? Second, if it is accompanied by this feeling in the relevant group, how do we determine whether the presence is effective or just an idle accompaniment?

I'm at a disadvantage here since by introspection I cannot, even with the best of will, discern a special feeling that accompanies my contemplation of the naïve comprehension axiom, Gettier cases and other alleged paradigms of the intuitive. When I contemplate naïve comprehension, for example, I recognize that I might have believed that it was true if I hadn't read some philosophy, but the contemplation and the recognition have absolutely no distinctive phenomenology for me. I would recognize this as a failure in myself if there were significant empirical research to establish a systematic presence of the relevant feeling in other people, but there is no such evidence. All we have is anecdotal evidence that some intuition-theorists have these special feelings when they contemplate certain propositions. Given these difficulties, I will focus on the second issue in my case studies: I will look for some evidence in the relevant texts (or the debate about the text) that the author and interlocutors find it important that the judgments that *p* are accompanied by a feeling of a certain kind. Clear evidence of this would be that participants say things like, "Note that the judgment that *p* is accompanied by the special and important phenomenology' or "I am not sure '*p*' can be an answer to this question since it is missing the relevant kind of phenomenology." This obviously isn't the *only* kind of evidence that could show the effective presence of the special feeling. However, absent clear evidence of effective presence, I will assume that the feeling is either absent or, if present, idle and so not significant to the argument presented.

7.3.2 *More on Rock, Non-inferential, Non-experiential and Evidence Recalcitrance*

It is difficult to precisely characterize the special status I've labeled Rock. I think something along the lines of what Weinberg writes might be what many intuition-theorists have in mind:

> In the extant practice of appeal to intuitions as philosophical evidence, one cites one's application or withholding of a concept from a given case, usually a hypothetical one, in defense of (or in order to attack) a particular philosophical claim. Such citations thus are meant to carry argumentative, evidential weight, but one is not usually required to offer any further argumentation for the intuition itself.[. . .] Although they are used to provide evidence, one does not, and need not, provide further evidence for them.[9] (2007, p. 320)

But this characterization, when not combined with F3, raises a number of tricky questions. How are we supposed to interpret the 'usually' in "one

---

[9] Often a comparison is made here with perceptual reports: according to some philosophers they have a kind of defeasible default justificatory status. It goes beyond the scope of this work to evaluate that view of perceptual reports. My own view is that if this is true of perceptual reports, it applies to a vanishingly small set of them. For example, it does not apply to *I see the US president sign the health bill into law*—that report relies on all kinds of beliefs about the world, and e.g. facts about what it says on the particular pieces of paper in front of Obama. Suppose we think there are some *very few* perceptual reports that have this status. It is then still an open empirical question whether they are appealed to and play an important role within a particular intellectual domain—for example: it is an open question whether debates between economists rely in any interesting sense on such perceptual reports. I am in effect arguing in this kind of way about philosophy and intuitions: there might be a few judgments that have the feature intuitions theorists like to appeal to when they appeal to intuitions (I'm neutral on that), but such judgments play no special role in philosophy.

is not *usually* required to offer any further argumentation for the intuition itself" (italics added)? How many exceptions are allowed? Do we need to do statistical analysis to find out whether a particular claim has this feature? One reason these questions are difficult is that the answers will require that we be able to distinguish claims with this alleged Rock feature from claims that are regularly in the common ground of conversations. Any argument has premises that are not argued for. That's an essential feature of all arguments. All conversations have propositions in the common ground—propositions that are taken for granted among conversational participants. So, for example, when I talk to my brothers it is common ground *that Eftang is located more than 1 mile outside Sandefjord*. I can rely on this as a premise in reasoning without backing it up in any way. But this doesn't mean that this proposition is Rock in the intended sense—the sense that's supposed to help us identify intuitions. Similarly, the claim *that the earth is not flat* is in the common ground of most conversations taking place these days. So it is *usually* not required that we justify that claim. Again, that proposition is not Rock in the intended sense. So we need to find a way to distinguish propositions that are not argued for *because* they are in the common ground, from the propositions that have this alleged Rock feature.

In response to this kind of concern,[10] it is tempting and natural for Rock proponents to get rid of 'usually' and substitute a normative or modal claim, i.e. to construe Rock along the lines of: 'an intuitive judgment doesn't *require* further justification—it *would be* justified even without inferential and experiential support'. Suppose p is a proposition that philosophers always provide arguments and evidence for. On the current construal, this doesn't show that p doesn't have Rock status. That is settled by whether p *requires* that justification, i.e. whether p *would* be justified even in the absence of the arguments and evidence presented in its support.

One difficulty with this proposal is that it is in tension with the emphasis on *effective* occurrences of F1–F3. As emphasized above, for the purposes of evaluating Centrality, presence of F2 that does not move and influence

---

[10] Of course, those who think only necessary truths can be judged intuitively, will have an easy answer. Rock is introduced as a way for Centrality proponents to back off from that strict requirement—it would be much easier to refute Centrality if I could assume that an intuitive judgment had to be of a necessary truth (since a large number of the putative intuitive judgments concern contingent matters).

philosophical practice is uninteresting. Hypotheses about how philosophical practice *could be* or *ought to be* done won't tell us what philosophical practice is really like (if those possibilities are not realized and the practice isn't the way it ought to be). In particular, suppose the claim that *p* is debated by philosophers: reasons are given and evidence is presented. *P* is accepted or rejected based on the strength of those reasons and that evidence. Then the fact that it *could be* endorsed without justification constitutes no support for Centrality.

One might think an appeal to Evidence Recalcitrance could help here. I included Evidence Recalcitrance, in part, as a kind of concession to those who construe Rock as a claim about what is *required* (rather than what is actually done). The idea is roughly this: we can notice that the *real* basis for *p* is its intuitiveness if philosophers are reluctant to give up *p* even when evidence is presented against *p*. If endorsement of *p* is resistant to refutation of the arguments given in favor of *p*, that's evidence of *p*'s Rock status. The suggestion is that even though philosophers spend a lot of time arguing for and against *p*, we will note that it doesn't *require* justification because it is evidence recalcitrant.

While I can see the motivation for this kind of suggestion, I think it raises more difficulties than it solves. It will be very hard to discover that a particular claim is evidence recalcitrant. First, suppose we find that in a context C, a proposition *p* is argued for—extensive evidence is presented for *p*. According to the proposal now under consideration, we should check whether the proponent of *p would* stick with *p* (or continue to feel disinclined to give up *p*) even if she came to believe that her justifications for *p* failed. If she sticks with *p* (or continues to feel disinclined to give it up) no matter what evidence for not-*p* she is presented with, the fact that she spends time arguing for and against *p* doesn't constitute evidence against *p*'s having Rock status (since *p* is evidence recalcitrant). However, note that in most actual cases this kind of counterfactual evidence is *extremely* hard (if not impossible) to come across since most philosophers just write one or two papers on a topic and don't often write about why their own previous arguments fail. Establishing that a particular judgment has this feature will require careful empirical research into the phenomenology that accompanies it among philosophers and into the reaction they would have had were they to be presented with opposing data. Since no one is likely to ever get funding to do the kind of large-scale research into the psychology and dispositions of philosophers that would be required to establish even a single case of evidence recalcitrance, the appeal to evidence recalcitrance is entirely unhelpful in practice.

A final problem with the appeal to Evidence Recalcitrance is that even if we had some kind of empirical evidence of the relevant kind, that evidence could support a number of alternative hypotheses. Not only is it hard to find out how a particular philosopher would react were she to recognize that her argument for *p* failed. Even if it turns out to be true that she would stick with *p* under such conditions that could have a number of intuition-neutral explanations. She could be a stubborn and intellectually dishonest person, unwilling to give up her views when faced with opposing data. Unfortunately, some philosophers are like that. But, surely, that feature of her character can't be evidence for *p* having a special evidential status. Alternatively, it could be that she genuinely thinks she has another argument for *p*, one that's better than the one she first presented—and that this argument then provides the basis for *p*. If so, sticking with *p* when shown that the original argument fails is a sign of intellectual resourcefulness—it doesn't indicate that *p* has this kind of Rock status.

In sum, I think appeals to Evidence Recalcitrance are likely to be impossible to substantiate and so it will be entirely unhelpful to rely on this diagnostic when evaluating Centrality. I should add (and this is a brief digression) that this illustrates a more general phenomenon: often Centrality proponents will appeal to features that are practically impossible to detect and as a result their claims are empirically unsupportable.

Where does all this leave us with respect to Weinberg's characterization, "Such citations thus are meant to carry argumentative, evidential weight, but one is not usually required to offer any further argumentation for the intuition itself"? I'll put aside most of the difficulties just mentioned and operate on the following Rough Guide to Rock Detection:

Rough Guide to Rock Detection: If in a context *C*, evidence and arguments are given for *p* and those arguments or evidence plays a significant argumentative role in *C*, that is evidence that *p* is not Rock relative to *C*. The existence of a context *C'* in which you can get away with claiming *p* without providing argument or other evidence is irrelevant to *p*'s status in *C*, unless there is some clear evidence in *C* that what goes on in *C'* matters for *p*'s status in *C*.

This is admittedly a *rough* diagnostic, but it will prove useful. Looking ahead: all the texts to be investigated, the philosophically significant claims are all extensively discussed and argued about. There is no evidence in any of those texts that the *possibility* of asserting *p* without evidential support is significant (so even if some of these claims have that property, it plays no effective role in the debates).

7.3.3 Thought experiments, Rock and abductive inferences

This rough diagnostic raises a question (one that was pressed by an anonymous referee for OUP): suppose an author makes a claim c about a thought experiment. Suppose that author goes on to present various principles and maybe even a theoretical framework T that implies (or increases the likelihood of) c. I'm suggesting that we should take such authors to be using T as arguments for c, and this again as indicating that c is not treated (in this context) as having Rock status. There is, however, another option: maybe the author is engaging in a kind of abductive reasoning, where, in effect, c provides evidence for T. She is, speaking loosely, arguing that since T is the best explanation of c, we should endorse T. So the direction of support goes from c to T, not the other way around. If this is what's going on, the presence of T in the paper gives us no good reason to think that c doesn't have the alleged Rock status (it is because c has Rock status that it can serve as the starting point of an abductive inference).

While this is an issue worth looking into, it is not a possibility that will substantially undermine the practical value of Rough Guide in the next chapter. When would we have reason to think that an author engages in abductive reasoning? Let's start with the obvious: if the author says that she is engaging in an abductive inference that would be evidence that she is. However, in none of the cases we will investigate is there any explicit statement like that. If, on the other hand, the author says that T is an argument or evidence *for* c (rather than the other way around) that would be a (defeasible) reason to think this is *not* an instance of abductive reasoning. In many of the cases we'll be looking at there are explicit such statements. However, in some of the cases I will look at, there are no explicit remarks about what kind of argument is being presented. For such cases, some of the following features are relevant. First, in an abductive inference with c as the *explanandum* and T as the *explanans*, the question of whether c is the case is typically not under discussion. C is taken for granted and the author is trying to figure out how best to explain that c (where, of course, it is a highly contentious issue how to understand 'explain' and 'best'). If, on the other hand, not-c is one of the salient options in the context and it is clear from the argumentative context that T

is used to eliminate not-c, we have some reason to think this is not an abductive inference. In practically all the cases I will look at in the next chapter, not-c is under consideration (it's a live option), and I take that to be some evidence that the author didn't intend to present an abductive argument. Second, in several of the cases, it's too simplistic to say that the thought experiment starts out with some easily identifiable judgment c about a described scenario. Often, figuring out *how* to best describe the scenario is part of the challenge. The thought experiments at the start of John Perry's "The Essential Indexical" provide good illustrations of what I have in mind. On the first page of that paper he describes his goal as follows: "My aim in this paper is to make a key point about the characterization of this change, and of beliefs in general" (1979, p. 3). And he means this literally: he is interested in *how we should characterize what happens to the agents in his mini-scenarios*. He doesn't start out with a claim about what has happened or how it is best described. He starts out noticing a potentially interesting phenomenon and then goes on to try to figure it out—he tries to understand it better. As we will see, this procedure is typical of philosophical thought experiments (even the notorious—and I think abnormal—Gettier case, see Chapter 9, note 3, below.) When this is what is going on, the abductive model is inappropriate. For a few of the cases I discuss in the next chapter, it's less obvious how to rule out the abductive model—the cases are open to being read in both ways (i.e. both as taking T as an argument for c and vice versa.) In these cases, it is fairly clear what the relevant judgment is (so it's not like the Perry case where the challenge is to figure out what to say about a case) and there's little pressure towards not-c (except maybe by the pressure exerted by general skepticism). In most of those cases the right reading is probably to take the writer's intention to be that support goes both directions: she sees T as providing support to c, and vice versa. If that's the right reading, this is still a context in which c is in need of justification and so the Rough Guide is relevant.

It is also worth noting that the abductive model tells us nothing relevant about c. Any kind of claim whatsoever can be used in an inference to the best explanation (i.e. propositions that have no Centrality-relevant properties, e.g. *that Nora and Rachel went to Paris this spring* can be so used.) So, that a proposition is used as a starting point for an abductive inference provides no evidence that it is intuitive (or has the Rock property). What we might be deprived of is a quick argument, relying on the Rough

Guide, against *c* having the Rock status. How, in such cases, do we settle whether Rock is present? I don't think there's an obvious answer, but I think the burden of proof often ends up being squarely on the proponent of Centrality. A natural first step is to investigate whether the other intuition features, F1 and F3, are present. If we find that they are not (as we will in *all* the relevant cases in the next chapter) then the proponents of Rock and Centrality owe us an answer to the question: why, in the absence of F1 and F3, should we think that the proposition in question should be classified as intuitive? None of those who explicitly defend Centrality in the now very extensive literature on intuitions in philosophy operate with a notion of the intuitive that relies *solely* on the Rock feature. There's always also an appeal to the *a priori*, to reliance on only conceptual competence or to distinctive phenomenology. More generally, those who think some propositions have the Rock feature (and that it is essential for being classified as intuitive) think this is a property a proposition (or judgment) has by virtue of having some other properties—it is not a brute property. So someone who rejects F1 and F3 as necessary conditions on the intuitive owes us some alternative story about Rock and how to determine that a proposition has it.

In sum: while it is true that Rough Guide to Rock Detection is somewhat simplistic and that when used uncritically it can, for example, overlook the presence of an abductive inference, it will, when used with care, serve us well in the cases considered in the next chapter.

7.3.4 More on intuitions and conceptual justification

Many intuition-theorists and Centrality proponents take intuitive judgments to be of conceptually justified propositions. Three facts about contemporary philosophy are important in this connection:

1. There is extensive disagreement in the philosophical community about the very existence of this kind of justification. Many philosophers think the idea is incoherent or if coherent then without an extension.
2. Among those who believe in conceptual justification, there is minimal agreement on just what concepts are, what conceptual competence is, and just what is required for conceptual justification.

3. Among those who believe in conceptual justification, there is minimal agreement about just which particular propositions have that status.

There is an important corollary of (1)–(3): no contemporary philosopher who hopes to engage constructively with her contemporaries can expect to get away with relying on asserting p simply because *she* thinks p is a conceptual truth. In contemporary philosophy you simply cannot get away with something like what A is trying in this exchange:

A: p.

B: I am not convinced that p. What's your argument—what's the evidence for p?

A: Oh, you see, I don't need arguments or evidence for p. p is special in that it is conceptually justified and so I don't need to provide arguments or evidence for it.

If A does not want to simply *stop* the conversation at this point, the best she can hope for is to engage with a small subset of philosophers who believe in conceptual justification as she construes it and agree that p has that property. However, given the many construals of 'conceptual justification' that are operative today and the extensive group of philosophers who deny that there's any such thing, this will be a very tiny group of philosophers. So the argumentative strategy A tries out in this exchange will have a very limited influence on the larger philosophical community. These points are relevant when trying to operationalize F3. Given the intense controversy over these issues, the idea that philosophers can *effectively* rely on this kind of justification without extensive and explicit theoretical backing is *prima facie* implausible. Even if those who believe some judgments are justified in this way are correct (and Quine, Williamson, *et al.* are wrong), the issue is so controversial that it is just not the kind of thing you can effectively rely on in contemporary philosophical debates without at least making it explicit what you are up to. So what we should expect from A is that she tells us what she thinks concepts are, what she means by 'conceptual competence', how she construes the relevant kind of justification, and that she then goes on to show that p satisfies these various conditions. We would also expect that in so doing, A would tell us how she has convinced herself that the various excellent arguments given against analyticity can be overcome (she doesn't need to spell out the arguments, but she should at least reference her favorite reply to those arguments).

This gives us some hints for how, when faced with a philosophical text, we can discern whether central claims in that text are taken to be conceptually justified by the author. We can look for the following:

- First, if the writer *says* that the judgment is based solely on conceptual competence, that would be good evidence in favor of the writer trying to rely on F3.[11] Looking ahead: *none* of the texts I look at include such explicit statements (and several of them explicitly deny it).
- Second, if there are explicit discussions of the following kind in a debate over the answer to some question Q that would constitute evidence of an attempt to rely on F3:

A: The answer to Q is *p*.

B: Are you basing *p* solely on your conceptual competence? It seems to me you are relying on experience and memory in a way that goes beyond what is required for conceptual competence.

A: I disagree. Let me explain: here is what I mean by concept: *Blah 1*. Note that these are the concepts involved in the judgment that *p*: *Blah 2*. Here is what I mean by 'based solely on': *Blah 3*. Putting all this together, you will note that the judgment that *p* is based solely on competence with its constituent concepts.

If we find in the case studies significant discussions of this form—where answers to questions are ruled out because they are not conceptual truths and where that topic is at the center of the discussion—we have evidence that F3 figures centrally in those case studies. The flip side of this is that if we *do not* find any such discussions, then we have evidence against the idea that a search for judgments with F3 status plays a significant role in the

---

[11] I am here talking about what philosophers are trying to do, since I don't want to assume that what such philosophers try to do is possible. My own view is that the notion of conceptual justification has never been satisfactorily worked out, and I suspect it *cannot* be respectably articulated and defended. But I don't want to rely on that view here. I will take it as support for Centrality if there is extensive evidence of philosophers *seeking* conceptually justified truths. I will come back to these points in Chapter 10.

discussion of thought experiments. Looking ahead: *none* of the texts I look at include such discussions. I take that to be evidence against an effective presence of F3.

- Third, we can look for the presence of F1 and F2/F2.1/F2.2.[12] According to many proponents of F3, F1 and F2 accompany conceptually justified judgments, so their absence is evidence of the absence of F3.
- Fourth, we can check whether the judgment in question is of a necessary truth. Most of those who believe there are conceptually justified truths also believe such truths are necessarily true.[13] If the judgment is of a contingent proposition, then we have reason to think it isn't a conceptually justified claim and hence evidence of the absence of F3.
- Finally, a helpful heuristic in some cases is to compare a candidate claim to alleged paradigms. I will use Vixen and Tall as paradigms of conceptually justified claims and Sick and Libro as paradigms of claims that are not so justified:

Vixen: Consider a case in which Mark walks around in the forest and then a vixen passes right in front of him. Question: Did a female fox pass right in front of him?

Tall: Consider three brothers, *A*, *B*, and *C*. *A* is taller than *B*. *B* is taller than *C*. Question: Is *A* taller than *C*?

Sick: "A 65-year-old man is admitted with pneumonia. He has a 2-year history of Parkinson's disease and is on treatment to control his symptoms. He is an ex-smoker of 20 cigarettes per day for 40 years. He claims he has never had a bad chest until recently but he admits this is his third attack of pneumonia in the last 6 months. Question: What is happening?" (Roper 2005, p. 131)

Libro: Mandy is walking down Russell Avenue in Buenos Aires from Thames. She walks two blocks and then turns left and walks two more blocks. Question: how many blocks away from Boutique del Libro is she?

---

[12] Though, for reasons given above, I doubt that F2.2. will be helpful.
[13] See again Section 6.1.3 above.

When we encounter a philosophical case/thought experiment we can ask: is there even a *prima facie* case to be made that they are like Vixen and Tall rather than Sick and Libro? While certainly not foolproof, this heuristic can help in a few cases. Looking ahead, the cases I will be investigating all strike me as clearly belonging with Sick and Libro.[14]

7.3.5 *General remarks about diagnostics: how to understand the hidden subject in 'p is intuitive'*

Intuitiveness is a feature of judgments. Judgments are made by people and they judge in different ways. So talk of 'the judgment that *p*' must often be taken to have a tacit subject. This could be the speaker, some larger set including the speaker (e.g. humans with certain kinds of cognitive make-up), or some group that does not include the speaker. In some of the recent debate triggered by experimental philosophers the issue of scope, and of the proper identification of the tacit subject, has come to the forefront. Should the scope include all competent speakers be they philosophers or not, from any culture, or is the scope more limited, say to experts in the field? Since this issue is a matter of debate, I will leave it open-ended at this point of the discussion, but at various junctures below it will be important to explicitly address this issue.

7.4 Summary and additional reflections on how to operationalize appeals to intuitions

It should be overwhelmingly clear by now that those who claim philosophers rely extensively on intuitions are not making it easy to support or criticize their view. All the key features they claim intuitions have are difficult to effectively detect in a particular text or philosophical exchange. This makes it puzzling, to put it mildly, how proponents of Centrality have managed to convince themselves that appeals to intuition are found extensively in the practice of doing philosophy (unless, as I conjecture, they have been tacitly influenced by AIT). Of course, this will also seem to

---

[14] There's another foundational question that I'm not sure how to answer on behalf of Centrality proponents: why think that F1, F2 and F3 accompany each other? In particular, what's the reason for thinking the distinctive phenomenology connects in significant ways with the other two features? It is hard to find clear answers to this in the literature and the question will not be explored further here.

be bad news for the kind of project I've set myself. However, in the next two chapters I claim that even if we operate only with these somewhat loose characterizations of the intuitive that I have attempted to articulate above, it will become very clear that philosophy is not a domain where anything like the intuitive plays an important role.

8
Case Studies

Those interested in the role of intuitions in contemporary philosophical practice should be deeply engaged in an empirical study of that practice and be concerned with how to detect the presence of an appeal to the intuitive. Given the amorphous and shifty understanding of the intuitive in the philosophical tradition, it is *not* helpful to just look at a text and ask: *Is there an appeal to intuitions in this text?* Given the many understandings of 'intuitions' found among philosophers, a debate over this question, without further precisification, is worse than pointless. To alleviate this problem, the previous chapter identified three features that can be used to identify a reliance on the intuitive:

F1: Seem True
F2: Rock
F3: Based Solely on Conceptual Competence

What I do in this chapter is look at ten case studies to see whether we can find evidence of the presence of those features. I focus on a part of philosophical practice where Centrality proponents typically claim we can find intuition-appeals: judgments about thought experiments.

The reader can reasonably wonder what could possibly follow from this. Even if I am right that these ten cases don't rely on intuitions, isn't that a very poor empirical basis for a claim about what goes on in philosophy more generally? In brief my answer is this:

(i) You have to start somewhere and those familiar with this literature will note that what I do in this chapter is very much more than what's done by any of those defending Centrality.
(ii) The cases are carefully chosen: they are exactly of the kind that proponents of Centrality mention (but don't carefully study).

(iii) The reader will soon notice that a pattern emerges—the pattern is one of complete absence of any of F1, F2 and F3. I predict that more detailed research of more cases will find more of the same.

Think of this chapter as a first attempt at a somewhat detailed study of philosophical practice guided by intuition-diagnostics. Philosophical methodology needs more studies of these kinds—maybe using alternative and more refined diagnostics. I'm engaging with a tradition in metaphilosophy that despite its enormous influence has been subject to hardly any empirical testing.[1] I want primarily to show how implausible the traditional picture is and how much of a *prima facie* misrepresentation of the actual practice it is.

Three remarks before turning to the case studies: First, in what follows I focus on philosophical practice as it is reflected in written texts. Ideally, such an investigation should be extended to verbal philosophical discourse and in particular to lectures and Q&A since these play an important role in philosophical practice. Since I don't know how to do that in a respectable way, I will, unfortunately, have to restrict myself to the written evidence of philosophical practice.

Second, in a way, what I have to say about all these cases is the same: if you read the text carefully and don't add to what is there, you'll find no evidence of presence of F1–F3. However, just repeating that over and over again doesn't make for very exciting reading, so for each case I consider some objections and sources of confusion. Many of those can be repeated for all the cases, but, again, that would be repetitive, so I trust the reader to be able to make the appropriate generalizations. Sometimes I will wait to discuss an objection until I get to a case where the objection most naturally arises. In other cases, particularly for objections that have a very broad scope, I will postpone the discussion until the next chapter. In that chapter I respond to a wide range of objections I have heard when presenting this material and from people who generously commented on early drafts of this book. Therefore, although I understand this can get frustrating, I ask the reader to be patient, and hopefully all the most

---

[1] Of course, experimental philosophers have emphasized the importance of empirical research into intuitions, but that is based on an uncritical endorsement of Centrality. Experimental philosophers are just as nonempirical in their description of philosophical practice as methodological rationalists. See Chapter 11 for a discussion.

prominent objections to my diagnosis of the cases will be addressed at some point, either in this chapter or the next.[2]

Third, as will become clear, I don't think it should be a goal to have a theory of thought experiments. What we call 'thought experiments' is not the kind of thing that one should have a theory of. I endorse a no-theory theory of thought experiments, if you will. That said, I think reflecting on the case studies justifies a few generalizations. In particular, thought experiments are devices for drawing our attention to philosophically interesting features of the world and for asking questions about those features. I spell this out in a bit more detail at the beginning of Chapter 9 and the first three case studies have an 'Observations' section where the relevant features are highlighted.

8.1 Perry on the problem of the essential indexical

If anything constitutes a paradigmatic use of the method of cases it is in John Perry's classic paper from 1979, "The Problem of the Essential Indexical." Perry starts by describing some cases. Robert Stalnaker describes these as "stories in which two agents had all the same relevant (objective) beliefs and desires, but nevertheless were rationally motivated to act in different ways because of their different perspectives on the world" (2011, p. 140). Perry's cases have triggered an extraordinarily extensive literature in many philosophical subfields and in neighboring fields such as linguistics. They are still topics of intense philosophical investigation and there is no consensus about what conclusions to draw from them.

Here is a famous passage from this paper, known to many contemporary philosophers from their undergraduate days:

---

[2] A reader for OUP raised concerns about presenting the material in this way, pointing out that "too many readers will be picking up the book not to read it cover to cover but to read the detailed discussion of the case they are interested in." Clearly, any such reader will be very unsatisfied, since the discussion of any one of these cases considered in isolation is incomplete and unsatisfactory. However, I find that the two alternative ways of proceeding—discussing just one case in enormous detail or repeating all the important points in connection with each case—both have more significant drawbacks. All I can do is encourage readers to at least complete all of this and the next chapter.

I once followed a trail of sugar on a supermarket floor, pushing my cart down the aisle on one side of a tall counter and back the aisle on the other, seeking the shopper with the torn sack to tell him he was making a mess. With each trip around the counter, the trail became thicker. But I seemed unable to catch up. Finally it dawned on me. I was the shopper I was trying to catch. I believed at the outset that the shopper with a torn sack was making a mess. And I was right. But I didn't believe that I was making a mess. That seems to be something I came to believe. And when I came to believe that, I stopped following the trail around the counter, and rearranged the torn sack in my cart. My change in beliefs seems to explain my change in behavior. My aim in this paper is to make a key point about the characterization of this change, and of beliefs in general. (p. 3)

This is but one of a range of examples in the paper. Immediately after presenting this case, he goes on to describe a hiker lost in the wilderness with a map transitioning into a belief expressed by "I am here" (accompanied by a pointing to the map); a professor transitioning from the belief that the departmental meeting starts at noon to a belief expressed by "The meeting starts now." Perry's goal is "to make a key point about the characterization of this change, and of beliefs in general." He ends up with a surprising conclusion: the cases *don't* involve a change in belief. The same proposition is believed before and after the transition. What has changed is the way in which that proposition is believed. In Perry's way of thinking, the way in which a proposition is believed plays an important role in explaining agency. While Perry's cases and his discussion have been enormously influential, his solution is controversial. In the more than thirty years since the publication of the paper, a wide range of solutions has been proposed and reflections on these cases and the questions they raise have made philosophers of language and mind rethink the nature of content, and the connection between propositional attitudes, semantic content, and agency.

8.1.1 *Observations about Perry's thought experiment*

The goal here is to determine whether F1, F2, or F3 play an important role in Perry's thought experiment. Before addressing that question directly, some general features of Perry's cases are worth highlighting (and we will see these recurring in the remaining cases to be discussed):

Fact focuser: the most useful way to think of Perry's cases is as a device for drawing our attention to some phenomenon or feature of the world that has philosophical significance. It presents us with the challenge of characterizing and explaining this feature of the world. At the most abstract level, the challenge raised by the first case is this: a certain kind of change happened when Perry went from thinking that *someone is making a mess* to thinking that *I am making a mess* and this explained his change in behavior.[3] The goal is to help us understand this kind of change better.

Generality requirement, plurality of cases, and abstraction: Perry's paper starts with *a range of cases*. As we will see, all the case studies involve a family of cases, not just a single case. Perry claims that these cases exemplify *the same phenomenon*. The question he asks us to focus on is not a question that has specifically to do with philosophers making messes in supermarkets, or even with first-person beliefs. According to Perry, the same phenomenon is involved in *locational beliefs* and *temporal beliefs*. This feature of the paper is important for at least two reasons:

(i) It is a requirement on proper understanding of e.g. the first case that the reader understands what the relevant features of the case are. In particular: it is important to understand that it is inessential to the case that it involves a so-called first-person belief.
(ii) To understand the question Perry asks about the first case, you have to understand that he takes it to be a requirement on a correct characterization of it that it generalizes to the other cases.

Plurality of questions: The case raises not just one question, but a whole range of questions: what is the connection between change in belief state and the content of a belief? Can a change in content of belief explain Perry's change in behavior? What is the content of a first-person belief? How do we articulate the change in content—i.e. how do *we*, who are not that person and so cannot use the first-person pronoun, articulate the change? These and many other questions are raised by the case.

Lack of clear conclusion: Perry ends the presentation of the case with a hedged observation about what happened, saying, "My change in belief **seems** to explain my change in behavior." As he keeps emphasizing throughout the paper, it is far from obvious what to say about what is going on in these cases, and it is even difficult to come up with a non-question-begging characterization of the case. According to Perry, it is, for example, a mistake to say that the agent underwent *a change in belief*. He says:

---

[3] This is a contentious description since it is unclear what the italics are supposed to indicate. Just how to interpret the role of those italics is at the center of the problem.

At first characterizing the change seems easy. My beliefs changed, didn't they, in that I came to have a new one, namely, that I am making a mess? But things are not so simple. The reason they are not is the importance of the word "I" in my expression of what I came to believe. (p. 3)

According to Perry's solution at the end of the paper, *what he believes*, the object of his belief, is the same before and after the change in behavior. The correct description of what happened in the supermarket ends up relying on highly complex issues in linguistics, metaphysics, philosophy of mind, philosophy of language, psychology and other disciplines.[4]

Justification requirement: Yes/No answers are excluded: Perry's paper illustrates one obvious feature of good philosophical questions about cases: no simple yes/no answer is sought. Even if it is correct to answer the question *Did a change in the content of Perry's belief explain his change in behavior?* by 'yes', this isn't the kind of answer Perry is looking for. Perry's questions (and philosophical questions more generally) come with a justification requirement. Any interesting answer has to be accompanied by an explanation of *why* this is the right answer.

8.1.2 Perry's case and the intuition features

I turn now to the question of the extent to which claims made by Perry about this case have any of the intuition features F1–F3. I will first state somewhat bombastically my view of how to characterize the case and then immediately consider some objections to my characterization.

Rock? Perry does not present any element of his case as one where we can have only a standoff of intuitions and where there is, by default, no need for argumentation or evidence. What I called 'Rock' in the previous chapter was an attempt to capture the following phenomenon: a proposition *p* is endorsed and treated as justified despite a complete absence of reasons and evidence given in support for it. It has some kind of default justificatory status. There is no evidence in Perry's text that any proposition of significance in the paper has this status. Perry continuously emphasizes how hard it is to even describe the case. No description of the case is uncontroversial. All the many characterizations he considers are evaluated by giving arguments for and against them. The characterization he

---

[4] For some recent work on the topic, see Ninan (2010), Anand (2006), and Stalnaker (2008).

ends up endorsing is extensively argued for, and is endorsed only tentatively.

Note also that when a philosopher presents a *range* of cases, as Perry does, in order to make the *same* point, that is evidence against the idea that the description of any one of those cases will have Rock status. As I pointed out above, a philosopher who presents a range of cases, typically challenges the reader to reflect on what they all have in common—in effect puts as a requirement on understanding any one of them that it is seen as illustrating the same point as the others. The writer is also (sometimes implicitly, sometimes explicitly) claiming that the judgment about one case should be, in some relevant respect, the same as the judgment about the others. So the writer is requiring the reader to engage in complex reasoning and inference in order to even understand the set of cases. This tends to undermine the proposal that any particular claim about any one of the cases has Rock status.

Seem True? Perry presents his cases as puzzling throughout—nothing about them strike us as *seeming true* in the way that de Morgan's laws do or the way the Gettier judgments do to some people. So we can put aside the background issue of whether this kind of 'seems-true' feeling exists at all: Perry's case is presented in a way that clearly doesn't attempt to appeal to—or put argumentative weight on—any such feeling: if any feeling is appealed to, it is the feeling of puzzlement. I am not aware of any contribution to the discussion of this topic that appeals to the evidential importance of a special phenomenology when a judgment about these cases is contemplated.

Conceptual justification? The discussion of Perry's cases over the last thirty years has drawn on evidence and considerations from many surprising areas: data from linguistics, psychology, and different areas of philosophy including action theory, philosophy of mind, metaphysics and the philosophy of language has been considered relevant. Perry is asking us how to explain a certain change in behavior. The facts appealed to along the way are, among other things, contingent features of human cognition (e.g. the connections between thoughts, ways of thinking thoughts, and features of English) and the connections between these and motivations for and rationalization of action. There is simply no evidence in Perry's text that he thinks of this as an a priori enterprise that one should engage in by relying on nothing but conceptual competence. No one working on these issues today takes him or herself to be constrained by the idea that the *only* relevant considerations when deciding how to describe the original cases are those that rely *only* on conceptual competence.

8.1.3 Objection to the characterization of Perry's case: you focused on the wrong proposition—you have overlooked the real intuitive judgment

I suspect in this (and the other cases to be discussed later in this chapter), many will respond by saying that there is *some* judgment in the case that does instantiate F1, F2, or F3, and I've just failed to identify it. The judgments that I say don't instantiate these features aren't the relevant judgments. This is of course very tricky. For each case we have to look through alternatives and there will always be indefinitely many candidates. Consider first P1 as a candidate judgment in Perry's case that I have, allegedly, overlooked (i.e. think of P1 as candidate for the judgment that is *really* the intuitive one):

P1: Some cognitive change happened to Perry and that change figures in an explanation of his change in behavior.

Reply: First note that on some interpretations of 'cognitive' P1 is already included in the initial description of the case, and just repeating a claim made directly in Perry's description of the case does not constitute an answer to any question we are interested in (if the setup of the case stipulates that *p*, then describing the case as one in which *p* is the case will not answer any interesting question about the case). Of course, it is true that many philosophers believe something they would express using a sentence like P1, but not because it has any of the intuition features F1–F3. It is simply an assumption shared by many of those who think about these kinds of cases—it is in the common ground among most conversational participants. Most of the philosophers who think about this case assume that the kind of change in behavior exhibited in Perry's cases is connected to some cognitive change. This is not a claim that has some kind of special epistemic status (other than simply being in the common ground). Participants in the debate would welcome challenges to it and when faced with those challenges would present evidence and reasons.

What about P1 and the special 'Seem-True' feature? As a matter of self-reporting, I have no such special sense at all when reflecting on P1. This could of course be a defect in me, but I note that there is no evidence that anything of argumentative significance in the debate over the *de se* hangs on whether the belief in P1 comes with a special feel. The issue of how certain judgments feel has played absolutely no role in any discussions of P1. So even though it is *possible* that some people feel a certain way when they contemplate P1, there is no evidence that this has had any discernible effect on the debate (and certainly no evidence in Perry's original text that he thought the phenomenology of P1 was significant).

Can an argument be made that P1 is conceptually justified? As we saw in Chapter 7, claims about conceptual justification are elusive and difficult to pin down, but using the rough diagnostics from the previous chapter, it seems implausible: P1 lacks F1 and F2 and insofar as those accompany conceptually justified claims, we have evidence against attributing that status to P1. Conceptually justified propositions are, according to the views surveyed in Chapter 6, necessary truths. P1 is not. It is *possible* for the kind of change in behavior to happen without a cognitive change. Moreover, at no point in the discussion of the *de se* over the last thirty years has the question of whether P1 is conceptually justified played a role. Had this been an important element of the case, we should expect there to have been discussions of what the relevant concepts are, what the relevant notion of concept possession is, and how the alleged instances of conceptual analysis lead to P1. Since none of those discussions has taken place, we at least have good reason to think the presence of F3 is not an effective element of the debate.[5]

A final remark on the suggestion that P1 is the real intuition relied on by those reflecting on Perry's case: many participants in the debate think Perry's focus on agency and change in behavior was a mistake. The real issue, according to these philosophers, has to do with whether we should characterize the agents as learning something new.[6] On this construal of the case, P1 is not important and maybe an incorrect or at least misleading

---

[5] See Chapter 7 for a discussion of the 'effective presence' of intuition features.

[6] For example, in David Lewis' (1979) version of Perry's cases involving two gods, there is no significant change in behavior—it is all about when, how and whether the two gods learn something new. Many think Lewis' version brings out the important elements of the phenomenon better than Perry's description of his original cases.

interpretation of the original case. Note that if this is right, Perry in effect misconstrued the significance of his own examples. This illustrates a further fact: we shouldn't take the original authors to be authorities on the cases they present. Someone could come up with an ingenious case, a case that enables us to see very important aspects of the world, but the person coming up with the case isn't necessarily an authority on how that feature should be articulated and certainly not on how it should be explained.

No doubt, some will find these remarks about P1 inconclusive. Some will pick a claim other than P1 as the intuitive judgment of the case. My suspicion is that whatever other options are presented they will lack F1–F3, or be irrelevant to the philosophical debate surrounding the case, but of course this is a point where I'm open to concrete constructive proposals on behalf of Centrality proponents.

8.2 Burge on individualism and the mental

My second case study is one of the twentieth century's most influential, original, and discussed cases in the philosophies of mind and language—Tyler Burge's arthritis case in his paper, "Individualism and the Mental" (1979). To remind the reader here is an overview of what goes on. Burge divides the case into three stages. Here is the first stage:

A given person has a large number of attitudes commonly attributed with content clauses containing 'arthritis' in oblique occurrence. For example, he thinks (correctly) that he has had arthritis for years; that his arthritis in his wrists and fingers is more painful than his arthritis in his ankles, that it is better to have arthritis than cancer of the liver, that stiffening joints is a symptom of arthritis, that certain sorts of aches are characteristic of arthritis, that there are various kinds of arthritis, and so forth. In short, he has a wide range of such attitudes. In addition to these unsurprising attitudes, he thinks falsely that he has developed arthritis in the thigh.

Generally competent in English, rational and intelligent, the patient reports to his doctor his fear that his arthritis has now lodged in his thigh. The doctor replies by telling him that this cannot be so, since arthritis is specifically an inflammation of joints. Any dictionary could have told him the same. The patient is surprised, but relinquishes his view and goes on to ask what might be wrong with his thigh. (p. 77)

Here is the second stage:

The person might have had the same physical history and non-intentional mental phenomena while the word 'arthritis' was conventionally applied, and defined to apply, to various rheumatoid ailments, including the one in the person's thigh, as well as to arthritis. (p. 78)

The third stage is an interpretation of the counterfactual situation, or an addition to it as so far described. Burge says that it is reasonable to suppose that:

In the counterfactual situation, the patient lacks some—probably all—of the attitudes commonly attributed with content clauses containing 'arthritis' in oblique occurrence. He lacks the occurrent thoughts or beliefs that he has arthritis in the thigh, that he has had arthritis for years, that stiffening joints and various sorts of aches are symptoms of arthritis, that his father had arthritis, and so on. (p. 78)

According to Burge, "the upshot of these reflections is that the patient's mental contents differ while his entire physical and non-intentional mental histories, considered in isolation from their social context, remain the same" (p. 79).

8.2.1 Observations about Burge's case

Complexity and plurality of cases: This is the most complex case of any of the ones to be considered in this chapter. For one thing, it is very long. The presentation of it starts on page 77 and ends on page 79. Several pages of terminological remarks precede it. After the presentation of the first case, there are several analogous cases presented—these are integral to the presentation of the first case since they are supposed to tell us what features of the first case are essential. Anyone who has struggled with this case in any detail knows that subtle differences in how the case is described can make a significant difference and so none of the details are superfluous.

It is very tricky to identify just what counts as 'the case' and equally tricky to get clear on exactly what questions we are supposed to ask about 'the case' once it is identified. It is open to many interpretations, no one of which is the unique correct one. This open-endedness is an important feature to keep in mind when using this as an example of a philosophical case. I will present the key question much as Burge does in Section III of the paper. Burge first observes:

I believe that common practice in the attribution of propositional attitudes is fairly represented by the various steps. This point is not really open to dispute. Usage may be divided in a few of the cases in which I have seen it as united. But broadly speaking, it seems to me undeniable that the individual steps of the thought experiment are acceptable to ordinary speakers in a wide variety of examples. (p. 88)

Burge points out that speakers of English utter sentences like 'She believes that she has arthritis in her thigh' under the circumstances described in the first step of the thought experiment. This is a straightforwardly empirical claim about our linguistic practice and according to Burge it's so easy to check on that it's not worth more discussion (you might find this a controversial interpretation of this step and I'll return to it below). Call this step '*Observation about Usage*'. He doesn't think discussing this observation is particularly philosophically interesting or useful. The philosophically interesting issue, according to Burge, is how to *interpret* this usage:

The issue open to possible dispute is whether the steps should be taken in the literal way in which I have taken them, and thus whether the conclusion I have drawn from those steps is justified. In the remainder of Section III, I shall try to vindicate the literal interpretation of our examples. I do this by criticizing, in order of increasing generality or abstractness, a series of attempts to reinterpret the thought experiment's first step. (p. 88, my italics)

He ends up rejecting all these alternative interpretations and defending what he calls 'the literal interpretation'. What is it to give an interpretation of the first step? It is to interpret utterances of e.g. 'She thinks she has arthritis in her thigh.' What Burge calls 'the literal interpretation' is disquotational according to which it means *that she has arthritis in her thigh*. Burge thinks many philosophers will resist such a literal interpretation. He says:

The first step, as I have interpreted it, is the most likely to encounter opposition. In fact, there is a line of resistance that is second nature to linguistically oriented philosophers. According to this line, we should deny that, say, the patient really believed or thought that arthritis can occur outside of joints because he misunderstood the word 'arthritis'. More generally, we should deny that a subject could have any attitudes whose contents he incompletely understands . . . .If a foreigner were to mouth the words 'arthritis may occur in the thigh' or 'my father had arthritis', not understanding what he uttered in the slightest, we would not say that he believed that arthritis may occur in the thigh, or that his father had arthritis. So why should we impute the belief to the patient?" Why, indeed? Or rather, why do we? The question is a good one. (p. 89)

According to Burge, these kinds of considerations could lead us to conclude that we should interpret the utterance of 'She thinks she has arthritis in her thigh' to mean, for example, *that she thinks she has something called 'arthritis' in her thigh* (this is the metalinguistic interpretation extensively discussed by Burge, especially on pp. 96–99).[7]

The point of this somewhat detailed description of Burge's case is to remind the reader that just talking about 'Burge's case' and the alleged intuitions it appeals to is simplistic.[8] Identifying what Burge takes to be of central philosophical interest is not simple. As I interpret the text, the central question raised is the *Interpretative Question*: how should we interpret attitude reports of the form "She believes she has arthritis in her thigh" in the kinds of contexts described in the first step of the thought experiment? For those who think the case relies, at its core, on an appeal to an intuition, it should be found somewhere in the reply to the Interpretative Question.

Fact focuser: The observations I made at the beginning of the discussion of Perry's case apply to Burge's as well. The function and purpose of Burge's case is to focus our attention on a philosophically interesting set of features of the world: the various ways in which an individual's thought content depends in complex ways on that individual's social setting. As Burge points out, this is a philosophically significant fact about thoughts and our mentalistic notions (it undermines what he calls the individualistic tradition in philosophy). As we have just seen, the case raises a number of interesting questions and, just as with Perry's case, we can construe the case as a device for raising those questions.

Generalization: As with other fact-focusing cases, one important challenge is to figure out how to generalize. The phenomenon he is interested in has nothing specifically to do with arthritis. For this reason, he, just like Perry, goes on to present many other cases that he claims make the *same* point and illustrate the *same* phenomenon. For example, he considers thought ascriptions about contracts and briskets to people who have false or incomplete

---

[7] Here is an alternative structuring of the case: what Burge refers to as 'the usage' is what the subject utters, i.e. they utter sentences like 'I have arthritis in my thigh' and 'I'm concerned that I have arthritis in my thigh' even under conditions of ignorance and lack of information. What's an open question is whether an informed reporter in such a circumstance says, 'She believes she has arthritis in her thigh' or says, 'She believes she has something called "arthritis" in her thigh.'

[8] For example, when Bealer (1996, p. 4) tells us that what he refers to as 'Burge's arthritis example' is a paradigm of intuition-based philosophy, it would be helpful to be told just what the example is and what the relevant intuitive judgments are. Only then can we properly evaluate the claim.

beliefs about contracts and briskets. Looking at the total set of cases we are supposed to get what they have in common and that will identify the general phenomenon that Burge wants to draw our attention to.

8.2.2 Burge's case and the intuition features

Anyone who engages seriously with Burge's example and the debate about it will realize that there is no interesting or philosophically significant judgment about it that can plausibly be characterized as having Rock status in the debate. Burge's case is exceedingly complex. Complicated theoretical vocabulary is used to describe it, and any philosophically significant judgment made about the case draws on knowledge we have and assumptions we make about a variety of theoretical and empirical issues. As pointed out in the section above, Burge first makes an initial set of Observations about Usage. These are observations about the kinds of sentences English speakers as a matter of fact use to report each other's thoughts under the kinds of conditions described by Burge. One can of course question Burge's description. Doing so involves empirical research into linguistic behavior. Having made his observation about usage, Burge goes on to ask the Interpretative Question: how do we interpret those reports? Is there evidence that 'arthritis' as it is used in such a report is ambiguous or context sensitive? Is there evidence that it is mentioned and not used in those reports? Again, answers to those questions will rely on knowledge of and assumptions made about the nature of context sensitivity, ambiguity, and quotational contexts. Finally, given an interpretation of the reports in question, we have to ask: are the reports so interpreted true or should we conclude that there are systematic errors made by those who make such reports in the circumstances Burge describes? In sum, there's a range of questions raised by Burge's case, and none of the answers to these questions are presented by Burge (or other participants) in this debate as not needing justification or as somehow constituting rock-bottom points of argumentation.

There are three elements of Burge's description of the case that can generate confusion on this point. First, as mentioned above, Burge says about the Observation about Usage that it "is fairly represented by the various steps. This point is not really open to dispute." This is not to say that this judgment has some kind of Rock status. What he means is that no interesting interlocutor would deny it. It is, Burge assumes, in the common ground of the conversation. Remember, the claim is that ordinary speakers utter sentences like 'She thinks she has arthritis in her thigh' even when the agent has incomplete or mistaken ideas about arthritis. That is an *empirical fact about speech behavior*. These are facts about linguistic practice that Burge has observed by being around speakers of English—the judgments are based on years of experience as a member of various linguistic communities.[9] As mentioned above, Burge thinks the interesting and difficult question is how to *interpret* utterances like 'She thinks she has arthritis in her thigh.' It is *not* obvious that it should be interpreted to mean *that she thinks she has arthritis in her thigh*. No answer to the Interpretative Question is presented by Burge as having the alleged Rock status.

Second, Burge talks quite a bit about beliefs he thinks *non-philosophers* will have about his case. What he says is instructive and easy to misinterpret if one doesn't read the text carefully. He says, for example:

I find that most people unspoiled by conventional philosophical training regard the three steps of the thought experiment as painfully obvious. Such folk tend to chafe over my filling in details or elaborating on strategy. (p. 87)

About this naïve reaction he adds: "I think this naïveté appropriate" (p. 87). But at no point in the paper does he treat that naïve reaction as evidence or give it evidential weight. He notes the naïve reaction and then goes on to argue, for another forty pages, against alternative, non-naïve, interpretations of the relevant phenomenon (and the objection isn't at any point, 'This is not sufficiently naïve').

Turning next to intuition feature F1, i.e. Seem True, there is no evidence that such a feature plays any role in the debate over Burge's case. If someone has the Seem-True feeling when reflecting on one answer to the question of how we should interpret the first step, there is no evidence in Burge's text or the extensive debate that it has triggered that this feeling is relevant to these arguments. At no point in the debate over Burge's case has a discussion of the phenomenology of the judgment played an important role.

---

[9] He also says that he has "presented the experiment as appealing to ordinary intuitions" (p. 88). Part I established that 'intuition'-talk provides no support for Centrality. The various strategies for Centrality-unfriendly interpretations of 'intuition' presented there apply to these passages.

The absence of F1 and F2 is reason for thinking there is no significance occurrence of F3, i.e. of conceptual justification (or analysis). Here are four further considerations that tell against thinking that F3 characterizes the judgments Burge make about the thought experiment. Burge's paper is filled with appeal to obviously empirical facts about the practice of ascribing beliefs to speakers and he encourages his readers to explore this highly complicated practice further. It's helpful in this connection to consider the actual details of the arguments that Burge engages with. Here is an illustration of what I have in mind: Burge considers the following objection to his interpretation of the first step in the thought experiment—an objection to the claim that the report should be interpreted to mean that the agent believes she has arthritis in her thigh. The imagined opponent says:

> If a foreigner were to mouth the words 'arthritis may occur in the thigh' or 'my father had arthritis', not understanding what he uttered in the slightest, we would not say that he believed that arthritis may occur in the thigh, or that his father had arthritis. So why should we impute the belief to the patient? (p. 89)

Note Burge's reply:

> The question is a good one. We do want a general account of these cases. But the implied argument against our attribution is anemic. We tacitly and routinely distinguish between the cases I described and those in which a foreigner (or anyone) utters something without any comprehension. (p. 89)

He then spends two pages going through various facts about how we react to speech by non-native speakers, people speaking 'regional dialects', tongue slips, Spoonerisms, malapropisms, radical misunderstandings, and related cases. These are empirical facts about linguistic behavior and Burge's goal in these passages is to "learn something about principles controlling mentalistic attribution" (p. 90). He notices that "common practice," i.e. how speakers commonly behave in these circumstances, is a mess (p. 91). However, he says, "I think any impulse to say that common practice is *simply* inconsistent should be resisted (indeed, scorned)" (p. 91). There are rough generalizations to be made from observations about common practice of reinterpretation:

> A person's overall linguistic competence, his allegiance and responsibility to communal standards, the degree, source, and type of misunderstanding, the purposes of the report—all affect the issue. From a theoretical point of view, it would be a

mistake to try to assimilate the cases in one direction or another. We do not want to credit a two-year-old who memorizes '$e = mc^2$' with belief in relativity theory. But the patient's attitudes involving the notion of arthritis should not be assimilated to the foreigner's uncomprehending. (pp. 91–2)

These observations about 'common practice' are just that, *observations*. At no point in these discussions does he give the impression of intending to rely solely on his conceptual competence and to avoid evidential sources that go beyond what can be obtained solely by conceptual competence. To someone who insists that we know everything there is to know about the different reinterpretation patterns for speech by foreigners, people who speak regional dialects, tongue slips, Spoonerisms, malapropisms, radical misunderstandings, less radical misunderstandings, etc. simply by being competent users of the concepts *misunderstanding, belief, tongue slip, regional dialect, foreigner,* etc., I have no good reply other than an incredulous stare. Someone who claims this without showing it in detail is simply refusing to engage seriously with the subject matter.

Second, it is worth noting in this connection that Burge himself rejects the notion of a 'purely conceptual truth' in the paper:

I do not believe that understanding, in our examples, can be explicated as independent of empirical knowledge, or that the conceptual errors of our subjects are best seen as "purely" mistakes about concepts and as involving no "admixture" of error about "the world." **With Quine, I find such talk about purity and mixture devoid of illumination or explanatory power.** (p. 88, my emphases)

Third, recall that we are looking for *effective* occurrences of intuition features (see Chapter 7, esp. 7.2). The question is therefore whether a search for F3-judgments guide or constrain the debate about Burge's case. Do those who discuss it disregard or downplay judgments when they are not a priori, conceptual truths? Is there evidence that participants in the debate find judgments that lack these features less valuable or somehow less likely to be of philosophical significance? The answer to both questions is 'No'.

A final piece of evidence against an F3-interpretation is that Burge does not put particular emphasis on judgments that are necessary truths. It is an interesting question whether some of the conclusions one might draw from reflecting on Burge's cases are necessary truths. It is an open question whether it is a necessary truth that the relevant utterances of 'She believes she has arthritis in her thigh' should be interpreted literally and not given one of the many alternative interpretations. Suppose a different reporting practice were instituted. Would that still be a practice where we reported beliefs? That's an interesting question, but what is striking is that it is not a question Burge is concerned with in the paper now under consideration. He painstakingly describes the practice as it actually is. He concludes that given the way our practice functions, we should not reinterpret in the first step of the thought experiment. He does *not*, at any place in the paper, address the question of whether these are necessary truths about belief reports. For all we know, he might think they are, but that is not stated in the paper.

8.2.3 Objection: Burge relies on intuitions about linguistic data

Objection: Again you have misidentified the point at which there is an appeal to the intuitive. While it is true that the Interpretative Question isn't answered by a simple appeal to an intuition, there are a number of other points in the paper where intuitions play a central role. As you point out above, Burge appeals to facts about the practice of reinterpretation of utterances involving words that are misunderstood by the speaker. He makes a number of claims about how we react to speech by foreign speakers who are not fully linguistically competent, people who speak 'regional dialects', our reactions to tongue slips, Spoonerisms, malapropisms, and so on. Those are the points where intuitions come in. Not on the big question of how to interpret the third step—but in all those apparently little claims about the practice. That's where Burge relies extensively on intuitions.

Reply: This objection has in effect been answered above, but since I find readers have an almost irresistible urge to return to it over and over again, it is worth repeating the answer in summary form: it is obviously true that Burge makes a number of claims about our linguistic practice, but there is no evidence that Burge thinks *intuitions*, i.e. judgments characterized by F1–F3, about the practice constitute the evidential base for those claims. He makes empirical claims about the practice, claims he takes to be known by anyone who has spent years participating in the practice of speaking English. He thinks these claims constitute common ground between him and his opponent, so he doesn't waste time arguing for them. If those claims were to be challenged, he would gather evidence about the practice—he would show that people who speak English actually do what he says they do. There is no reason to think that Burge thinks the way to figure out how people react to e.g.

spoonerisms is to appeal to intuitions, i.e. to judgments characterized by F1–F3. Consider an example from Burge's paper: a case of someone who makes a more radical mistake than the agent in his thought experiment (pp. 90–1). In this case someone believes that 'orangutan' applies to a fruit drink. Burge notes we would be reluctant to take this agent's utterance of "I drank orangutan for breakfast" to indicate *that she thinks she has been drinking orangutan for breakfast*. This is a claim about what speakers would be reluctant to do. Here is something Burge takes to be a fact: *members of group P would be reluctant to take such a speaker's utterance to indicate that she thinks she has been drinking orangutan for breakfast*. Call this presumed fact *f*. Suppose someone asks Burge to provide evidence that *f* is the case. We have no reason to think that in response to such a challenge, Burge would put particular weight on judgments not backed up by evidence or arguments, or judgments accompanied by a special feeling, or judgments generated by relying only on conceptual competence. What we need to figure out is whether speakers are, as a matter of fact, reluctant in these cases to say that the speaker drank orangutan for breakfast.

8.3 Thomson's violinist in "A Defense of Abortion"

My third and fourth cases are both from Judith Jarvis Thomson. The first involves an example of a person being hooked up to an unconscious violinist in her paper, "A Defense of Abortion" (1971). The second is one of the first and most cited papers on so-called 'trolley cases'. Like the first two thought experiments, these have both been enormously influential and have triggered a great deal of literature. By fairly wide consensus they are paradigms of important thought experiments in moral philosophy.

To see the role of the example some stage setting is needed. Thomson starts by granting for the sake of argument that the fetus is a person. She then asks whether it follows from this that abortion is morally impermissable. Here is how she describes her goal:

I suggest that the step [from the claim that the fetus is a person to abortion is morally impermissible] *they* [opponents of abortion] *take is neither easy nor obvious, that it calls for closer examination than it is commonly given and that when we do give it this closer examination we shall feel inclined to reject it.* (p. 48, emphases added)

Note right away that Thomson, like Perry, is quite careful about the kind of claims she makes: she says the step "calls for closer examination than it is commonly given" and implicates that we will not reach a stage of clear conviction in either direction—merely an inclination to reject the anti-abortion argument. Her goal is to undermine confidence in what I will call the *Target Argument*, which Thomson describes as follows:

Target Argument: [Assume a fetus is a person.] Every person has a right to life. So the foetus has a right to life. No doubt the mother has a right to decide what shall happen in and to her body; everyone would grant that. But surely a person's right to life is stronger and more stringent than the mother's right to decide what happens in and to her body and so outweighs it. So the foetus may not be killed; an abortion may not be performed. (p. 48)

The famous example is supposed to show *that something is wrong with the Target Argument*, though just what it shows to be wrong is an open question. The example itself is a bit hard to individuate since after presenting the initial case, Thomson immediately considers a number of variations, and it is indeterminate what to count as 'the case'. Here is the initial setup:

You wake up in the morning and find yourself back to back in bed with an unconscious violinist. A famous unconscious violinist. He has been found to have a fatal kidney ailment, and the Society of Music Lovers has canvassed all the available medical records and found that you alone have the right blood type to help. They have therefore kidnapped you, and last night the violinist's circulatory system was plugged into yours, so that your kidneys can be used to extract poison from his blood as well as your own. The director of the hospital now tells you, 'Look, we're sorry the Society of Music Lovers did this to you—we would never had permitted it if we had known. But still, they did it, and the violinist is now plugged into you. To unplug you would be to kill him. But never mind, it's only for nine months. By then he will have recovered from his ailment, and can safely be unplugged from you. (pp. 48–9)

Thomson then asks, "Is it morally incumbent on you to accede to this situation?" It is interesting that she does *not* reply to this question right away. She first adds various elements to the original case. She asks, "what if it were not nine months but nine years? Or longer still?" She doesn't directly answer that question either, she goes on to elaborate even further on the case:

150   THE ARGUMENT FROM PHILOSOPHICAL PRACTICE

What if the director of the hospital says, "Tough luck, I agree, but you've now got to stay in bed, with the violinist plugged into you, for the rest of your life. Because remember this. All persons have a right to life, and violinists are persons. Granted you have a right to decide what happens to your body, but a person's right to life outweighs your right to decide what happens in and to your body. So you cannot ever be unplugged from him." (p. 49)

This last question Thomson finally gives a reply to: "I imagine you would regard this as outrageous, which suggests that something is really wrong with that plausible sounding argument I mentioned a moment ago" [i.e. the Target Argument] (p. 49).

There are two elements of the conclusion she seems to endorse here. First C1:

C1: "You would regard this as outrageous."

C1 can be interpreted in at least three ways, one focusing on the emotion of outrage and two on an evaluation of the argument. Here is the first:

C1a: If you were the person hooked up to the violinist and were told that you would have to spend the rest of your life in this situation, you would react with outrage.

To evaluate C1a we have to make a prediction about the emotional response we would have had had we found ourselves in this unusual situation. An alternative interpretation of C1 is:

C1b: If you were the person hooked up to the violinist, you would find the hospital director's *argument* to be outrageous (where this means, roughly: you would think it is a *very, very* bad argument).

To evaluate C1b we have to make a prediction about how we would evaluate an argument were we to find ourselves in a very unusual and unpleasant situation. Finally, C1 can be interpreted as:

C1c: You (i.e. the reader) think that the hospital director's argument is outrageous, i.e. a *very* bad argument.

I am going to assume that something like C1c is the correct interpretation. A natural interpretation of C1c is to treat it as a *reductio*: The conclusion of the argument, i.e. *that the person should spend her entire life in bed hooked up to a violinist*, is false.[10] Therefore the argument is either invalid or has a false premise.

To this Thomson adds:

C2: If the hospital director's argument is unsound or invalid, then so is the Target Argument.

However, and this is important, she immediately and very explicitly qualifies C2. She says that this is merely *suggested*. She makes the rather modest claim that someone who finds fault with the hospital director's argument might *suspect* that some analogous mistake can be found in the Target Argument.

8.3.1 Observations about Thomson's violinist case

Thomson's case patterns with Perry and Burge's in at least three important respects.

Generality requirement: The goal is to get the reader to learn something of relevance to the question of whether abortion is morally permissible. So to understand the case, the reader has to understand what a kidnapped woman hooked up to a violinist has in common with a pregnant woman contemplating abortion. This will typically require complex reasoning and careful thought. In this case, it is particularly hard to see just how the analogy is supposed to go. Does it for example matter how *long* she is hooked up to the violinist (Thomson seems to think it does)? Does it matter that she was kidnapped? Does it matter that it is a *famous* violinist? Does it matter that she is treated by doctors in a hospital? Does it matter that she will have to spend her entire life in a bed? These are complicated questions that must be settled for anyone who wants to use the conclusions drawn about the violinist to draw conclusions about the Target Argument and whether abortion is legitimate.

Fact focuser: I said that a primary function of Perry and Burge's cases was to draw our attention to certain philosophically significant features of the world. You might not like to characterize rights, obligation and permissions as 'facts', but putting that issue aside, Thomson's purpose is closely related. One of Thomson's goals is to draw our attention to ways in which a person's right to control what happens to and in her body interacts with

---

[10] If you don't think claims about what people ought to do can be true or false, then substitute the appropriate evaluative term for 'false'.

the rights persons have to life. The goal of reflecting on the thought experiment is to help us understand those relations better.

Lack of clear conclusion: I emphasized that Perry's conclusion was tentative: he reacts to the initial cases with a kind of puzzlement and says he thinks it is extremely difficult to even decide how to describe the cases. This is also true for Thomson. She is confident that the person in the thought experiment would react with outrage to the hospital director's argument, but she doesn't think that anything specific or clearly articulable follows about what is wrong with the Target Argument. We are supposed to get a sense that *something* has gone wrong, but at this point in the article, exactly *what* has gone wrong is underdetermined. That is settled by a wide range of further complex arguments.[11]

8.3.2 *Thomson's violinist case and the intuition features*

There is no evidence in Thomson's text that she thinks that someone's immediate, unjustified claim about the violinist case has any particular significance or special epistemic status, i.e. that she takes a special interest in judgments with Rock status. Consider again C1a, C1b, C1c:

> **C1a**: If you were the person hooked up to the violinist and were told that you would have to spend the rest of your life in this situation, you would find it outrageous, i.e. you would react with outrage.
>
> **C1b**: If you were the person hooked up to the violinist, you would find the hospital director's *argument* to be outrageous, where this means, roughly: you would think it a very bad argument.
>
> **C1c**: You (i.e. the reader) think the hospital director's argument is outrageous, i.e. a very bad argument.

That C1a and C1b are true is common knowledge: we all know that other things being equal, a normal person would be outraged finding out that we had been kidnapped and hooked up to a violinist in a hospital. It is also common knowledge that under such circumstances, we would react with outrage to the hospital director's argument. These are empirical

---

[11] One kind of case that plays an important role in the subsequent argument is that of a woman trapped in an extremely tiny house with a very rapidly growing child who will be crushed to death unless she stops the child from growing further. It seems to me this case actually plays a more important argumentative role in the article than the violinist example, though it is not as frequently mentioned as a paradigm of a thought experiment.

claims about typical human reactions and there is no need to appeal to anything like Rock status to explain their argumentative role. Consider next what I take to be the more relevant conclusion, i.e. C1c. Thomson is assuming that C1c is in the common ground among participants in the debate. In particular, she assumes, quite reasonably, that C1c is endorsed even by proponents of the Target Argument. Again, there is no need to appeal to any kind of special epistemic status of the kind characterized by Rock (more on this in Sections 8.3.3 and 8.4.2 below).

Next consider C2:

C2: If the hospital director's argument is unsound or invalid, then so is the Target Argument.

Thomson recognizes that this is a more problematic claim, one that is much less likely than C1c to be in the common ground. This is why she says it is only 'suggested'. To establish C2 you need to reflect on whether the fact that this was a kidnapping is important, whether the length of time is important, whether it being a *famous* violinist is important. Those questions cannot be settled without giving further arguments and there is no evidence in Thomson's text that she has any illusions about this. She goes on to argue in all kinds of ways for her preferred conclusion, i.e. that in certain important respects, there is a shared mistake in the hospital director's argument and the Target Argument. There is no evidence that she treats C2 as having Rock status.

There is also no textual evidence that Thomson thinks any of the relevant judgments come with a special phenomenology. If, for some people, some of these judgments come with a special phenomenology, there is no evidence in Thomson's text that she takes this to be of any argumentative significance.

C1a and C1b are obviously not candidates for being conceptually justified claims—they are empirical claims about how people would react under certain very strange circumstances. The truth of C1c and C2 depends, as I have emphasized, on all kinds of complex questions about what the relevant features of the case are (kidnapping, time span, famous violinist, etc.)—and there is no evidence that Thomson thinks that settling these issues is *only* a matter of inspecting or analyzing your concepts. To see how *prima facie* implausible it is to classify C1c as a conceptually justified claim, note the extent to which our commitment to C1c depends on our knowledge of contingent facts about human lives and preferences. Our knowledge that most people like to move around independently of another person's movements is important for our judgment. So is our knowledge that most people's quality of life would be significantly reduced if they had to spend their entire life in a bed. It is very likely that knowledge of these kinds of contingent facts about human lives plays a central role in our judgment about the case and so it is implausible to claim that any interesting version of the claim that we rely solely on conceptual competence will get a foothold here. Finally, note that even if a philosopher has a theory of concepts according to which, say, C1c can be classified as a 'conceptually justified' claim, this status does, as a matter of fact, play no role in Thomson's discussion of this case. So it is not an effective presence of F3, i.e. even if it were true that on some construal of 'conceptually justified', C1c has that property, that's an idle feature that plays no effective role in the debate over this case.

In sum, I conclude that a third paradigm of a philosophical thought experiment, this time from ethics, fails to exhibit any of the key features standardly taken to be characteristic of the intuitive.

8.3.3 First objection to the characterization of Thomson's violinist case: Appeal to what's in the common ground is irrelevant—what matters is why a proposition is in the common ground

> Objection: Appeal to propositions being in the common ground is cheating: they are in the common ground because they are intuitive. You assume that claims such as P1 are simply in the common ground of the conversation:
>
> **P1**: It is impermissible to hook the agent up to the violinist for the rest of her life.
>
> But there's an alternative view: it has the kind of default justificatory status characterized by Rock and that is why it is in the common ground. More generally how do we tell whether a claim c is best characterized by (i) (as you maintain) or (ii)?:
>
> (i) C is not argued for because it is a non-Rock claim that happens to be in the common ground.
>
> (ii) C is not argued for because it has a special epistemic status of the kind characterized by Rock and other intuition features, and that also explains why it is in the common ground of most conversations.

How can these options be distinguished? What is the argument for choosing (i) over (ii)?

Reply: This is a difficult issue primarily because the characterization of Rock is elusive and those who believe that certain propositions have this special property don't do a good job helping others identify it. Most of the arguments in favor of there being such propositions conclude that *some* propositions have this status, but provide minimal guidance about how to identify them in actual texts. So there is an important dialectical argument in favor of (i): (ii) appeals to a controversial and elusive category. There is no such controversy over the phenomenon appealed to in (i). It is not controversial that conversations have propositions in the common ground. Nor is it controversial that all arguments start with premises that are not argued for. These are facts all participants in this debate will agree on. It is also agreed among all participants in this debate that *not* everything that happens to be in the common ground of some conversation or is used as a premise in an argument has the special kind of epistemic status that Rock tries to capture.[12] Given this, it is fair to say that the challenge is for the believer in Rock status (and its particular significance in philosophy) to tell us how to distinguish those elements of the common ground that have the special status from those that don't have it.

Two further considerations count heavily against hypothesis (ii):

- First, for many philosophers, the alleged Rock status is accompanied by F1 and F3, i.e. something has the special status if it is accompanied by special phenomenology and is based solely on conceptual competence. I have argued against the effective presence of any of these in the relevant cases. If those arguments succeed, we have evidence in favor of (i) and against (ii).
- Second, if asked why we endorse P1 we can all with minimal effort give answers, and we are not likely to react with puzzlement or surprise at being asked (and we're very unlikely to respond with 'You know what, I don't really need to justify that; it's not the kind of claim that stands in need of justification.') We know that it

---

[12] Recall that F2 is an attempt to describe a feature of the intuitive. No intuition-theorist wants to classify every proposition in the common ground as intuitive.

is awful for most people to be hooked up to another person in a bed for the entirety of a life. We know that this restricts your movement and that again restricts freedom of choice and prevents you from leading a full, rich, and autonomous life. We know that close proximity over a long period of time to another person can be particularly dreadful if you don't get along with the other person. In this particular case the person would be hooked up to a violinist and would have to listen to violin practice for long periods of time. That would be an added burden. These are the kinds of reasons all of us could come up with on a moment's notice. There is no reason to think we all just have a brute unjustified insight into the impermissibility of hooking someone up to another person for a long time.[13]

8.3.4 Second objection to the characterization of Thomson's violinist case: You should be looking at the real (underlying) logical form of thought experiments, not their surface structure

> *Objection: You're missing an extremely important feature of how thought experiments are constructed (and this remark applies equally to your other case studies). In constructing thought experiments we build all the material that you rightly label contingent, worldly knowledge into the characterization of the case as follows:*
>
> *Paradigmatic Thought Experiment (PTE): If it were the case that BIG-C, would P be the case?*
>
> *On the proposal you fail to consider, 'BIG-C' doesn't include just the elements explicitly mentioned by Thomson when she describes the case in the first few pages*

---

[13] A reader for OUP objected to this reply, saying that "given the point of Thomson's paper on the whole, there is no way she could offer such an argument—since it's an argument that, if it could be legitimate to appeal to in this debate, the pro-choice person could *mutatis mutandis* offer to the pro-life person. Pregnancy is even more dangerous and, in the long run, burdensome than the hypothetical situation with the violinist. If such discomfort, danger, and general disutility were sufficient grounds to justify unplugging from the violinist, then they'd already be sufficient grounds to justify abortion. In which case, it's hard to see what Thomson thinks she is supposed to gain from all this wacky rigamarole with the violinist!" It might be right that if this is the basis for the judgment we make about the violinist's predicament, that will make trouble for Thomson's dialectic. But that's not sufficient reason for thinking that we don't, as a matter of fact, rely on these kinds of considerations when making the judgment (nor is it reason for thinking we wouldn't provide them as reasons if asked for reasons). It simply shows that Thomson's argumentative strategy is problematic.

of her paper. i.e. 'BIG-C' doesn't include just the fact that you were kidnapped and then hooked up to a famous violinist for life in a hospital bed. An enormous amount of additional assumptions about human life and psychology is added to get BIG-C. It is, for example, part of BIG-C that humans in general and you in particular don't like to spend an entire life in a hospital bed listening to someone practicing the violin, that there are lots of arguments against allowing kidnapping on a large scale, that being able to exercise choices about where to go and what to do when getting there is an important component of a rich human life, etc.[14] What you are asked to judge, according to this proposal, is of the form: Suppose BIG-C were the case, then would the act be permissible? The claim that we don't rely on contingent facts to make that judgment is less implausible, since the worldly knowledge that you claim we draw on in making judgments about Thomson's case has now been built right into the characterization of the case. Something with the form of PTE is therefore more likely to have features F1–F3 and be the kind of thing Centrality proponents characterize as intuitive.

Reply: The question Thomson asks us isn't of the PTE form. Answering and investigating that question is not answering and investigating the question asked by Thomson. To think it is, is to ignore the fact that figuring out what goes into BIG-C is at the center of engaging with a case like Thomson's (or any of the other cases I am considering here). To see this point, note how implausible an analogous move with respect to Libro would be:

Libro: Suppose Mandy is walking down Russell Avenue in Buenos Aires from Thames. She walks two blocks and then turns left and walks two more blocks.

Libro-Question: How many blocks away from Boutique del Libro would she be?

This is a paradigm of a question that cannot be answered using a priori strategies of the kind envisaged by the objection now under consideration. Suppose someone said that, contrary to appearances, the Libro

---

[14] A version of this view is defended by Ichikawa and Jarvis (2009). See also Williamson (2007, 2009a) and Ichikawa (2009) for discussion. Weinberg seems to be endorsing this controversial view of thought experiments when he writes: "In particular, no empirical evidence is required, because one is presumed to have stipulated all the contingencies in the construction of the hypothetical, and one is thus applying only one's mastery of the concepts involved and not any empirical knowledge" (2007, p. 320).

question isn't one that requires careful investigation of empirical matters. Using the strategy outlined above we could turn this into something that appears to be accessible to a priori theorizing. We first gather all the relevant contingent information about the geography of Buenos Aires—including where Boutique del Libro is located and how that location relates to all other streets in Buenos Aires. Call these facts 'BIG-BA-FACTS'. Then add BIG-BA-FACTS to the description in Libro, and we get something that no doubt will look much like how a proponent of this reply thinks a paradigmatic philosophical thought experiment looks like. For example Libro+:

Libro+: Suppose Mandy is walking down Russell Avenue in Buenos Aires from Thames, she walks two blocks and then turns left and walks two more blocks, and suppose also that: *BIG-BA-FACTS*.

Libro+-Question: How many blocks away from Boutique del Libro would she be?

Arguably, this is the kind of question we can answer without doing empirical research and without drawing on any worldly knowledge. No doubt some would be tempted to say that the judgment instantiates F1–F3 and that it is a good candidate for a necessary conceptual truth, known a priori. I'm not going to address the question of whether this is correct, since the point I want to emphasize here is an obvious one: the Libro+-Question is not the same as the Libro-Question. To investigate the first is not to investigate the second. The same point applies in the philosophical case. Thomson's question isn't the question articulated by something like PTE. Thomson presents a brief story and what we have to do as philosophers is, in part, to figure out: *What would that be like?* Included in that challenge is figuring out whether the act would be permissible. The reason it is an interesting and challenging case to reflect on is that we have to use philosophical judgment and skill to determine what facts are included in BIG-C. This challenge is not in any relevant respect like trying to answer the question asked by PTE (where BIG-C is already fixed).

8.4 Thomson and Foot on trolley cases

Judgments about the so-called trolley cases are often mentioned as paradigms of the intuitive. I will consider Judith Jarvis Thomson's presentation of the cases in her classic paper, "The Trolley Problem" (1985). The first pages are devoted to a presentation of two cases from Philippa Foot (1967). Here is Thomson's presentation of the cases:

> Suppose you are the driver of a trolley. The trolley rounds a bend, and there come into view ahead five track workmen, who have been repairing the track. The track goes through a bit of a valley at that point, and the sides are steep, so you must stop the trolley if you are to avoid running the five men down. You step on the brakes, but alas they don't work. Now you suddenly see a spur of track leading off to the right. You can turn the trolley onto it, and thus save the five men on the straight track ahead. Unfortunately, Mrs. Foot has arranged that there is one track workman on that spur of track. He can no more get off the track in time than the five can, so you will kill him if you turn the trolley onto him. Is it morally permissible for you to turn the trolley? (p. 1395)

Thomson remarks that everyone she has asked this question has answered in the affirmative: "Everybody to whom I have put this hypothetical case says, Yes, it is." She then immediately goes on to consider a second case:

> Now consider a second hypothetical case. This time you are to imagine yourself to be a surgeon, a truly great surgeon. Among other things you do, you transplant organs, and you are such a great surgeon that the organs you transplant always take. At the moment you have five patients who need organs. Two need one lung each, two need a kidney each, and the fifth needs a heart. If they do not get those organs today, they will all die; if you find organs for them today, you can transplant the organs and they will all live. But where to find the lungs, the kidneys, and the heart? The time is almost up when a report is brought to you that a young man who has just come into your clinic for his yearly check-up has exactly the right blood-type, and is in excellent health. Lo, you have a possible donor. All you need do is cut him up and distribute his parts among the five who need them. You ask, but he says, "Sorry. I deeply sympathize, but no." Would it be morally permissible for you to operate anyway? (p. 1396)

Thomson remarks that, "Everybody to whom I have put this second hypothetical case says, No, it would not be morally permissible for you to proceed." Note that so far what we have are two questions and consensus among Thomson's interlocutors about their answers. So the two answers are in the common ground of the conversations she has had about this topic.

What is interesting for our purposes is that she—like Foot in the original paper Thomson is discussing—*immediately* goes on to *question* these

160   THE ARGUMENT FROM PHILOSOPHICAL PRACTICE

answers. She *asks for reasons* (i.e. arguments) for why these should be the correct answers. She says:

> Here then is Mrs. Foot's problem: "Why is it that the trolley driver may turn his trolley, though the surgeon may not remove the young man's lungs, kidneys, and heart?" In both cases, one will die if the agent acts, but five will live who would otherwise die—a net saving of four lives. What difference in the other facts of these cases explains the moral difference between them? (p. 1396)

The trolley case is in effect presented, at least in part, as a puzzle in much the same way Perry's case was presented as puzzling. A central goal of Thomson's paper is to *question* the answers given to questions asked about the cases. There is a tension between the two answers and that tension shows further reflection and investigation is needed. Thomson and Foot articulate the reasons that can be given for the initial answer. Here is Thomson's first proposal for a justification of the initial judgments:[15]

> Look, the surgeon's choice is between operating, in which case he kills one, and not operating, in which case he lets five die; and killing is surely worse than letting die—indeed, so much worse that we can even say
>
> Killing one is worse than letting five die.
>
> So the surgeon must refrain from operating.
>
> By contrast, the trolley driver's choice is between turning the trolley, in which case he kills one, and not turning the trolley, in which case he does not let five die, he positively kills them.
>
> Now surely we can say
>
> Killing five is worse than killing one.
>
> But then that is why the trolley driver may turn his trolley: He would be doing what is worse if he fails to turn it, since if he fails to turn it he kills five. (pp. 1396–7)

8.4.1 *The trolley case and the intuition features*

Of all the thought experiments that Centrality proponents typically parade as paradigms of intuition-based philosophy, I think the trolley case is the best illustration of how they fundamentally misrepresent philosophical practice. Just cursory reading of the passages above should make it clear

---

[15] This is not an argument Thomson accepts, but it illustrates the kinds of considerations that are at the center of the paper.

how far the real text is from the caricature. Take, as an example, the answer to the question, 'Is it morally permissible for you to turn the trolley?' Thomson's answer immediately appeals to what is in the common ground or pre-theoretically accepted ("Everybody to whom I have put this hypothetical case says, Yes, it is."). What she doesn't do is treat this answer as having Rock status. She certainly doesn't treat it as a point where justification gives out, where philosophers don't require reasons, or where we have reached rock bottom and can have nothing but a clash of intuitions. The whole point of the paper is to question this conclusion by contrasting it with the judgment about the doctor. So within two pages, that initial, pre-theoretic judgment is called into question. The goal of the paper is to look for reasons and evidence beyond the pre-theoretic judgment. There is also no evidence in this text that a special phenomenology plays a significant argumentative or evidential role. Maybe some people have special feelings when they contemplate certain answers to some questions about these cases, but there is no evidence in the text that Thomson thinks that the presence of these feelings is argumentatively significant. Finally, at no point in the text is there evidence that Thomson is relying solely on her conceptual competence or that she puts particular emphasis on that kind of justification. She never claims that this is what she is trying to do and there is no direct evidence in the text that she disavows descriptions of the case (or answers to questions asked about the case) that draw on experience that goes beyond what is required for conceptual competence.

In short, not even a prima facie case can be made for the claim that Thomson's presentation of the trolley case appeals to intuitions, where these are construed as judgments with any of features F1–F3.

8.4.2 Objections to my characterization of the trolley case: that arguments are given for p in a text doesn't show that p doesn't have Rock status[16]

> Objection: You seem to be assuming that just because someone gives an argument for p, p can't have the kind of status described by Rock. Surely, something can have default justificatory status (and other special epistemic properties in this

---

[16] An alert reader will note that this objection and the reply were already discussed in Chapter 7; I thought it useful to give here an illustration of the dialectic linked to the interpretation of an actual text.

neighborhood) even though some philosopher in some paper happens to present an argument for p.

Reply: All I am assuming is that if in a context C, someone presents a set of premises R from which a conclusion p follows, and indicates full commitment to the premises and the validity of the inference, then, other things being equal, we should take that argument to be what justifies p in C. That doesn't mean there aren't other contexts in which p is given another justification or asserted without any justification at all. The conclusion I draw is fairly limited. Let C be the context consisting of these important papers in moral philosophy. There is no evidence in C that the conclusions about the cases are treated as not being in need of justification or having a kind of privileged epistemic status. As I emphasized in the introduction to this chapter, this is an inductive enterprise and I welcome further careful case studies. It is useful, I find, to start with the original and most cited papers in a debate since some of the groundwork for later work is presented there. It is certainly likely that if someone writes a groundbreaking paper on topic T with some very good arguments for a conclusion p, then later papers will find it unnecessary to argue for p (since the original argument is considered so good). This can lead p to be included in the common ground of later discussions (and that, as we have seen, is not on its own evidence of p being based on an intuition). It is also worth noting (as an anonymous reader for OUP did) that "the seminal papers in a debate (such as many of the papers discussed in this chapter) often get morphed into caricatures by the literature they spawn; participants forget that the proponent of a case in the seminal paper hedges and says they're puzzled about what to say, and they forget that arguments are often given for key claims that later participants take as assumptions."[17] As we have seen, the trolley case illustrates this point very vividly.

Second Objection: Some of those who contribute significantly to the literature on trolley cases, for example Frances Kamm (1998, 2007), describe this and related cases as being based on intuitions. She and other contributors to the debate make explicit methodological remarks that contradict your description. This objection

---

[17] The quote is from the anonymous reader for OUP.

generalizes since in many of the cases you discuss you can find contributors that explicitly say that their contributions rely on intuitions about cases.

Reply: Being good at thinking about trolley cases doesn't imply that you are good at thinking about what you do when you think about trolley cases—no more so than being a good mathematician implies being good at thinking about the nature of mathematical reasoning. As a result we sometimes find authors who make excellent contributions to a topic saying false things about how they go about making those contributions. As I emphasized in Chapter 1, endorsement of Centrality is part of many analytic philosophers' self-conception. Since Centrality is false, many philosophers will say false things and have false beliefs about what they do when they philosophize, which is no more incompatible with being an excellent philosopher than being confused about metamathematics is incompatible with being an excellent mathematician.

8.5 Three epistemology cases: Lotteries, Truetemp, and fake barns

Epistemology is a subfield of philosophy in which participants in various debates tend to think of themselves as engaged in a practice that relies heavily on appeals to the intuitive. So epistemologists who think about how epistemology is done often describe the activity as a paradigm of a field that provides support for Centrality. However, I think even in this philosophical subfield that description is mistaken. (As I pointed out in the reply right above, this isn't a particularly serious indictment of epistemology, since an epistemologist can have mistaken beliefs about meta-epistemology and still be good at answering first-order epistemological questions.) My next three cases, Stewart Cohen on lottery propositions, Keith Lehrer on Truetemp, and Goldman on fake barns, illustrate these points.

Brief remark about how I will proceed in the remaining case studies: many of the points I'm about to make have already been made in connection with the previous case studies—the structure of the cases and the reasons for the lack of the intuition features are closely analogous. So rather than repeat the same structural points I will often refer back to previous discussions and rely on the reader to see the relevant similarities.

8.5.1 Stewart Cohen on lottery propositions

It is often assumed that epistemologists who rely on so-called lottery cases appeal to intuitions when they do so. Here is Stewart Cohen in one of the early and most discussed papers on the topic, "How to be a Fallibilist" (1988). Cohen starts by asking a fairly simple question:

> Suppose S holds a ticket in a fair lottery with n tickets, where the probability n-$1/n$ of S losing is very high. Does S know that his ticket will lose? (p. 92)

He immediately gives us a hedged answer: "Although (if n is suitably large) S has good reasons to believe he will lose, it *does not seem right* to say that S *knows* he will lose. This remains true for arbitrarily large n" (p. 92, my italics). Note that 'seem' is used as a hedging term and so this is not a full-out endorsement of the answer. Cohen goes on to discuss a related case, where he gives another hedged answer in reply to a question:

> Now, suppose S learns from Jones, the person running the lottery, that Jones intends to fix the lottery so S will lose. Does S, then, know that he will lose? Better still, suppose S reads in the paper that another ticket has won. In both of these cases *we are inclined to say* that S does know that he loses. (p. 92, my italics)

The pattern here follows that found in several of the cases discussed above and it patterns particularly closely with the trolley case. Cohen immediately goes on to point out that the answer he is inclined to give to the second question is in tension with the answer he is inclined to give to the first question:

> In the first case, *it seemed*, contrary to fallibilist assumptions, that as long as there is a chance that S wins, no matter how small, he does not know that he loses. But the other two cases *indicate* otherwise. There we said that S can know, on the basis of his reasons, that he will lose. But surely his reasons do not entail that he loses. Generally reliable sources lie, have their intentions thwarted, make mistakes, etc. The probability that S loses conditional on *these* reasons is less than 1. (p. 92, my italics)

The case is presented as a puzzle. Pre-theoretically we find ourselves with both C1 and C2 in the common ground (these are the replies we are inclined to give prior to theorizing):

> C1: If S holds a ticket in a fair lottery with n tickets, where the probability n-$1/n$ of S losing is very high, S does not know that her ticket doesn't win.

C2: If *S* learns from Jones, the person running the lottery, that Jones intends to fix the lottery so *S* will lose, (or reads in a newspaper that another ticket has won) then *S* knows that she will lose.

The reaction of puzzlement is significant: it explains why the replies have to be hedged. C1 and C2 are *not* presented as starting points for theorizing. *They are tentatively presented as claims we are likely to find in the common ground prior to theorizing and we are presented with tentative arguments for endorsing them.* The tentative argument for C1 is C1A and the tentative argument for C2 is C2A:

C1A: As long as there is a chance that *S* wins, no matter how small, he does not know that he loses.

C2A: *S* can know, on the basis of being told about the fixed lottery or reading that another ticket has won, that he will lose even though his reasons do not entail that he loses.[18]

Cohen's lottery cases and the intuition features. The claim that philosophers rely unquestioningly on default justified, immediate reactions to these cases is simply unfounded: the moment the cases are presented, they are *questioned*, they are *not endorsed*, and they give rise to *puzzlement*. This response indicates that the Rock feature is absent. The reaction most readers have when first presented with the cases is to consider options such as: (i) reject both C1 and C2 (the skeptic), (ii) reject neither (Cohen), or (iii) figure out if there's some relevant difference between them such that one can be preserved and the other rejected. To repeat a point from the discussion of Thomson's trolley case: the reason we start with C1 and C2 is that many participants in the discussion are inclined to endorse them pre-theoretically—they can, tentatively, be characterized as being in the common ground prior to theorizing ('tentative' is important, since Cohen hedges when presenting and so doesn't present them as propositions he endorses). But there's no evidence they are pre-theoretically in the common ground *because they have the intuition features* (and to repeat a point made many times already, being in the common ground pre-theoretically

---

[18] Some might be inclined to classify C2A as an observation and not an argument. I am using 'argument' somewhat loosely here—philosophers don't typically present deductively valid arguments, but rather considerations that in some way lend support to their conclusions. C2A provides such support for C2.

is not to be intuitive; that we start with propositions in the common ground is not a defense of Centrality). Not only is intuition feature F1, i.e. Rock, absent, but so is F2, Seem True. At no point does Cohen implicitly or explicitly indicate that he thinks the phenomenology of C1 and C2 are argumentatively significant. As pointed out repeatedly above, maybe some people have distinctive phenomenology when they contemplate one or both of them, but that phenomenology plays no effective argumentative role in this discussion. With respect to F3, Cohen does *not* say that he aims to avoid any information that goes beyond what can be obtained by relying solely on his competence with the concept of *knowledge*. He does not present us with his view of what concepts are, what competence is, how competence can be relied on to justify claims about knowledge, and how such justification is related to the intuitive. Surely, if Cohen saw himself as restricted to this kind of methodology, he, being knowledgeable about the philosophical tradition and the controversial nature of these views, would tell us (at least in a footnote).

Objection to my characterization of Cohen's lottery case: Evidence Recalcitrance

> *Objection:* The key thing to focus on with regards to this and other case studies is Evidence Recalcitrance. Roughly speaking, what shows that C1 and C2 are intuitions is that we are extremely reluctant to give them up. Even when given evidence against one of these two claims, we feel inclined to continue accepting it and are reluctant to give it up. That is what drives this debate and makes it challenging and interesting.

> *Reply:* First, this is a psychological hypothesis about participants in a certain debate and it requires empirical evidence: we would need studies of the inclinations of the participants in these debates in order to confirm it. No such studies have ever been conducted. Certainly, no such evidence can be found by reading Cohen's text. That said, it is hard to see why anyone would want to conduct such studies since even if you found a bit of support for the hypothesis, the debate about C1 and C2 is easy to understand without any appeal to Evidence Recalcitrance. Here is a plausible description of what is going on. Lots of people believe both C1 and C2 because they are both true and there are good reasons for endorsing both. But the data is confusing—there are puzzles in this domain. In particular, the reasons for endorsing C1 seem to be in conflict with the reasons we give for endorsing C2. Cohen's

solution preserves both. In other words, to understand why philosophers want to resolve the puzzle there is no need to appeal to special psychological biases of the kind described by Evidence Recalcitrance. That is not to say there is no such bias—that's an open empirical question—it's only to point out that there is no evidence that an understanding of these biases is important for understanding the dialectic or dynamics of the debate surrounding fallibilism.[19]

8.5.2 Keith Lehrer on Mr. Truetemp

My second example of a classic case from epistemology is Keith Lehrer's (2000) case involving Mr. Truetemp. This is cited extensively as an example of an epistemologist constructing a thought experiment and then relying on an intuition about the case to draw wide-reaching conclusions. It is the subject of one of the most cited papers in experimental philosophy, Swain *et al.* (2008). Swain *et al.* say that Lehrer's judgments are based on intuitions and then they go on to argue that those intuitions are unreliable. Are they right? Is this finally a paradigm of a case where there is extensive reliance on the intuitive? Answer: No. Anyone who thinks this either hasn't read the text carefully or has misinterpreted it. Here is Lehrer's initial setup:

Suppose a person, whom we shall name Mr. Truetemp, undergoes brain surgery by an experimental surgeon who invents a small device which is both a very accurate thermometer and a computational device capable of generating thoughts. The device, call it a tempucomp, is implanted in Truetemp's head so that the very tip of the device, no larger than the head of a pin, sits unnoticed on his scalp and acts as a sensor to transmit information about the temperature to the computational system of his brain. This device, in turn, sends a message to his brain causing him to think of the temperature recorded by the external sensor. Assume that the tempucomp is very reliable, and so his thoughts are correct temperature thoughts. All told, this is a reliable belief-forming process. Now imagine, finally, that he has no idea that the tempucomp has been inserted

---

[19] I should point out that Cohen does use 'intuition'-talk in this paper. He says, for example, "The burden of the fallibilist is to resolve these puzzles and paradoxes in a way that preserves the truth of our everyday knowledge attributions. But a satisfying resolution requires an explanation of why the paradox arises—an explanation of why we have the intuitions that saddle us with the paradox" (p. 94). It was the burden of the first part of this book to deflate such talk and show that it typically is not Centrality supporting. One option mentioned was to interpret 'intuition' as 'pre-theoretic commitment'. I take that to be a charitable way to reinterpret the use of 'intuition'-talk in this passage.

in his brain, is only slightly puzzled about why he thinks so obsessively about the temperature, but never checks a thermometer to determine whether these thoughts about the temperature are correct. He accepts them unreflectively, another effect of the tempucomp. Thus, he thinks and accepts that the temperature is 104 degrees. It is. Does he know that it is? (p. 187)

Mr. Truetemp and the intuition features. Does Lehrer's reply to his question, "Does he know that it is?," fit the model of what Centrality proponents think of as an appeal to the intuitive? Is the answer presented as a rock-bottom starting point for which arguments are not needed? Is it presented as a response that justifies, but stands in no need of justification? Is there any evidence that an appeal to special phenomenology plays a significant role in the argument? Is there evidence that Lehrer is attempting to appeal to nothing but his conceptual competence?

The answer to each of these questions is an unequivocal 'no'. The first thing Lehrer does after asking the question, "Does he know that it is?," is to present several arguments for responding with 'No.' The primary argument goes something like this: "More than possession of correct information is required for knowledge. One must have some way of knowing that the information is correct" (p. 188). Since Mr. Truetemp has no way of knowing that the information is correct, he doesn't know. In the text, the negative answer to the question, "Does he know that it is?," is derived from this more general principle. So the answer is not presented as a basic, unjustified but justifying starting point in argumentation. There is no evidence in the text that the phenomenology of the judgment plays an important role in the argument. As usual, the question of whether all these judgments are based solely on our possession of the relevant concepts is difficult to investigate. What is clear from simply reading the text is that Lehrer doesn't say that this is what he is trying to do, he never tells us that he has no interest in an answer that relies on information that is not required for concept possession. Had he imposed such a constraint on his theorizing we should expect him to tell us that and to tell us what he takes concepts to be, what he takes concept possession to be, what he takes the relevant kind of justification to be. I am assuming here that Lehrer knows that many of the twentieth century's leading philosophers deny that there is anything like conceptual justification and so assuming that there is such justification would be controversial. Given this, it would be uncharitable to interpret him as tacitly making the assumption and expecting his readers to pick up on that.[20]

An objection to my characterization of the Truetemp case: abduction and direction of support: This objection is from a reader for OUP: "HC writes: "In the text, the negative answer to the question "Does he know that it is?" is derived from this more general principle." This strikes me as a rather poor reading of Lehrer's text. Lehrer earlier on in the chapter asserts that such a principle would make trouble for the externalist, and that's what he's looking to do. If he could already help himself to such a principle, then he'd also already have the argument he wants against the externalist—he wouldn't need to bother with the thought-experiment. . . . It is in order to argue for the principle that Lehrer appeals to the Truetemp case, not the other way around" (my emphases).

Reply: This kind of concern has already been addressed in Chapter 7, but since it is an important and tricky point it is worth revisiting here. According to the objection, the argument that I claim Lehrer gives for his judgment about the case (*that Mr. Truetemp doesn't know*, call this *L*) isn't an argument for *L*. Instead, *L* serves as evidence for the premise of that argument. I have a two-part reply to this.

First, I think the proposed abductive reading is implausible (and the implausibility in this case illustrates the implausibility more generally in these kinds of cases). Consider the actual text. (It's important to focus on the original text, not the argument as it is idealized in the later literature.)[21]

---

[20] That said, it is unclear whether the relevant judgment about this case is of a kind that methodological rationalists could appeal to. If, for example, the judgment is something like: *If someone S were to stand in the relation described by the Truetemp case to some proposition p, then S would not know that p*, it would not support their account. One account that might suit them is a strict (not a counterfactual) conditional along the lines of: *Necessarily, for all S and p, if someone S stands in the relation described by the Truetemp case to the proposition that p, then S does not know that p* (for discussion of these issues, see e.g. Williamson 2007, Ichikawa and Jarvis 2009, and Malmgren 2011). Thanks to Margot Strohminger for discussion here. Keep in mind that the goal here is not to argue that there are no analytic or conceptual truths. The goal is to show that the thought experiments under consideration can be appreciated (and serve their argumentative purpose) even though we stay neutral on that issue. In the terminology of Chapter 7: it is not an effective element of Lehrer's argument.

[21] Not only are seminal papers often morphed into caricatures in the literature they spawn (as the anonymous referee for OUP helpfully put it), but argumentative mistakes found in the original texts are forgotten and what remains in memory is some kind of idealized and sanitized version of the original (fixed up after many years of refinement in an ongoing debate).

Having described the Mr. Truetemp scenario (2000), Lehrer asks, "Does he know that it is [104 degrees]?" He answers:

Surely not. He has no idea whether he or his thoughts about temperature are reliable. What he accepts, that the temperature is 104 degrees, is correct but he does not know that his thought is correct. His thought that the temperature is 104 degrees is correct information, but he does not know this. Though he records the information because of the operation of the tempucomp, he is ignorant of the facts about the tempucomp and about his temperature-telling reliability. Yet the sort of causal, nomological, statistical, or counterfactual relationship required by externalism, may all be present. *Does he know that the temperature is 104 degrees when the thought occurs to him while strolling in Pima Canyon? He has no idea why the thought occurred to him or that such thoughts are almost always correct. He does not, consequently, know that the temperature is 104 degrees when that thought occurs to him. The correctness of the thought is opaque to him.* (p. 187, italics added)

Focus on the italicized part of this quote. I don't know how to read this other than as Lehrer giving an argument in favor of a certain answer to the question. And it gets worse for the abductive-inference proposal. Lehrer continues, right after the passage quoted: "It might be useful to add a bit to the story to reinforce the conclusion that Mr. Truetemp does not know that the temperature is 104 degrees when the tempucomp causes him to have the thought that the temperature is 104 degrees which he accepts" (p. 187). He goes on to modify the scenario so that even the doctor who introduced the device into Mr. Truetemp is ignorant of its effects and reliability. Why would Lehrer go on to develop ways of reinforcing the conclusion, if he wasn't in the business of giving arguments for it?

Second, as pointed out in Chapter 7, even if certain passages in certain philosophy papers are best read as engaging in an inference to the best explanation, that doesn't show much that's helpful to Centrality. If in a text a proposition p, is presented as the starting point of an inference to the best explanation, that tells us nothing about the epistemic status of p. Inference to the best explanation plays an important role in empirical sciences and any kind of proposition can be a starting point. What would the Centrality proponent have to show about p? Since Centrality is such an unclear thesis, that is unclear, but the previous chapter collected some suggestions from the literature: that it is important to the arguments in question that p has intuition features F1–F3. Surely, no matter how sympathetic the reader is to the idea that Lehrer is engaged in abductive reasoning, that alone will provide no positive argument for the claim that Lehrer's description of Mr. Truetemp has these features. The next case study illustrates this point: it is one where something like an inference to the best explanation perhaps takes place, but where there's no good reason to think that the *explanandum* has the intuition features.

8.5.3 Goldman on fake barns

My final example of a case central to much theorizing in epistemology is Alvin Goldman's fake-barn example (1976). Here, to remind the reader, is the initial setup:

> Consider the following example. Henry is driving in the countryside with his son. For the boy's edification Henry identifies various objects on the landscape as they come into view. "That's a cow," says Henry, "That's a tractor," "That's a silo," "That's a barn," etc. Henry has no doubt about the identity of these objects; in particular, he has no doubt that the last-mentioned object is a barn, which indeed it is. Each of the identified objects has features characteristic of its type. Moreover, each object is fully in view, Henry has excellent eyesight, and he has enough time to look at them reasonably carefully, since there is little traffic to distract him. (p. 772)

Goldman then asks: does Henry know that the object is a barn? The answer, Goldman gives, is of the usual hedged kind, "Most of us **would have little hesitation in saying this**, so long as we were not in a certain philosophical frame of mind" (p. 772, emphases added). He then contrasts this case with the following:

> Suppose we are told that, unknown to Henry, the district he has just entered is full of papier-mache facsimiles of barns. These facsimiles look from the road exactly like barns, but are really just facades, without back walls or interiors, quite incapable of being used as barns. They are so cleverly constructed that travelers invariably mistake them for barns. Having just entered the district, Henry has not encountered any facsimiles; the object he sees is a genuine barn. But if the object on that site were a facsimile, Henry would mistake it for a barn. (pp. 772–3)

He then asks whether Henry knows in the modified scenario, and replies that we "**would be strongly inclined** to withdraw the claim that Henry knows the object is a barn" (p. 773, emphases added). The challenge of the paper is to answer the question, "How is **this change in our assessment** to be explained?" (p. 773, emphases added).

Fake barns and the intuition features. Two claims are candidates for being intuitions at the core of Goldman's fake barn case (and I'm formulating these claims loosely here, not meaning to take a stand on the various competing theories of logical forms):

A1: In the first scenario, Henry does know.

A2: In the modified scenario, Henry doesn't know.

Here is the kind of deflationary interpretation of the role of A1 and A2 that I favor, which follows the pattern found in the earlier case studies. A1 and A2 are presented as being pre-theoretically in the common ground between Goldman and his readers. He thinks they are indicative of something important about knowledge and that figuring out why A1 and A2 are the case will be illuminating. Articulating the reasons and evidence that support our pre-theoretic commitments is sometimes a difficult task. Explaining why Henry knows in the first scenario but not in the second has proved to be not just difficult, but also enormously fruitful for those trying to understand what knowledge is. To see what I mean by saying that Goldman attempts to articulate arguments and evidence in favor of pre-theoretic commitments, consider his brief discussion of what he calls Unger's non-accidentality analysis:

> According to this theory, S knows that p if and only if it is not at all accidental that S is right about its being the case that p. In the initial description of the example, this requirement appears to be satisfied; so we say that Henry knows. When informed about the facsimiles, however, we see that it is accidental that Henry is right about its being a barn. So we withdraw our knowledge attribution. (p. 773)

Putting aside Goldman's objection to this view,[22] it illustrates what Goldman is doing. If Unger's view were correct, it would provide a reason for A1 and A2. That is the goal of the paper: to answer the question, 'Why A1 and A2?' What makes A1 and A2 special is not that they have some kind of privileged and hard-to-articulate epistemic status, it's that trying to figure out the answer to the question, 'Why A1 and A2?', has proved to be significant in thinking about the nature of knowledge. This, however, doesn't require attributing any kind of privileged epistemic properties to A1 and A2.

According to the alternative Centrality-friendly account of A1 and A2, A1 and A2 are not like, say, A3:

---

[22] Goldman says about Unger's view: "The 'non-accidentality' analysis is not very satisfying, however, for the notion of 'non-accidentality' itself needs explication. Pending explication, it isn't clear whether it correctly handles all cases" (p. 773).

A3: Barack Obama knows that he was born in America.

A3 is true, it's in the common ground among most sensible human beings, and so we can use it as a starting point/premise in most conversations. A1 and A2 might also be in the common ground of most conversations but, the Centrality proponent suggests, that is because they have the intuition features. They are, so to speak, special and glowing members of the common ground. They are in the common ground of conversations because they have Rock Status, are accompanied by special phenomenology, or can be justified by relying on nothing but one's conceptual competence.

As in the previous case studies, careful reading of the text reveals no evidence that the propositions in question have these features, and so we should stick with the simpler deflationary account. I trust the reader can go through the text in much the same way I've done in the previous case studies, so I'll just briefly summarize: there is no evidence that such feelings play an important role in the argument. Goldman does not say he restricts his answers to those that are based solely on his conceptual competence. He doesn't relate his favored theory of concepts and concept possession to any particular argument in this paper. Given that Goldman is familiar with the debates around these issues, we would expect him to do that if it were important to his arguments.[23] The overall point to focus on is that the detailed arguments in the paper lose none of their force, if we treat A1 and A2 as suggested by the more deflationary reading.

An objection to my characterization of Goldman's case: psychological language in Goldman's text

> Objection: You keep saying we should stick carefully to the texts, but here you are blatantly ignoring salient parts of what Goldman says. His presentation of the

---

[23] In other work (e.g. his 2007), Goldman has discussed philosophical methodology extensively. He is a proponent of Centrality and he has theories of intuitions, concept possession, and the connections between these that support Centrality. Some of those views are discussed and criticized in Chapter 10. The point to emphasize here is that those who disagree with Goldman's metaphilosophical views should not for that reason alone dismiss his other contributions to epistemology and philosophy more generally. What he does in his non-metaphilosophical papers is open to many metaphilosophical interpretations. Those who reject Centrality (and Goldman's views of conceptual analysis) can still find those papers persuasive and important. Goldman (1976) is a good example of this: it's hard to find any particular argument in that paper that relies essentially on metaphilosophical assumptions developed by Goldman in other papers. Similar points apply to several of the authors discussed in these case studies.

cases crucially makes use of expressions such as "would we say...," "would have little hesitation in saying," "Contrast our inclination here with the inclination we would have...," "we would be strongly inclined to withdraw." This shows that Goldman's goal is not to find arguments for A1 and A2, but to explain some features of our psychology—to explain the kinds of feelings and inclinations we have when we reflect on these cases. You've stripped away all the psychologizing language found in Goldman's text, and that makes the anti-intuition line deceptively easy to defend.

Reply: I think it is more charitable to take Goldman to literally mean that he is interested primarily in why A1 and A2 are true. If his real interest were in why we have certain psychological inclinations and speech dispositions, then literally *all* the arguments he presents are invalid, irrelevant to the question under discussion, or radically incomplete. From none of the arguments does anything directly follow about our inclinations or speech dispositions. Take Unger's theory as an example. What it shows, if correct, is that A1 and A2 are true. It doesn't show anything about what we feel like or what we are inclined to say. In order to get to those kinds of conclusions many additional premises are needed connecting truth to speakers' dispositions and inclinations. So we have a choice: we treat the body of the paper as missing obvious and important argumentative steps or we reject the psychological reading of the initial remarks. I suggest we pursue the latter strategy, since we have no reason to think that Goldman would either overlook huge gaps in his arguments or intentionally include such gaps in his papers. The various interpretative strategies outlined in Part I will serve us well here. Recall, if in response to the question, 'Why didn't Louise come to the meeting?', you answer, 'I/we think she's in Sweden, 'Sam says she is in Sweden', or 'I am'/we're inclined to say she's in Sweden.' You are not saying that Louise is absent because you or the group thinks she is in Sweden or because you, Sam or the group are inclined to say certain sentences. You are instead using the propositional attitude verb to hedge your assertions. That's the natural and charitable interpretation of Goldman's use of psychological vocabulary. As a result we shouldn't treat the final question in the passage I quoted from Goldman, "How is this change in our assessment to be explained?," as a request for an explanation of the difference between two acts of judging, but rather for an explanation of the judged contents, i.e. A1 and A2. Note that this interpretation of Goldman's goal is compatible with there being all kinds of interesting connections between the truth of A1, A2, our inclinations to have certain beliefs, and our inclination to perform certain sayings. The point is just that we shouldn't take the goal of this paper to be to specify what those connections are.

8.6 Cappelen and Hawthorne on disagreement, predicates of personal taste, and relativism about truth

The next case study is from Cappelen and Hawthorne's book, *Relativism and Monadic Truth* (2009).[24] Cappelen and Hawthorne are concerned, in part, with disagreement verdicts about predicates of taste such as 'delicious' and 'fun'. In the debate about this topic in particular and in other debates between contextualists, minimalists and relativists, there is often extensive use of 'intuition'-terminology and it is common to find participants describing their methodology using Centrality-friendly language. Nonetheless, when we look carefully at the texts and the arguments presented, those characterizations turn out to be mistaken.

The starting point for many of the arguments in the current debate between relativists and contextualists is the observation that if *A* says, '*X* is fun', and *B* says, '*X* is not fun', we are inclined to think that *A* and *B* disagree. Suppose that 'fun' is a context-sensitive predicate that somehow incorporates the standard of the speaker into the content, and so means, roughly speaking, something like 'fun for *A*' when *A* speaks and 'fun for *B*' when *B* speaks. Then it is hard to explain how the disagreement between *A* and *B* is generated: *A* would have said *that* X *is fun for* A, and *B* would have said *that* X *is fun for* B—this is not a disagreement. On the other hand, it is also hard to see how the predicate 'fun' can be associated with one invariant and universal standard. Many contemporary versions of relativism were developed to deal with this kind of data.[25] Cappelen and

---

[24] I should emphasize that there is no presumption here that this case study belongs in the distinguished company of the other cases *qua* influential piece of philosophy. It is chosen as a case study because I, as co-author, am well positioned to report on what the authors regarded as relevant considerations and how they intended the cases to be interpreted.

[25] See Lasersohn (2005), MacFarlane (2007), Stephenson (2007), and Chapter 4 of Cappelen and Hawthorne (2009).

Hawthorne claim that the relativist's presentation of the disagreement data is simplistic and in response to it they consider a range of cases involving disagreement judgments that run counter to the pattern predicted by relativistic semantics. The emphasis throughout the book is on the complexity of the data. More than fifty examples are examined, different kinds of disagreement are distinguished, and various procedures for diagnosing disagreements are proposed. The overall goal is *to show how careful reflection reveals that certain quick, unreflective judgments about disagreement, which appear to be troubling for contextualists, are mistaken.*

Here are some illustrations of how Cappelen and Hawthorne proceed. They ask us to consider "a concoction, chica mascada, enjoyed in some cultures, which is produced by a group of people blending their saliva with maize, with the individual outputs being mixed together in a pot and allowed to ferment" (p. 116). Cappelen and Hawthorne note that many Westerners, when this is described to them, "are inclined to the judgment 'That's disgusting!' Some will no doubt be inclined to supplement that verdict with a claim of disagreement with this or that chica-loving group" (p. 116). Crucially, Cappelen and Hawthorne advocate that we *do not* take these initial, unreflective disagreement judgments at face value—they point out that such initial judgments are subject to revision:

> When there is *prima facie* conflict there are various procedures we can go through that make us question whether the disagreement is real. Many of the relevant reflections are aptly described by Sextus: we reflect on the situation dependence of judgments using a predicate of personal taste—how it is controlled by background factors of depression and elation, intoxication and sobriety, youthfulness, and the various mixtures of humors that shape the contours of our dispositions; we reflect and find it arbitrary to assign a 'power of distorting objects' to one set of background factors and not others. (p. 117)

Cappelen and Hawthorne claim that the result of such "Pyrrhonian" reflections hardly ever is what Sextus predicts: a suspension of judgment. What does happen, according to Cappelen and Hawthorne, is that we lose any sense of disagreement. Cappelen and Hawthorne think that is what will happen in the case of apparent disagreement about chica mascada. Here is a second illustration of how the sense of disagreement evaporates as a result of Pyrrhonian reflection. They say:

> We have often witnessed the following kind of chauvinism exercised by people from hot climates. It is 95 degrees, and a person from Arizona overhears someone

from Boston say 'This is hot'. The Arizonan, in a fit of primitive machismo, says 'He's totally mistaken. It's not hot at all. He needs to be in Phoenix in the summer. Then he'll know what it really is to be hot'. (p. 117)

Their diagnosis is that the Arizonan thinks her own threshold for heat tolerance manifests a kind of superiority over the Bostonian. She then makes the mistake of projecting her own standards onto others. That kind of mistake is exhibited in the dialogue above. But, they say,

[S]uch an attitude is hard to maintain for very long. The force of the relevant Pyrrhonian reflections is not hard to appreciate. And the result is that insofar as one judges 'It is not hot', one no longer hears the content expressed as in conflict with the Bostonian's speech. Ascription of a mistake to a Bostonian will either be altogether withdrawn or else will have a ring of playfulness (or else will be a self-indulgent means of imposing one's own standards on certain predicates that appear in some conversation). (p. 118)

Using a range of such examples, Cappelen and Hawthorne aim to undermine the starting point for relativism; the kinds of disagreement verdicts that are used to motivate relativism are shown to be naïve, confused and easily rejected.

8.6.1 Disagreement and the intuition features

Cappelen and Hawthorne's discussion of disagreement is typical of the way such mini-scenarios are treated in the current literature on contextualism and relativism about knowledge, epistemic modals, tense, pronouns, quantifiers, adjectives, future contingents, conditionals and related issues. These discussions draw on a very large range of examples—some of them real, some of them imaginary. Cappelen and Hawthorne are typical in that they treat immediate, unreflective reactions to the cases with a high degree of suspicion. In this respect they align themselves with an extensive current literature that argues that initial reactions to certain kinds of cases in this domain often confuse different levels of semantic and non-semantic content and can also be subject to systematic psychological biases. They advocate the view that speakers are systematically inclined to make mistakes in their judgments about certain cases in certain kinds of settings. Careful reflection and theorizing is required in order to get it right. Naïve and spontaneous reactions not based on arguments should be bracketed.

Note also that Cappelen and Hawthorne rely extensively on claims about what typically happens to people's judgments once they have made what they label "Pyrrhonian reflections" (pp. 117ff.). These claims are empirical conjectures—armchair empirical psychology, anthropology, or what have you. They are obviously subject to further empirical investigation.

More or less as a corollary of the above points, Cappelen and Hawthorne's cases fail to exhibit any of F1-F3:

- At no point in *Relativism and Monadic Truth* does special phenomenology of judgments play any role. Both the authors are unaware of any such special phenomenology and so *they* certainly didn't put any weight on it. In none of the by now considerable literature on the book, does phenomenology of particular claims made by Cappelen and Hawthorne make any discernible difference. In short, there is no evidence that F1 plays a significant role in that work.
- I am not aware of any claim about a case made in that book that the authors treat as having the kind of special epistemic status characterized by Rock. The claims we make about the various cases discussed are either assumed to be in the common ground between Cappelen and Hawthorne and their interlocutors or claims that require evidential backing or inferential support. Cappelen and Hawthorne treat no claim about the many cases they discuss as being by default justified (as required by F2). So there is no evidence that claims characterized by F2 play a significant role in these discussions.
- The absence of F1 and F2 is already evidence against the effective presence of F3. Putting that aside, it would come as a big surprise to both Cappelen and Hawthorne that any of their claims about the many cases they discuss in the book are based solely on their conceptual competence. First, neither of them believes *anything* has the F3-property, so they certainly didn't intend for any of their claims to be based solely on their conceptual competence and they didn't have as a goal to find claims characterized by F3. This isn't decisive, since it is *possible* that unbeknownst to Cappelen and Hawthorne, they relied on F3-claims. Is it plausible, on any construal of 'concept', 'conceptual competence' and 'justified', that their claim *that the two imagined utterances of 'Chica mascada is delicious' and 'Chica mascada is disgusting' don't express disagreement*, is justified simply by their competence with *disagreement, delicious, disgusting and chica mascada*? As we have seen, it is hard to find proof for or against any such hypothesis given the vague

and variable characterizations of F3, but, speaking now as one of the co-authors, I can report that the work that led up to those claims did not resemble anything that we know as being described as conceptual analysis: we read anthropology books about disgust reactions in various cultures, we tried to learn a bit about the cultural variations in disgust reactions, their various physical expressions, and the various hypotheses about the evolutionary source of disgust reactions. It would just be silly to insist that this entire process should be characterized as 'relying solely on our conceptual competence'.[26] Of course, none of this is conclusive evidence against the presence of F3: a proponent of conceptual competence could say that what we did was learn more about our concept, or that we developed our conceptual competence by doing all this empirical research. But the point is that at no point did that goal guide the activity we were engaged in. At no point did either of us say to the other, 'Hold on, this isn't a conceptually justified claim, so we shouldn't make it.' So it certainly wasn't a feature that played an *effective* role in this particular instance of philosophical practice.

8.7 Bernard Williams on personal identity and the fear of the prospect of torture

In "The Self and the Future" (1970), Bernard Williams develops an influential and ingenious thought experiment that is paradigmatic of much literature on personal identity. Williams' case is complex and importantly involves asking us to imagine the same scenario in two different ways—once from the first-person point of view and once from the third-person point of view. I will focus here on the first-person description and the judgments we are asked to make about it.

(i) *Someone in whose power I am tells me that I am going to be tortured tomorrow.*

BW says: I am frightened, and look forward to tomorrow in great apprehension.

---

[26] And equally silly to insist that it was an 'armchair activity', unless Googling in one's armchair counts as engaging in armchair activity.

(ii) He adds that when the time comes, I shall not remember being told that this was going to happen to me, since shortly before the torture something else will be done to me which will make me forget the announcement.

BW says: This certainly will not cheer me up.

(iii) He then adds that my forgetting the announcement will be only part of a larger process: when the moment of torture comes, I shall not remember any of the things I am now in a position to remember.

Williams says: This will not cheer me up either.

(iv) He now further adds that at the moment of torture I shall not only not remember the things I am now in a position to remember, but will have a different set of impressions of my past, quite different from the memories I now have.

Williams says: I do not think that this would cheer me up either.

(v) Nor do I see why I should be put into any better frame of mind by the person in charge adding lastly that the impressions of my past with which I shall be equipped on the eve of torture will exactly fit the past of another person now living, and indeed I shall acquire these impressions by (for instance) information now in his brain being copied into mine.

Williams says: Fear, surely, would still be the proper reaction (all from pp. 167–8).

As with Perry and Burge, it is difficult to identify 'the case' here. There are a number of judgments we are asked to make:

(i) Whether we agree with Williams about whether any of these modifications would cheer him up;
(ii) What judgment each one of us would have made had we been the agent in the thought experiment; and
(iii) Whether he, i.e. BW, is the person that has the body undergoing these changes (call this 'the Body Person').

His answer to (iii) is a tentative 'yes'. He thinks that if he, i.e. BW, feels fear for what will happen to the Body Person, those fears must be *his* fears, so he has some reason to think the Body Person is him. This, however, is a conclusion he reaches only tentatively. Assuming that he is the Body Person is, he says, "risky: that there is room for the notion of a risk here is itself a major feature of the problem" (p. 180).

CASE STUDIES 181

One striking and original aspect of Williams' case is that he is asking us to check on an *emotional* response to the prospect of certain sequences of events. He is not, primarily, asking us to make truth-value judgments. It is also important to the evaluation of the case that it is done in the first person—you cannot just read Williams' text and relate to what he says about his reaction to it. We are encouraged to actually *go through the case from the first-person perspective*. On one construal you are supposed to do that in order to *predict* the emotional response you would have had in the described scenario.

One of the questions Williams wants the reader to focus on is just how the case generalizes. In the very same paper, Williams presents what he in some places describes as the same case but which is described from a third-person perspective. According to Williams the reaction we are inclined towards differs between the two presentations, and this is a puzzling and philosophically significant aspect of the case. It also raises the question of whether, strictly speaking, we are considering 'the same scenario' or whether the change in perspective changes what we are considering.[27]

8.7.1 Williams' case and the intuition features

Williams puts no weight on either the Seem-True feature or the Rock feature. First, the initial question is not obviously about the truth value of a proposition: we are asked the check on an emotional response—whether we think these various changes to the hypothetical torture would cheer us up. There is of course something truth-evaluable in the vicinity: predictions about an emotional response. Maybe the candidate for F1 and F2 status is a proposition like: *Such-and-such a change would not cheer me up*. So understood, the claim is a prediction about an emotional response under extremely strange circumstances. If that is the judgment we focus on, there is no evidence in the text that we are encouraged by Williams to judge the truth value of this prediction without relying on evidence or reasoning, or that a special 'seem-true' phenomenology of the judgment plays an argumentative role. On the contrary, Williams' emphasis is on the complexity of the case and the mystery of the different judgments we get when evaluating the case from different perspectives. What Williams goes on to do is show that our inclinations about the case changes depending on

[27] See again Ninan (2010) on this issue.

whether the case is presented from a first-person or third-person perspective. A central theme of Williams' paper is that we have to reflect carefully about *why* our inclinations differ. Like Cappelen and Hawthorne's cases, Williams' is a paradigm of a case where we are encouraged to be skeptical of the immediate unreflective reactions we might have.

Consider next whether reflections on this case rely solely on conceptual competence. That idea is so implausible it is hardly worth considering. The question of how one would react emotionally under such circumstances is hardly accessible to us simply by relying on conceptual competence. Whatever the correct prediction is about how I would respond under such circumstances, it is not a necessary truth that I would have had that response. I could have been different emotionally—in particular my fear responses could have been different. For those who think propositions based only on conceptual competence are necessary truths, this should settle the case. As in all the cases discussed earlier in this chapter, further evidence is provided by the fact that no significant contribution to the debate over these cases rules out a reply simply because it fails to fit some theorists' conception of a conceptually justified statement.[28]

8.8 Chalmers on zombies

The so-called zombie argument plays an important role in David Chalmers' *The Conscious Mind* (1996) and more generally in contemporary discussions of consciousness. When I presented early versions of this material at various institutions, I was often encouraged to pick this as a case study. Many thought it would be a particularly tricky case for my purposes—one that seems to fit Centrality's picture of philosophizing almost as hand to glove. As it turns out, I think it's a good illustration of

---

[28] As in all the other cases, indefinitely many questions are raised by the case and one could object that I have focused on the wrong one. I have heard the suggestion that the 'real' question for each stage of the thought experiment is something like *Is that me?* I.e. we are supposed to, in the first person, ask ourselves whether we identify with the agent in the case as described at that stage. I agree that on some construal, this is one question we could ask at each stage, but it is even more obvious that the answer to this does not have the various intuitions features, i.e. does not have F1–F3. One central purpose of the thought experiment is to argue for a particular answer to the question, *Is that me?* That I feel fear at the various stages is supposed to constitute evidence for a positive answer to the question. So the answer is not presented as something we can access immediately without giving reasons.

many of the points I've made in previous sections and so serves well as a final case study.

In Chapter 3 of *The Conscious Mind*, Chalmers asks us to consider

> ... the logical possibility of a *zombie*: someone or something physically identical to me (or to any other physical being), but lacking conscious experiences altogether. At the global level we can consider the logical possibility of a *zombie world:* a world physically identical to ours, but in which there are no conscious experiences at all. (p. 94)

About this possibility, Chalmers goes on to add:

> The logical possibility of zombies seems... **obvious to me**. A zombie is just something physically identical to me, but which has no conscious experience— all is dark inside. While this is probably empirically impossible, it certainly seems that a coherent situation is described; I can discern no contradiction in the description. In some ways an assertion of this logical possibility comes down to a **brute intuition**.... **Almost everybody, it seems to me, is capable of conceiving of this possibility.** (p. 96, my emphases)

> [T]he only route available to an opponent here is to claim that in describing the zombie world as a zombie world, we are misapplying the concepts, and that in fact there is a conceptual contradiction lurking in the description.... But then the burden is on the opponent to give us some idea of where the contradiction might lie in the apparently quite coherent description. If no internal incoherence can be revealed, then there is a very strong case that the zombie world is logically possible.... I can detect no internal incoherence; **I have a clear picture of what I am conceiving when I conceive of a zombie.** (p. 99, my emphases)

The conceivability of zombies is used as an argument against materialism. I'll sketch the argument below, but keep in mind that the goal here is not to evaluate the argument; it is, rather, to determine whether a claim that is properly called 'intuitive' plays a central role in it.

8.8.1 Comments on Chalmers on zombies

In many cases, and this is a particularly good illustration, metaphilosophical remarks are integrated into the articulation of first-order philosophy in a way that makes disentangling them difficult. Chalmers says he relies on 'a brute intuition' and that he is engaged in a project broadly described as that of investigating a concept. So if we are to take his remarks about what he is doing at face value, the text lends support to Centrality. However, if one is approaching such a text from the point of view of someone skeptical of the metaphilosophical views of the author, it is worth trying to disentangle the metaphilosophy from the first-order arguments. In many cases, this is worth doing, even though difficult. Suppose you don't agree with Goldman's views about metaphilosophy (e.g. his views on the nature of intuitions and conceptual analysis). Even so, there are important lessons to be learned from what he has to say about knowledge. Suppose you don't agree with Timothy Williamson's views on metaphilosophy; you can still learn things from reading his work on vagueness, knowledge, and second-order modal logic. In the same way, there are important lessons to be learned from reading Chalmers, and his version of the zombie argument in particular, when his metaphilosophical commitments are set aside. So I'll try to do that. It means, first, ignoring his explicit claim that he is relying on nothing but an intuition and that he is engaged in an analysis of the concept of a zombie.[29] What is left when the metaphilosophical remarks are removed? What are the candidate intuitive claims that, allegedly, play a central role in this argument? Here, first, are some claims that are *not* reasonable candidates and should be set aside as irrelevant:

Chalmers has tried to conceive of a zombie world.

Chalmers has failed to find an internal incoherence in the description.

While readers will no doubt be willing to grant Chalmers these introspective reports without further argumentation, they are not serious candidates for the relevant intuitive claims (they are, rather, contingent empirical reports of cognitive efforts by Chalmers). We should also immediately make clear that the following possibility claim is not the relevant intuitive claim:

The zombie world is possible.

That we can go from conceivability to (some kind of) possibility is a theoretical claim that stands in need of argumentation, not a claim Chalmers or others in this debate are willing to rest on so-called appeal to intuition. The more serious candidate is the conceivability claim,

CI: The zombie world is conceivable.

---

[29] Alternatively, reinterpret those remarks according to one of the strategies outlined in Part I. For reasons that will become clear at the end of this section, an interpretation of 'intuition' as meaning something like 'pre-theoretic' can work well here.

Is CI a claim that can plausibly be characterized as an intuitive foundation for the argument? The answer I'll give is: clearly not—at least not if being intuitive requires having some combination of the intuition features F1, F2, and F3. The first thing to note is that in subsequent work Chalmers went on to clarify and elaborate on this argument and in particular on the notion of conceivability involved. Chalmers (2002) distinguishes between eight sorts of conceivability. He starts with three initial distinctions:

Prima facie vs. ideal conceivability,
Positive vs. negative conceivability, and
Primary vs. secondary conceivability.

He emphasizes that "[t]hese distinctions are independent of each other, [and] so there may be up to eight sorts of conceivability in the vicinity: prima facie primary positive conceivability, and so on." (p. 146). As a result there are eight versions of CI, and eight versions of the so-called zombie argument—one for each notion of conceivability. According to Chalmers (2002) it is *ideal primary positive (negative) conceivability* that is appealed to in CI. Chalmers reconstructs the earlier zombie argument as follows:

...let P be the conjunction of physical truths about the world, and let Q be a phenomenal truth. The zombie argument claims that zombies, and therefore P∧~Q, are primarily positively conceivable. (Here, Q might be 'someone is conscious'.)... If we use the current framework to analyze these arguments, a first pass might yield something like the following:

(1) P∧~Q is ideally primarily positively (negatively) conceivable.
(2) If P∧~Q is ideally primarily positively (negatively) conceivable, then P&~Q is primarily possible.
(3) If P∧~Q is primarily possible, materialism is false.
(4) Materialism is false. (p. 196)

In this context the focus isn't on the soundness of this argument, but rather whether (1) has the hallmarks of the intuitive. Is it the kind of judgment that proponents of Centrality claim lies at the center of philosophical method? Even just casual familiarity with Chalmers' work should make it clear that the answer to this question is 'no'. Consider his notion of 'ideal conceivability'. Here are some representative passages in which this notion is elaborated on:

S is ideally conceivable when S is conceivable on ideal rational reflection. It sometimes happens that S is prima facie conceivable to a subject, but that this prima facie conceivability is undermined by further reflection showing that the tests that are criterial for conceivability are not in fact passed.... The notion of ideal rational reflection remains to be clarified. One could try to define ideal conceivability in terms of the capacities of an ideal reasoner—a reasoner free from all contingent cognitive limitations.... Alternatively, one can dispense with the notion of an ideal reasoner and simply invoke the notion of undefeatability by better reasoning. Given this notion, we can say that S is ideally conceivable when there is a possible subject for whom S is prima facie conceivable, with justification that is undefeatable by better reasoning.... I will not try to give a substantive characterization of what good reasoning consists in, or of what counts as a cognitive limitation to be idealized away from. I suspect that any such attempt would turn out to be open-ended and incomplete. (pp. 147–8)

In light of this account of what ideal conceivability might consist in, consider again, "(1) P∧∼Q is ideally primarily positively (negatively) conceivable." Is it even prima facie plausible that the intuition features F1–F3 play a central role in the debate over and justification for this claim? Note first that both F1 and F2 are absent. What is conceivable on ideal reflection is not something that we can settle without careful reflection and argumentation and so will be a conclusion we reach inferentially.[30] At no point in this work does Chalmers claim that the phenomenology that accompanies (1) has argumentative significance. As pointed out above, Chalmers is committed to views about the centrality of conceptual analysis in philosophizing, which have figured prominently in the discussion of his work, and so it's hard to deny that F3 plays an important role. However two points are important here. First, not even Chalmers thinks that these commitments about the role of conceptual analysis are sufficient to make (1) into a claim justified solely by an intuition. Second, many if not most philosophers don't endorse Chalmers' construal of what he is doing—they don't think conceivability claims like (1) are claims that rely solely on conceptual competence (as this is construed by Chalmers and other proponents of two-dimensional semantics). Most philosophers of mind think that the zombie argument is important even though they reject or are agnostic about the metaphilosophical views that Chalmers advocates. In short, Chalmers'

---

[30] Since we are not ideally rational, we will have to engage in very careful reasoning to try to figure out what an ideal reasoner would conclude—presumably all our conclusions about this would be tentative.

meta-views about how to construe conceivability arguments are optional. They are not essential elements of premise (1) or the argument it is a part of. When the zombie argument is looked at in the larger context of Chalmers' work on consciousness, the nature of conceivability, and the connection between conceivability and possibility, it looks implausible to think that any one premise in that argument is based primarily on what Centrality proponents would label 'an intuition'. The model that seems more appropriate is that of John Perry's cases in "The Essential Indexical." Perry draws our attention to a phenomenon that is philosophically significant and the debate over the last thirty years has consisted in attempts to figure out how to correctly describe those phenomena and their significance. None of those reflections have the hallmark of the intuitive. The same goes for Chalmers' discussion of the conceivability of zombies. There's an interesting phenomenon that we pre-theoretically would characterize as the prima facie conceivability of a zombie world. Then significant philosophical work has gone into theorizing about the nature of conceivability, it's connection to what is possible, and the particular details concerning zombies. Again, none of these further reflections appear to fit Centrality's model of the intuitive.

8.9 Conclusion

Okay, that's it. I could go on and on, but I won't. For some, this will no doubt be too much. For others, it'll be too little. For those who think it's been too much, I hope that's because they recognize a pattern: actual instances of philosophical argumentation hardly ever exhibit signs of relying on intuitions. For those who think too little I encourage further exploration. What I predict will be found is widespread misuse of 'intuition'-terminology but hardly any argumentation that has the hallmark of the intuitive. The next chapter articulates further generalizations that these case studies warrant and considers some objections.

9

Lessons Learned, Replies to Objections, and Comparison to Williamson

This chapter draws some general lessons from the case studies in the previous chapter. I start with seven observations about what cases *are*, and then nine observations about what cases *are not*. I use these observations to argue that a version of Centrality, Centrality$_{(M)}$, is false. I then consider a number of objections to my treatment of the case studies and the conclusions drawn. Finally, I compare my view to some aspects of the view defended by Williamson in *The Philosophy of Philosophy*.

9.1 What cases are: some generalizations

An unattractive feature of Centrality is that it makes a broad and generic claim about a group as varied as that of philosophers and an activity as varied as philosophizing. That said, were I to indulge in those kinds of generalizations, I would say something like the following:

- *Range of questions*: The function of philosophical cases is to raise a range of questions about some philosophically significant features of the world. (Contrast this with the idea that their function is to answer questions.)
- *Justification requirement*: Answers to questions about philosophical cases come with a *justification requirement*. The questions have this form, '*P*? Justify your answer.' Suppose in reply to one of Perry's questions about his case, e.g. "How should we characterize the transition from the belief expressed by 'someone is making a mess' to the belief expressed by 'I am making a mess?'" (1979, p. 3), someone replies

with only, 'His beliefs changed.' This isn't a good answer, even if it happens to be true. The questions we ask about philosophical cases come with justification requirements and the value of an answer to questions raised by a philosophical case depends on the quality of the justification.

- *Good philosophical cases are puzzling*: They are *difficult* and *challenging* and so we hardly ever conclusively settle on one answer to the various questions raised by a case. (Contrast this with the view that even though the goal of philosophy is to answer extremely hard questions, we have a relatively simple and non-theoretical starting point: judgments about cases. This is a mistake—the judgments about cases are as hard as the 'big' questions we try to answer.)
- *Philosophical cases come in groups and with a generality requirement*: Understanding a case requires an ability to abstract away from the irrelevant components of the case and construct other cases that illustrate the same point. This is why the seminal papers we have looked at in the previous chapter almost always present groups of cases. For example, you don't understand Perry's supermarket example if you don't understand that only a very abstract feature of the case is essential to it. It's a feature it has in common with the hikers lost in the wilderness and the professor going to his meeting. Often, as in this case, it is extremely hard to say what they have in common and so extremely hard to really understand the cases.
- *Reflection on cases is a hyper-rational, epistemically hyper-demanding context*: Philosophers question assumptions that in a non-philosophical context would be considered part of the common ground—assumptions that in a typical non-philosophical context would be accepted by the conversation partners without a demand for further justification. This tendency to question everything is part of philosophers' self-conception. Centrality and the false metaphilosophical theories it is embedded in have obscured the fact that this tendency applies equally to the questions we ask about cases. As Burge points out, in a non-philosophical context, no one would question his literal, disquotational interpretation of the belief attribution in the first step of his thought experiment. Nonetheless, he spends about twenty pages defending it and other philosophers have spent thirty years questioning his defense. And so it goes. Even when it comes to our

description of cases, we philosophers are hyper-rational and epistemically hyper-demanding.
- *Variety of evidential sources*: Philosophers are promiscuous in the kinds of data and evidence they allow themselves to draw on when answering philosophical questions. There are no self-imposed constraints on allowable evidential sources. Whatever you think counts as an evidential source, you will find some philosopher drawing on it.
- *Answers to philosophical questions come in a variety of modalities*: The answers we give to philosophical questions vary in the kind of modality they invoke. Rather than looking for a particular modality in their answers (metaphysical necessity, conceptual necessity, nomological necessity or what have you), they look for answers that can help them understand certain features of the world better and what counts as 'better understanding' varies a lot. Sometimes we are happy with understanding how something works in this world (e.g. how quantifiers or names actually function in English, whether there is a language of thought, what special relativity tells us about the nature of time). On the other end of the spectrum, some philosophers seek truths that hold in all metaphysically possible worlds. But there is no privileged modality that is characteristic of philosophical answers to questions asked about thought experiments.
- *The so-called method of cases is not a method*: When one realizes the variety of what philosophical methodologists tend to call 'the method of cases', it is hard not to be struck by how misleading the label 'method' is. When we say *that philosophers appeal to cases*, what we mean is that they draw our attention to philosophically significant features of the world (or ways the world could have been). Perry noticed interesting features of self-locating beliefs. Burge noticed important connections between mental content and social environments. Describing such interesting features of the world is hardly a method. I also suspect talk of 'cases' fuels an unfortunate misunderstanding: it encourages a kind of meta-linguistic construal of what goes on in these examples—it lends itself to the idea that the subject matter is the so-called case, which is some kind of philosophical construct. It encourages the view that when we discuss cases, the subject matter is *the description given of the world* or some kind of theoretical construct, not *the described feature of the world*. But that, of

course, is deeply mistaken. Philosophers like everyone else use language to describe the world. Their subject matter is whatever feature of the world they are describing. The representational device is not the subject matter. Of course, sometimes what we describe are the representational devices themselves, but then the focus is not on the device for representing the representational devices, but on the representational devices.[1] Of course, occasionally, we will object to someone's way of representing a particular feature of the world—and in that way make someone's representation into the subject matter, but in none of the cases discussed in the previous chapter is the representation itself the subject matter.

If I were in the business of making broad generalizations about philosophers' appeal to cases, those are the ones I would start with. This is obviously just a very brief beginning. There are, for example, important avenues of research that explore the effects of examples, illustrations, and thought experiments more generally (not just in philosophy). It might very well be that, as Tamar Szabó Gendler has emphasized (see Gendler 2007 and 2011), that "by presenting content in a suitably concrete or abstract way, thought experiments recruit representational schemas that were otherwise inactive, thereby evoking responses that may run counter to those evoked by alternative presentations of relevantly similar content" (2007, p. 69). Gendler, talking about thought experiments in moral philosophy, describes them as "devices of persuasion" and suggests that at least some of them function to identify "images that will bring the readers to reframe their experience of some morally valenced situation, in such a way that their apprehension of the morally relevant features of it are re-experienced in light of the scenario presented" (p. 83). She specifically addresses one of the case studies in the previous chapter, Thomson's violinist case, and describes its purpose as follows:

Thomson's thought experiment "works" if it brings about a reframing of the subject's attitudes in the domain it is intended to illuminate—if he comes, either reflectively or unreflectively, to represent the question of the fetus–mother relationship in ways akin to those that he represents the violinist–patient relationship. (p. 86)

---

[1] This again is not to deny that sometimes the focus is on the representational devices used to represent representational devices (see Cappelen and Lepore 2008). The general point here applies to every iteration of levels.

Just as it is extremely hard to give a systematic account of the effects of metaphor (and how it is related to literal content), it will be very hard to say anything systematic and general about the cognitive effects of examples, illustrations and thought experiments (and the relation of these to the general principles they illustrate), but those are still important issues to explore. What is important in this context is that such a topic can be pursued independently of anything that Centrality proponents would call 'intuitions'. It also has very little to do specifically with philosophy—these are general issues about the connection between form and content.

If the generalizations above are right (in whatever sense such generalizations can be right) it shows that an endorsement of Centrality has led to significant misconceptions about philosophy. The misconceptions include these:

- Judgments about cases are rock-bottom points in philosophical discourse—they are not points where reasons/arguments/justifications run out.
- Judgments accompanied by special phenomenology play a particularly significant role in philosophical theorizing.
- Philosophers seek conceptual truths and try to restrict their theorizing to what can be based solely on conceptual competence.
- Philosophers seek essences (where this is construed e.g. as Bealer construes it)[2] or necessary truths.
- Philosophers seek a priori knowledge.
- Philosophers appeal to 'what non-philosophers would say' about cases as evidence.

All of these generalizations are false. Finally, and most importantly in this context, Centrality$_{(M)}$ is false:

Centrality$_{(M)}$: Philosophers rely (in some epistemically significant way) on intuitions when they make judgments about cases.

---

[2] Recall that Bealer writes: "In being interested in such things as the nature of mind, intelligence, the virtues, and life, philosophers do not want to know what those things just happen to be, but rather what those things must be, what they are in a strong sense" (1996, p. 3).

I take this to be evidence that the Argument from Philosophical Practice fails. The first part of this book showed that the Argument from 'Intuition'-Talk fails. In other words, the two main arguments for Centrality both fail. So I conclude that Centrality is false.

In the remainder of this chapter I first consider a series of objections to my treatment of the cases and the conclusions drawn from them. I end the chapter with a discussion of two themes central to Timothy Williamson's book, *The Philosophy of Philosophy*. First, I discuss Williamson's claim that philosophers have a tendency to psychologize evidence. Second, I discuss Williamson's motivation for engaging in an extended discussion of whether there are any conceptually justified claims.

9.2 Objections and replies

The procedure I have used to investigate Centrality is somewhat unorthodox—most of those making claims about philosophical practice and methodology do so without careful investigation of case studies. In part as a result of this, there is no extensive tradition of detailed and careful reflection on how to interpret thought experiments. I can imagine a great number of objections to the way I have gone about doing it. I can also imagine a large number of alternative strategies. What follows are some brief responses to some of these objections and brief justifications for not pursuing some of the alternative strategies.

> *Objection: Your choice of cases is biased. I'll grant, at least for the sake of argument, that your cases don't have features F1–F3, but that just showed that you picked the wrong cases. The right selection, a truly representative selection of philosophical cases, will support Centrality.*

> Reply: We could play this game and I would welcome it. I would like to see such replies worked out. Proponents of Centrality$_{(M)}$ should come up with a set of paradigmatic cases and try to show by careful detailed study of the texts, that they really exhibit F1–F3. I predict failure. But it is a challenge to proponents of Centrality$_{(M)}$ that I would be delighted if someone tried to meet. Only by detailed study of a wide range of examples will we understand philosophical method better.

> *Objection: What about the Gettier case? You didn't investigate that case and it is a philosophical thought experiment par excellence. No discussion of*

philosophical methodology can be respectable without talking extensively about the Gettier case.

Reply: I find the focus on the Gettier case to be counterproductive. It is typically the only case discussed in the literature on these topics and that is dangerous: suppose it turns out that the Gettier case is significantly different from the cases I discussed in the previous chapter. That would provide evidence that the Gettier case is non-representative and so damage has most likely been done by the almost pathological focus on it. However, my view is that the case is typically misrepresented in the literature and that careful study of it and the discussions it has triggered will reveal close similarity to e.g. Perry's case. Since I want to downplay the importance of that case, I will pursue that issue in a footnote.[3]

Objection: Even if not all (or even most) cases discussed by philosophers have features F1–F3, surely some do. The charitable thing to do is to interpret proponents of Centrality as saying no more than that some philosophers sometimes rely on intuitions (about cases) as evidence in their theorizing.

---

[3] Several points are worth noting about Gettier's original paper (1963). First, there is no talk of any intuitions about the case or about Gettier's inclinations to believe, his judgments or other psychological states. All he talks about is whether Smith knows. Second, when stating that Smith doesn't know in the first case, he immediately, in the next sentence, goes on to explain why. He says: "But it is equally clear that Smith does not *know* that (e) [The man who will get the job has ten coins in his pocket] is true; for (e) is true in virtue of the number of coins in Smith's pocket, while Smith does not know how many coins are in Smith's pocket, and bases his belief in (e) on a count of the coins in Jones's pocket, whom he falsely believes to be the man who will get the job" (p. 122). Gettier does not present the claim that Smith doesn't know as based on an intuition, he presents it as based on an argument. For further exploration of how the Gettier case was treated when it was first presented I suggest careful reading of the papers by Clark (1963), Lehrer (1965) and Sosa (1965) (Thanks to Derek Ball for drawing my attention to these early replies to Gettier.). Again, we find the same pattern: they present arguments for why we should deny knowledge to Smith. They don't appeal to intuitions. What makes Gettier's case significantly different from other famous cases and therefore unrepresentative is that practically all philosophers agree with his conclusion. This is because Gettier was right—Smith doesn't know. This observation triggered what Williamson calls the "failed" project of trying to come up with necessary and sufficient conditions for knowledge (2000, p. 50). If Williamson is right, this was an enormous waste of intellectual energy. Putting that issue aside, note that the consensus generated about Gettier's cases is extremely unusual in philosophy and so in this respect the Gettier case is an anomaly. That wide consensus combined with the obsessive focus on that case in philosophical methodology (caused no doubt partly by the fact that epistemologists have dominated the debate) could, at least in part, explain some of the common misconceptions about how philosophers treat cases. Many of these points about Gettier's case are laid out in more detail by Max Deutsch (2010).

Reply: This is like the suggestion that we should interpret the false claim, 'Philosophers take their undergraduate degrees in Finland', to mean the true claim, 'At least one philosopher took her undergraduate degree in Finland.' That's not an admissible interpretation of the original statement. There is no way to downplay the fact that all the passages quoted in the first chapter are false. They say false things about philosophy and philosophers. If some of those philosophers who made those claims would like to backtrack, that's good, but it is not good to present it as an interpretation of the original statement. That said, I think it would be immense progress if all methodologists stopped making generic claims about what philosophers do. If someone grants me that all the passages from Centrality proponents that I quoted in the preceding chapters are false and then goes on to make very specific and carefully investigated claims about the status of particular claims made in a particular argument, we would have made progress.[4]

Objection: What about simple counterexamples? Surely, they are typically quick appeals to intuitions. This is a variation on the earlier objections: the claim is that I have been focusing on the wrong kinds of cases. Maybe, the objection goes, the kinds of very deep, puzzling and rich cases that I have focused on are special. They contrast with the kinds of quick and unreflective judgments we make when we give quick counterexamples. The real focus should be on judgments about such cases. Those, the proponent of Centrality might say, rely on intuitions.

Reply: The response is similar to the one given to the first two objections: I would welcome a careful investigation of the practice of giving counterexamples, and if evidence is found that the features that characterize intuitions are present in a large number of judgments about counterexamples, that would be an interesting result. It would count in favor of some restricted version of Centrality. However, I predict no such evidence will be forthcoming. First, it is obviously false that counterexamples *in general* rely on anything like what proponents of Centrality call 'intuitions'. To give a counterexample to a generalization of the form, 'All *F*s are *G*s', is to present an instance of an *F* that is not a *G*. It certainly is not in general the case that anyone who presents a counterexample in this sense is relying on anything that can be properly

---

[4] In the next chapter I consider in detail one example of this strategy: namely, restricting Centrality to just those philosophers who engage in conceptual analysis.

called an intuition. Example of generalization: *All Norwegians like fish.* There are many counterexamples to this, including my brother Alexander. When I use Alex as a counterexample, it would be silly to even suggest that I rely on anything properly called 'intuitions'. I rely on testimony and forty years of experience and memories of his eating habits. This is what counterexamples typically are like. The same point applies to modal claims, e.g. *Necessarily, all Norwegians like fish.* Alex would serve as an actual counterexample, but I can also just think about a possible Norwegian being averse to fish. That would suffice. Again, that non-actual counterexample (maybe some would call it a thought experiment) would be based on my experience with humans of various nationalities and their variable taste preferences.

Objection: Surely some claims must have the Rock feature—otherwise we have an infinite chain of justifications (or it all goes in a circle). Your denial that judgments about cases have the Rock feature in the previous chapter seems to indicate that you think it's arguments all the way down.

Reply: No, I'm not saying that. I'm just saying that paradigmatic philosophical cases don't involve judgments that are rock-bottom. In order to make that claim I don't need to take a stand on the larger question of how chains of justification eventually end. Maybe there are judgments with the Rock feature and maybe those are needed in order for chains of reasoning to be *properly* grounded. All I am saying is that the place to look for such starting points is not in philosophical appeal to cases—those judgments are, as we have seen, typically puzzling and rely on a range of empirical data embedded in theorizing. If there is a rock-bottom point of justification, philosophers who discuss cases don't operate at that level.

Objection: If not intuitions, then what? If philosophers don't rely on intuitions, then how is philosophy possible?

Reply: As should be clear by now, this is a very, very silly question. Philosophers rely on all kinds of data—they are promiscuous and unconstrained about the kinds of considerations and sources of evidence that they consider relevant to the questions they try to answer. This is in part because philosophy is such a spectacularly broad topic—we ask questions that intersect with issues in economics, linguistics, logic, psychology, biology, physics, computer science, mathematics, art history, theology, etc. We draw on data from all these domains, common sense, and whatever else we can lay our hands on. The objection imagined here will often be accompanied by other silly remarks and questions such as these: *Philosophy is an armchair activity, it's an a priori enterprise and so we need special evidential sources—those that are available a priori. What can those be, if not intuitions?* It is of course true that philosophy can be done by people who sit in armchairs, but I'll assume those who make such remarks don't think we can make inferences from furniture preferences to the nature of the arguments developed while using that furniture. So these kinds of remarks about philosophers require empirical backing by careful studies of what philosophers do. And the data doesn't support such generalizations. It is not true that philosophers are correctly characterized by such remarks. Maybe there are a few philosophers who really only are interested in answers that rely on nothing but their conceptual competence. They are very atypical and I have some things to say about such philosophers in the next chapter.

Objection: Recently a number of philosophers[5] have made proposals about what the hidden logical form of thought experiments is. You have been operating on the surface level—maybe things would look different had you investigated the real, underlying logical form those thought experiments have.

Reply: I have stayed away from making assumptions about the underlying logical form of thought experiments because I don't know what status these logical forms are supposed to have. The notion of a logical form is familiar from syntax and semantics. In those domains, it is also a very tricky notion, referring, roughly, to the form the sentence is assigned in a correct syntax and semantics for the language. It is then a controversial issue whether that level of representation is psychologically real, some think it is, others not. Clearly, this is not what is going on when e.g. Williamson (2007) hypothesizes that thought experiments in general have the argumentative form he assigns to the Gettier case:

$\Diamond \exists x \exists p \, GC(x, p)$
In English: "Someone could stand in the relation described in the Gettier story to some proposition" (p. 184).
$\exists x \exists p \, GC(x, p) \; \Box\!\!\rightarrow \; \forall x \forall p \, (GC(x, p) \rightarrow (JTB(x, p) \, \& \, \neg K(x, p)))$.

---

[5] See e.g. Williamson (2007), Ichikawa and Jarvis (2009), Malmgren (2011).

In English: "If there were an instance of the Gettier case, it would be an instance of justified true belief without knowledge" (p. 186).

Therefore,
◇∃x∃p (JTB(x, p) & ¬K(x, p))
In English: "[S]omeone could have a justified true belief in a proposition without knowledge" (p. 184).[6]

Note that the actual sentences that are written in the papers by Perry, Thomson, Burge, Williams, etc., don't, on any view, have this syntactic or semantic form. It is also implausible that any such formalization can succeed in picking out what all or most of those who present cases *had in mind* (or meant to communicate, but just didn't make explicit). I don't know of any evidence that what Perry, Thomson, Burge, Williams, etc., had in mind really had this format. Speaking on behalf of Cappelen and Hawthorne I can say for sure that this isn't what we had in mind when presenting cases involving agreement and disagreement. Maybe the idea is that the proposed formalizations are attempts to *improve* on all the arguments presented by all those thousands of philosophers who appeal to cases in their arguments. Maybe the idea is that if all the texts we looked at in the previous chapter had contained arguments that fit e.g. Williamson's pattern, those arguments would be better than they actually are. Two points in reply to this: first, Centrality as it is discussed in this work is a descriptive thesis, not a normative one. I'm interested in how philosophers as a matter of fact present and argue about cases. So this normative claim is largely irrelevant to the concerns of this book. Second, even if one's interest is in the normative issues, the claim is immensely implausible. How can one in one fell swoop improve on all the thousands of papers that discuss cases without even looking at the actual text, the purpose of the case, the subject matter, and the kind of conclusion reached? It doesn't seem, for example, that any of the many discussions of Perry's cases have been hampered by a lack of proper formalization of Perry's appeal to cases. At no point in that discussion has it been a pressing issue to find an improved logical form for the cases

---

[6] Williamson tentatively suggests that this be used as a model for other thought experiments: "This chapter analyses the logical structure of Gettier-style thought experiments. The discussion can be generalized to many imaginary counterexamples which have been deployed against philosophical analyses and theories in ways more or less similar to Gettier's. Far more extensive investigation would be needed to warrant the claim that all philosophical thought experiments work in that way, but one must start somewhere" (p. 180).

discussed. None of those working on the *de se* have picked up on Williamson's suggested formalization of thought experiments and made progress on the issue by an improved formalization of the various cases. Surely, evidence that this would be an improvement of the arguments should come from the literature that actually discusses these issues. In general, I think we should be skeptical of the idea that a methodologist can manage to improve every philosophical argument that contains a reference to a case without detailed study of those arguments and the great variety of topics they are about.

Objection: Rock, as you have articulated it, is vague and your dismissal of this feature has played on that vagueness. A more precise articulation of Rock would have made dismissing it more difficult.

Reply: I agree that the articulation of Rock is imprecise and that it would be an advantage to have an improved set of criteria and diagnostics. It is important here to recall the reasons why I went with the Rough Guide to Rock Detection in Chapter 7 (see 7.3.2):

Rough Guide to Rock Detection: If in a context C, evidence is given for *p* and that evidence plays a significant argumentative role in C, that is evidence that *p* is not Rock relative to C. The existence of a context C' in which you can get away with claiming *p* without providing argument or other evidence is irrelevant to *p*'s status in C, unless there is some clear evidence in C that what goes on in C' matters for *p*'s status in C.

Chapter 7 discussed alternative articulations of Rock and concluded that they were either useless as a practical guide (they didn't tell us what to look for in a text) or took us too far away from what those who endorse Centrality as a matter of fact hold.

Objection: As you point out in Part I, some philosophers who describe their assumption as 'intuitive', simply mean that they are pre-theoretic or propose to place them in the common ground. Doesn't that suffice to establish Centrality? Isn't this a 'thin' version of Centrality that should be acceptable despite the lack of intuition features?

Reply: Some early readers of this material were pulled towards this kind of reply and I include it here simply to remind the reader that this issue was discussed in Chapter 4, esp. 4.6.

Objection: In not a single one of the cases discussed have you conclusively proved that on no Centrality-friendly interpretation of 'There is a reliance on intuition' can that sentence be used to describe some element of the case.

Reply: True. There is no proof here, but I don't think that should give comfort to those who believe in Centrality. The various amorphous and imprecise characterizations given of the intuitive by Centrality proponents make it difficult to conclusively prove that there is an absence of the intuitive in any particular case. But rather than consider this an advantage for Centrality, it should be seen as a serious indictment of the view. If it turns out that the claims Centrality proponents make about philosophical practice are so vague that it is impossible to determine whether they are accurate descriptions of particular instantiations of the practice, that's a problem for Centrality's proponents, not for its opponents.

9.3 Williamson on Evidence Neutrality, psychologizing the evidence, and analyticity

I end this chapter with some remarks on two central themes in Timothy Williamson's work, *The Philosophy of Philosophy*. That work inspired many components of this book, but here I want to highlight some important differences in emphasis and maybe in substantive commitments.

9.3.1 Comparison to Williamson's arguments against analyticity

The question of whether there are any analytically justified truths is central to Williamson's arguments in *The Philosophy of Philosophy*. Three of the chapters in the book address this issue. He goes to great length to show that there are no such propositions. I end this chapter by outlining some of the connections between Williamson's argumentative strategy and the strategy pursued in this work. First, note that before Williamson enters into his discussion of whether there are any conceptually justified truths he first points out that many philosophical truths are not conceptually or a priori justified on *any* construal of such notions. Some examples (from Williamson 2007, pp. 49–50):

E1: In arguing against subjective idealism, a defender of common sense metaphysics says that there was a solar system millions of years before there was sentient life.

E2: A defender of common sense epistemology says that he knows that he has hands; it is no conceptual truth that he knows that he has hands, for it is consistent with all conceptual truths that he lost them in a nasty accident.

E3: Some philosophers of time argue that not only the present exists by appeal to Special Relativity.

E4: Philosophers of mind and language dispute whether there is a language of thought; whatever the answer, it is no conceptual truth.

E5: Naturalists and anti-naturalists dispute whether there is only what there is in space and time; again, the answer is unlikely to be a conceptual truth.

E6: Moral and political philosophers and philosophers of art appeal to empirically discovered human cognitive limitations.

Williamson takes it to be indisputable that E1–E6 are not analytic and that the debates about these claims are not debates about how to analyze concepts. This is, he assumes, so obvious that he doesn't even need to argue for it. He is clearly right. Here is a thought that underlies the approach in this work: *E1–E6 are representative of philosophical claims/arguments/debates. As a consequence, we don't need to rule out that there are any analytic truths in order to show that it is false that philosophy is based on a priori conceptual insights.* That, however, is not how Williamson continues. He immediately goes on to consider the following option (I will call it 'Core'):

Core: "it may be thought that philosophy has a central core of truths which are all conceptual, perhaps with the rest of philosophy counting as such through its relation to the central core. Let us charitably read this restriction into the appeal to analyticity or conceptual truth in the epistemology of philosophy" (p. 50).

It is in response to Core that Williamson argues that *no* claims are justified by relying solely on conceptual competence. He argues that not even claims like 'All vixens are female foxes' belong in that category. This strategy, while I think it is ultimately successful, has some problematic effects:

- First, Williamson's strategy leaves open the possibility that even though there are no analytically justified truths, philosophers *seek* such truths (and so many of those who write on Centrality are right about what philosophers have as their goal). Maybe, if Williamson is right, what he has shown is that philosophy as it is actually practiced is based on the false tacit assumption that there are analytically justified claims and that they are relevant to philosophy in much the way described in Core.
- Second, no matter how sophisticated the arguments against analyticity are, many will retain the sense that there is something special

about sentences like 'All vixen are female foxes'—they have a kind of connection to conceptual competence and a lack of connection to empirical evidence that is striking, even though it may be difficult to make precise.[7] And so, if you think philosophers at least aspire to something that makes Core true, Williamson's arguments might trigger more attempts to defend a notion of the priori and its connection to conceptual competence. If so, Williamson's strategy might in effect promote the idea that we philosophers for the most part engage in activities that are at least *candidates* for something like conceptual analysis. It gives the impression that the issue of whether there are conceptual truths is crucial to an understanding of philosophical method.

To avoid these effects, I suggest that Williamson's strategy should be combined with the kind of empirical attack on Centrality pursued in this work. Suppose that we grant for the sake of argument that there are conceptual truths and a priori truths and that e.g. 'All vixens are female foxes' is a paradigm of those. Suppose we don't fuss, for now, about how to make those ideas precise. We can then ask: Does data about the practice make it even *prima facie* plausible that philosophy contains a core of claims that might belong in the same category as 'All vixens are female foxes'? I take the evidence from the case studies to support an unambiguously negative conclusion: *There is not even a* prima facie *case to be made for the existence of a conceptual a priori core. Claims like Williamson's E1-E6 are at the center of philosophy (and the Core thesis is false).* So: even if there are conceptual a priori truths, exemplified by 'All vixens are female foxes', those are irrelevant to philosophical practice. (This and related topics are pursued further in the next chapter.)

9.3.2 Evidence Neutrality and philosophers' alleged tendency to psychologize evidence

Timothy Williamson spends a chapter of *The Philosophy of Philosophy* arguing against what he describes as a 'pressure', 'temptation' and 'tendency' to psychologize evidence in philosophy. As a result of these temptations and pressures, Williamson says, many of us "think that, in philosophy, ultimately

---

[7] There is even some evidence that Williamson thinks this—cf. his notion of 'armchair' knowledge I discussed in Section 6.2.5.

our evidence consists only of intuitions" (p. 235). On one reading, this is the suggestion that the belief in Centrality is generated by the pressure to psychologize evidence. Williamson goes on to argue that we should reject this pressure. I agree with Williamson that we should reject the pressure and resist the temptation, but I find hardly any evidence that anyone doing first-order philosophy has given into it. So I want to, briefly, consider whether Williamson is right that analytic philosophers, generically, have been 'pressured' into psychologizing evidence. Here is how Williamson sees the temptation being generated. First, philosophers are, Williamson says, tacitly committed to what he calls "Evidence Neutrality":

> As far as possible, we want evidence to play the role of a neutral arbiter between rival theories. Although accidental mistakes and confusions are inevitable, we might hope that whether a proposition constitutes evidence is *in principle* uncontentiously decidable. Call that idea *Evidence Neutrality*. Thus in a debate over a hypothesis *h*, proponents and opponents of *h* should be able to agree whether some proposition *p* constitutes evidence without first having to settle their differences over *h* itself. Moreover, that agreement should not be erroneous: here as elsewhere, 'decidable' means correctly decidable. Barring accidents, if they agree that *p* constitutes evidence, it does; if they agree that *p* does not constitute evidence, it does not. (p. 210)

Evidence Neutrality combined with the threat of skepticism pushes us to psychologize evidence. Using the Gettier propositions as an illustration, Williamson imagines us engaging in debate with someone who takes the Gettier judgment as no more than a cultural prejudice. In such a debate, Williamson predicts, we will be pressured (or tempted) as follows:

> In order to argue for the conclusion that knowledge is not equivalent to justified true belief, I must go back a step to less contentious premises. What can they be? My opponent allows that I *believe* the Gettier proposition, and may even admit to feeling an inclination to believe it too, while overriding it on theoretical grounds (I am not merely idiosyncratic). Thus Evidence Neutrality tempts one to retreat into identifying evidence with uncontentious propositions about psychological states, that I believe the Gettier proposition and that both of us are inclined to believe it. (p. 211)

In this way, "The dialectical nature of philosophical inquiry exerts general pressure to psychologize evidence, and so distance it from the non-psychological subject matter of the inquiry" (p. 224). As a result, the alleged commitment to Evidence Neutrality narrows our evidence base:

One result is the uneasy conception many contemporary analytic philosophers have of their own methodology. They think that, in philosophy, ultimately our evidence consists only of intuitions (to use their term for the sake of argument). Under pressure, they take that to mean not that our evidence consists of the mainly non-psychological putative facts which are the contents of those intuitions, but that it consists of the psychological facts to the effect that we have intuitions with those contents, true or false. On such a view, our evidence in philosophy amounts only to psychological facts about ourselves. (p. 235)

Williamson goes on to argue that this is a bad development. We shouldn't psychologize evidence, Williamson claims: "Our evidence in philosophy consists of facts, most of them non-psychological, to which we have appropriate epistemic access" (p. 241).

All I want to note here is that the case studies in the previous chapter provide no evidence that the dialectical nature of philosophical inquiry tempts us to retreat to the (presumed) safety of psychological claims. We have found no evidence that judgments about cases rely on appeals to the writers' psychological states. Burge make claims about beliefs and belief reports (not about his beliefs about beliefs and belief reports), and Perry talks about how to explain his change in behavior (not how to explain his beliefs about his change in behavior.) This is the pattern found in all the cases studied in the previous chapter. Williamson might think the extensive use of 'intuition' and cognate terms in philosophical texts provides evidence of philosophers giving into the pressures to psychologize evidence since he takes such expressions to denote beliefs or inclinations to believe. However, that interpretation of such expressions should be rejected.[8] When such usage is seen for what it is, the description of analytic philosophers giving into pressure and temptation to psychologize is revealed as yet another example of methodological prejudice about real philosophical practice. We typically do exactly what Williamson says we *should* do.[9]

---

[8] I argue for this at length in the Appendix to Chapter 4.

[9] I should add that these passages from Williamson could maybe more charitably be interpreted to say only that metaphilosophers are giving into the relevant pressure and temptation—not that typical first-order philosophers do. (Thanks to Daniele Sgaravatti for pointing this out.)

10

Conceptual Analysis and Intuitions

In this chapter I address someone who grants me that all the bold claims on behalf of the intuitive made by Centrality proponents in Chapter 1 have been shown to be false. A question then arises: Can a more limited role be found for intuition in philosophy? One suggestion often made is that the intuitive shows up *whenever philosophers engage in conceptual analysis*. We find, for example, Goldman and Pust in more cautious moments saying:

> [W]e restrict our present inquiry to the role of intuitions in philosophical "analysis." This is not to suggest that philosophical analysis exhausts the mission of philosophy, nor that it comprises the most important part of philosophy. (1998, p. 179)

We are not told what falls under the category of what they call "philosophical 'analysis'" (and we're not told why 'analysis' is scare quoted), but the rest of the paper supports an interpretation along the lines of Centrality$_{(CA)}$:

> **Centrality$_{(CA)}$**: Philosophers who engage in conceptual analysis rely on intuitions as evidence (or as a source of evidence).

10.1 Hyperbole about intuitions leads to hyperbole about conceptual analysis

Hyperbole about the significance of intuitions in philosophy, e.g. Centrality, is typically accompanied by hyperbole about the significance of conceptual analysis in philosophy. Those who think philosophers appeal to intuitions when they make judgments about cases also tend to see philosophers as engaged in conceptual analysis when they appeal to cases and *vice versa*. The case studies show that both views are mistaken. Recognition of the marginal (or non-existent) role of intuitions in philosophical practice goes hand in hand with recognition of the marginal (or non-existent) role of anything reasonably labeled 'conceptual analysis' in philosophy. In our case studies we found no evidence of philosophers attempting to restrict their evidence to what was available only through 'analysis'. Just as philosophers in moments of confused meta-reflection will often describe what they do as relying on intuitions, they will often mistakenly describe what they do as 'analysis', but this turns out to be yet another instance of the familiar phenomenon of someone engaging in an activity he or she is not particularly good at giving a description of.

I said in Chapter 1 that this book is not about how philosophy *could* or *ought to* be done. The goal has been to investigate Centrality as a descriptive claim about contemporary philosophy. This chapter will diverge from that focus and briefly consider this claim: suppose someone agrees that conceptual analysis plays a marginal role in contemporary philosophy, but insists *that if someone were to engage in that activity, then she would have to rely on intuitions*. Anyone who advocates this kind of restricted version of Centrality faces three serious challenges:

1. **First Challenge**: Show that conceptual analysis (and cognate notions such as conceptual possibility and conceptual necessity) are coherent notions.
2. **Second Challenge**: Show that if conceptual analysis is a coherent notion and there are some conceptual truths, those truths have philosophical significance.
3. **Third Challenge**: Show that if there are conceptual truths that have philosophical significance, intuitions play an evidential role in the study of concepts.

The goal of this chapter is limited to making some largely sociological observations about the status of Centrality$_{(CA)}$. Someone endorsing it will have to defend a range of views few contemporary philosophers would be willing to endorse. Centrality so construed is a claim that will appeal to only a *very* small subset of philosophers—it's on par with, say, Davidson's paratactic theory of quotation or James' pragmatism about truth. Those are controversial claims, a few people still defend something like them and they certainly have some historical interest, but they in no way constitute common ground among contemporary philosophers. Centrality is interesting, in part, because of its peculiar status as a kind of neutral common core of how we conceive of philosophy. It's a view endorsed by philosophers who otherwise differ along more or less *all* theoretical dimensions (recall Weinberg saying, "It can seem that analytic philosophy without intuitions just wouldn't be *analytic* philosophy" (2007, p. 318)). The goal of this chapter is to point out that something like Centrality$_{(CA)}$ cannot have *that* kind of status. It is a highly controversial claim based on at best dubious assumptions that will appeal to a very small minority of philosophers who hold views that are marginal in the profession. In sum, it's a sectarian thesis. I will start with the third of the challenges mentioned above and then add some all too brief reminders about the first and second.

10.1.1 Suppose for the sake of argument that there are conceptual truths and that they have philosophical significance. Why think intuitions are involved in studying them?

Conceptual analysis is the presumed home of aprioristic philosophy, if it has a home. But no one can seriously engage in any activity labeled 'conceptual analysis' without a theory of what concepts are, and the philosophical debate about that topic is one of the least aprioristic fields of philosophy. It's a field where practically all serious contemporary participants engage with the results from empirical studies of concept possession, concept acquisition and related topics. In particular, the question of whether things properly labeled 'intuitions' play an important role in the study of concepts is an empirical question. Proponents of Centrality$_{(CA)}$ assume some version of a Bridge Principle:

> **Bridge Principles**: Those who engage in conceptual analysis *should* rely on intuitions in so doing./ Intuitions play a *significant* role in conceptual analysis./ Intuitions play an *essential evidential* role in conceptual analysis./ Appeal to intuitions is an *efficient* method for analyzing concepts./ Appeal to intuitions is a *reliable* method for analyzing concepts.

To defend a Bridge Principle, a proponent of Centrality$_{(CA)}$ will need to tell us what she takes concepts to be, what she takes 'intuition' to denote, and what she thinks concepts are. I start with the latter question. There are a number of options here, none of which are particularly attractive for proponents of Centrality$_{(CA)}$. It will go beyond the scope of this work to go through all the options. I will instead use the view proposed by

Goldman and Pust (1998) and some of the powerful objections from Kornblith to that view, as my illustration of how difficult it is to defend the relevant kind of Bridge Principles.

10.1.2 Kornblith's challenge to the Bridge Principles[1]

Alvin Goldman, and Goldman and Pust defend the standard justificatory procedure (more or less as described by Bealer, which I discussed in Chapter 6, esp. 6.1.2). They think philosophers should study concepts, and they should do so by appeal to, among other things, intuitions. They are explicit about wanting to be naturalists about the nature of concepts: they take concepts to be psychological states with significant causal-explanatory roles. Kornblith in a paper on Goldman's work asks the following excellent question:

> If someone believes, as Goldman does, that concepts are psychologically real, and also that there is a well established tradition in experimental psychology which studies them, then what room is left for the armchair methods of philosophers, methods designed to illuminate the very same target? (2007, p. 30)

Goldman (2007) and Goldman and Pust (1998) have a reply to this, and the inadequacy of that reply illustrates just how hard Kornblith's challenge is to meet. Goldman and Pust tell us that "there **might well** be an appropriate counterfactual dependence between e's satisfaction or nonsatisfaction of the concept expressed through 'F' and what the intuition 'says' about e" (1998, p. 188, my emphasis). Their argument for this goes as follows:

> The concept associated with a predicate F will have many dispositions, but among them are dispositions to give rise to intuitive classificational judgments such as 'example e is (is not) an instance of F.' Thus, it is not only **possible, but almost a matter of *definition*,** that if the concept possessor were fully informed about the relevant features of e, then if e satisfied the concept he expresses through 'F,' his intuitive response to the question of whether e satisfies this concept would be affirmative; and if e did not satisfy the concept he expresses through 'F', then his intuitive response to the question of whether e satisfies this concept would be negative. In other words, a concept tends to be manifested by intuitions that reflect or express its content. (p. 188, my emphases)

---

[1] The central argument in this section is based on Kornblith's (2007) response to Goldman (2007) and Goldman and Pust (1998).

I'll focus on the "almost a matter of definition" component of their claim. The claim that it is "almost a matter of definition" is hard to evaluate since Goldman and Pust don't tell us what they mean by "fully informed about the relevant features of e." In particular, we are not told whether the F-ness of e is one of those relevant features. Also, we are not told whether this is supposed to apply also to natural-kind terms like 'elm' and 'water' or to socially constructed objects like 'contract', or more generally how the claim is restricted. I will put those concerns aside, and raise three issues that will be relevant no matter how the view is further developed and clarified. First note that what dispositions a particular psychological state gives rise to depend on just what *kind* of state it is. Just calling it a concept doesn't tell us much about the nature of this state. Psychologists disagree widely about just what concepts are—one thing they don't disagree about is the rejection of the view that concepts are represented as neat little bundles of necessary and sufficient conditions inside the speakers' heads. The discovery of typicality effects has, as Kornblith points out in this context, led to a universal rejection of this view of concepts.[2] Suppose, as an improved toy theory, that concepts are represented via a set of exemplars and some dimensions of similarity along which new candidates are evaluated. Now ask: is it a matter of *definition* that what philosophers call 'intuition' will provide true applications of the concepts to arbitrary objects (when the subject is 'fully informed')?[3] It might be true, but it is surely not a matter of *definition*. So Kornblith's challenge hasn't been met—talk of definitions provides no reason to think that it can be met. This holds no matter what one takes as one favorite theory of concepts—the theory theory, atomism, or the prototype theory—and whether one is an empiricist or a nativist.

Second, the claim that it is an almost-definitional truth that something called 'intuitions' will correctly determine whether an arbitrary object is in the extension of a concept when the subject is 'fully informed about the

---

[2] As Kornblith points out, "The manner in which concepts are represented will do more than dictate the class of individuals which are members of the kind; it will also have implications for the manner and speed at which information about the category is processed. There are a number of different views available today about the way in which concepts are represented. But the importance of typicality effects, and a number of other results, have led to the demise of the Classical View. As Gregory Murphy notes in his recent book, 'To a considerable degree, it has simply ceased to be a serious contender in the psychology of concepts' (Murphy 2002: 38)".

[3] Of course, if F-ness is included in the relevant features, this is arguably true, but then the claim about the role of intuitions is irrelevant to any philosophical applications.

relevant features' is even more puzzling when we take into consideration what Goldman and Pust take 'intuition' to mean. Here is what they say:

> [W]e assume, at a minimum, that intuitions are some sort of spontaneous mental judgments. Each intuition, then, is a judgment "that p" for some suitable class of propositions p. (p. 179)

How can it be a definitional truth that *spontaneous* judgments as opposed to *careful and reflective* judgments are particularly effective for those determining whether an object is in the extension of a concept? Surely, that must be an empirical issue, not something to be settled by definition.

Finally, note that Goldman and Pust give us a necessary condition, not a sufficient condition, for being an intuitive judgment. Without being given a sufficient condition, it is hard to even evaluate the claim that the connection is definitional. Presumably lots of judgments that are spontaneous are not intuitive, and how can they know, before giving the sufficient conditions, that those that qualify as intuitive are the ones that 'manifest' or 'express' the content of the concept? Indeed, it is hard to see how anything can be definitional in this area when all we have to go on is a necessary condition.

These considerations are meant merely to illustrate how challenging it will be to establish one of the Bridge Principles. Appeal to what is definitionally true will not help. What is needed will vary from case to case, depending on what the lover of conceptual analysis takes concepts to be. In the case of Goldman and Pust, they will have to tell us in detail what kind of psychological state they take concepts to be, what they mean by 'fully informed about the relevant features of e', what they mean by 'intuition' and then show that what falls under the extension of the latter can play the role described by the Bridge Principles.

10.2 Are there any conceptual truths, and, if so, are they philosophically significant?

An influential tradition in philosophy of the last century starts with Quine and continues up to the present with Timothy Williamson. It forcefully argues that there is no philosophically interesting phenomenon plausibly labeled as a conceptual truth or analyticity.[4] For example,

---

[4] There is a plethora of terminological options when discussing these issues. One important distinction, going back to Boghossian (1996), can be drawn between metaphysical

Williamson (2007, Chapter 4) considers a range of variations on the idea that in order to possess a concept C (or understand a word W) an agent has to assent to certain propositions involving C or be justified in believing certain propositions involving C (or assent to certain sentences containing W or be justified in assenting to certain sentences containing W).[5] He presents powerful arguments against such views. This book will assume familiarity with these moves on behalf of the reader and they will not be considered in detail here. Suffice it to say that I am one of the many who find those objections very convincing and I have nothing original to add to them. Those who intend to seriously defend the activity of conceptual analysis owe the philosophical community a convincing reply to Williamson. If Williamson is right, the activity they advocate that people engage in is impossible to engage in. The search for conceptual justification is like the search for unicorns. The initial responses on behalf of conceptual analysis are not encouraging. Consider for example Frank Jackson's (2009) reply to Williamson. The problem with the reply is that it underestimates and misconstrues the seriousness of Williamson's challenge. Jackson first describes what he calls "the conventional wisdom" about thought experiments: "their role is to make trouble for one or another proffered conceptual analysis" (p. 101). Jackson goes on to describe Williamson's objection as follows: "Williamson isn't telling us that we cannot learn anything about what's conceptually possible. The idea rather is that the important putative messages from these kinds of thought experiments concern what's metaphysically possible" (p. 101). Jackson goes on to say that the disagreement between them is simply a matter of dividing thought experiments into those that tell us something about conceptual possibility and those that tell us about metaphysical possibility. He says,

---

analyticity and epistemic analyticity. Williamson characterizes metaphysically analytic sentences as those that are "true simply in virtue of their meaning", and likewise metaphysically analytic thoughts as those that are true "simply in virtue of their constituent concepts" (2007, p. 52). He characterizes epistemic analyticity as "a privileged status in respect of knowledge or justification which a sentence or thought has in virtue of the conditions for understanding its constituent words or possessing its constituent concepts" (p. 52). In the discussion of Centrality and intuitions more generally, the more fine-grained distinctions are hardly ever made and so I won't rely on them here.

[5] See also Boghossian (1996, 2003, 2011) and Williamson (2003, 2011).

I agree with Williamson that the utility of thought experiments is not confined to the theory of concepts.... But that doesn't mean that Gettier and Block's thought experiments are not primarily concerned with elucidating concepts. The conventional wisdom is a thesis about one class of thought experiments, the class of which Gettier and Block's are prime examples. It isn't a thesis about thought experiments across the board. (p. 101)

This is unhelpful as a reply on behalf of those advocating conceptual analysis since it fundamentally misconstrues and underestimates the force of Williamson's arguments. It fails to confront the real challenge from Williamson: *there is no such thing as conceptual possibility or conceptual necessity, and it is impossible to engage in what Jackson calls 'conceptual analysis'*.[6]

Jackson's response to Williamson contrasts with that of Paul Boghossian and this contrast will help introduce the second challenge mentioned at the beginning of this chapter: it is a distinct possibility that even if there are a few conceptual truths, none (or very few) of them have any relevance to philosophy. Think of this challenge as having at least three elements: Expansion, Evidence of Success, and Motivation. I discuss these in turn.

10.2.1 Expansion

In influential work, Paul Boghossian has defended an epistemology for logic based on the idea that a necessary condition on understanding the logical constants is that one be willing to assent to certain inference patterns. According to this view an understanding of 'if' require willingness to assent to Modus Ponens and an understanding of 'and' requires willingness to go from 'P and Q' to 'P'. Boghossian's work is one of the most sophisticated and most cited recent defenses of analyticity and it is one of the primary targets of Williamson's arguments in *The Philosophy of Philosophy*. Boghossian's reply to Williamson helps illuminate why the second challenge is pressing. In earlier work, Boghossian's primary example has been a willingness to endorse Modus Ponens as a condition on

---

[6] This is the point Williamson makes in reply to Jackson: "the longest chapter in the book (2007: pp. 73–133) is an attack on exactly the sort of epistemological conception of analyticity on which Jackson's appeals to conceptual modalities rely: the idea of matters on which we must agree in order to share a meaning or concept. Although he provides no explanation of the phrases 'conceptually possible' and 'conceptually necessary', his use of them makes clear that he has something of the sort in mind. In effect, my book argues that there is no such thing as conceptual necessity" (2009b, p. 128).

understanding 'if'. In the reply to Williamson, he does not defend those earlier claims about 'if', but instead focuses on a defense of (A):

A: "Necessarily, whoever understands 'and' is prepared to infer from any sentence of the form 'A and B' to 'A'" (2011, p. 492).

This isn't the place to consider Boghossian's reply and Williamson's reply to the reply (both 2011) in detail. I simply want to point out that it is highly contentious that even (A) can be defended against Williamson's objections (and I suggest the reader study the Boghossian-Williamson exchange to make up his or her mind on the matter). Now, suppose for the sake of argument that Boghossian succeeds in his defense of (A). Then the next, even harder challenge, is to do the same for Modus Ponens and 'if'. It will be harder yet to do it for *all* the logical constants. What is interesting here is that Boghossian has not made grandiose claims about the importance of analytic truths to philosophy more generally—he has not claimed that such truths will help us understand *truth, freedom, knowledge, reference, causation, consciousness, forgiveness, personhood*, etc. There is a striking contrast here: on the one hand, philosophical methodologists who don't defend in detail their notion of analyticity, tend to make very grand and sweeping claims about the philosophical value of such truths. On the other hand, those who engage in detailed defense of the idea that there can be analytic truths don't make such sweeping claims—they typically restrict their claims to boring statements like (A). So, even if Boghossian or another proponent of analyticity can defend the status of (A) as analytic in some interesting sense, it is a distinct possibility that hardly any philosophically interesting claims belong in this category.[7] Think of this as the Expansion Challenge:

Expansion Challenge: Even if we grant, for the sake of argument, that (A) is a conceptual truth, someone who wants to justify the appeal to conceptual analysis in philosophy needs to expand from the paradigmatic cases to a range of *interesting and substantive philosophical claims*.

---

[7] I don't mean to deny that (A) could be of interest to philosophical logic, but I do assume that if *the only* philosophically interesting results conceptual analysis yields is (A), it's not particularly important.

Boghossian's own argument indicates that this challenge might be impossible to meet. The argument he calls "the argument from above" (2011, p. 495) is one of the two main arguments in favor of his view. According to this argument,

> [I]t's hard to see what else could constitute meaning conjunction by 'and' except being prepared to use it according to some rules and not others (most plausibly, the standard introduction and elimination rules for 'and'). Accounts that might be thought to have a chance of success with other words—information-theoretic accounts, for example, or explicit definitions, or teleological accounts—don't seem to have any purchase in the case of the logical constants. (2011, p. 490)

So Boghossian thinks the kind of argument he offers applies to a very restricted range of terms and at no point in his work has he even tried to extend his view to concepts like *truth, freedom, knowledge, reference, causation, consciousness, forgiveness, personhood,* etc.

10.2.2 A Posteriori Evidence of Success and motivations

An adequate attempt to meet the Expansion Challenge should provide *evidence from philosophical practice* that truths that belong with (A) have led to philosophical progress in some way (even loosely defined). Call this requirement, 'A Posteriori Evidence of Success':

> **A Posteriori Evidence of Success**: Those who advocate that philosophers engage in conceptual analysis should provide some empirical evidence that this activity pays off for philosophers. It's an empirical question what kinds of methods work well in philosophy—is there any evidence that conceptual analysis delivers the goods?

The case studies in the previous chapter provide evidence against this: a very wide range of philosophical topics and traditions was surveyed and in none of those paradigmatic cases were conceptual truths appealed to, sought, or in any way considered significant. All those debates moved along fine without any attempt to engage in analysis, so why think we need to do it in other areas?

In addition to A Posteriori Evidence of Success, we should expect advocates of conceptual analysis to tell us *why* they think such truths are worth pursuing. There are many kinds of truths that we *could* seek, but have no reason to seek. Examples of truths that it would, without further justification, be pointless for philosophers to seek are truths that are derived from results in algebraic topology and truths that are discovered on a Thursday. If some philosophers said she wanted to pursue such truths, we would be puzzled. For some reason we are less puzzled when someone tells us they seek conceptual truths. I think we should be puzzled. Here are some of the justifications that are sometimes given, all of them entirely unsatisfactory:

Motivation 1: Conceptual truths are worth seeking because they are necessary truths.

Comment: Someone advocating this view owes us an argument for why necessary truths should be particularly valuable to philosophers. It is easy to see why actual truths are important: they tell us what the world we live in and engage with is like. The necessary truths are a small subset of the actual truths and the claim that those are particularly interesting requires an argument. Just pointing out that conceptual truths are necessary is not to provide a motivation for taking an interest in them. It just makes it even more puzzling: why should we think necessary truths are more interesting than contingent truths or truths that hold in worlds that are similar (along certain relevant dimensions) to ours?[8] Suppose, for example, we find out that Burge's version of social externalism about content is true about us, but that there are remote possibilities in which externalism is false (maybe even about creatures somewhat similar to us). Would that make the thesis of social externalism less significant? I think not.

Motivation 2: Conceptual truths are worth seeking because they are a priori.

Comment: As we have seen, good philosophers draw freely on empirical results from various sciences, they are interested in facts about human cognition, natural language, physics, biology, economics; some of us participate extensively in interdisciplinary work. It would be bizarre in the extreme to insist that truths with the label 'a priori' have some kind of intrinsic value. To seek such truths is as unmotivated as searching for truths that are discovered on a Thursday.

---

[8] Of course, not all necessary truths are conceptual, so even if you had decided that necessary truths are particularly titillating to you, we are owed an argument for why the conceptually necessary truths are particularly important.

Motivation 3: Conceptual truths provide the foundation for philosophy; without such truths, philosophy floats without a solid starting point.

Comment: There are deep and puzzling questions about the foundations of human knowledge, but these questions no more push philosophers to do conceptual analysis than it pushes psychologists or linguists or economists or anyone else to do it.

Motivation 4: This is an annoying question. I'm interested in concepts, just as some people are interested in medieval cartography. It's no worse a topic than a lot of other topics people work on.

Comment: This is of course fine, but if someone really is interested in conceptual truths for their own sake—not because they are particularly important to philosophy or have some kind of special epistemic status—then she should be engaged deeply in collaborative work with empirical scientists working on concept possession, concept acquisition and a range of related topics.

This isn't meant to exhaust the possible motivations a person might have for looking for conceptual truths, but simply to make the reader aware of how apparently arbitrary it is to treat the label 'conceptual truth' as in some sense laudatory. We need an argument that such truths are worth seeking for philosophers and I know of no good such argument.

No doubt, some proponents of Centrality$_{(CA)}$ will think it a glaring omission to not talk about the post-Gettier research on how to analyze the concept of knowledge. Maybe some will suggest that this is exactly what I've been asking for: a posteriori evidence of a successful research project in conceptual analysis. This is a high-risk strategy since there is no consensus among those most deeply immersed in that debate that any progress whatsoever has been made. Timothy Williamson, for example, cites the "failure" of the post-Gettier research program attempts to analyze the concept of knowledge as one of the central motivations for his knowledge-first program in epistemology (2005, p. 434). He construes the post-Gettier program as motivated by the idea that since knowledge requires both truth and belief, there has to be a further condition we can add to these two such that the three conditions combined will be necessary and sufficient for knowledge. However, Williamson points out:

[I]t is a fallacy to assume that necessary conditions can always be 'subtracted' to leave a further necessary condition that, added to them, gives a noncircular necessary and sufficient condition for what one first thought of. Being coloured is a necessary condition for being red, but if one asks what must be added to being coloured to give being red, one comes up only with answers stated in terms of being red: being red itself, or being red if coloured. There was no good prior reason to expect non-circular necessary and sufficient conditions for knowledge in terms of truth, belief and other factors. Moreover, the failure of the extensive post-Gettier research programme over several decades to come up with such conditions provides posterior inductive reason to think that there are none. (2005, p. 434)

A proponent of the post-Gettier programme could point out that at least it succeeded in showing that the concept of knowledge *cannot* be analyzed into more basic components. It paved the way for the knowledge-first movement. That, however, is hardly advertisement for the project of engaging in conceptual analysis in philosophy. Instead, we should see the post-Gettier literature as a cautionary tale—alerting us to the extraordinary potential for wasted intellectual energy when philosophers go down that road.

10.3 Conclusion: Centrality as a *sectarian* thesis

The remarks in this chapter are meant largely to summarize and remind the reader of the challenges facing the proponent of Centrality$_{(CA)}$. The main points are these:

- The case studies showed no evidence of conceptual analysis being an activity philosophers actively try to engage in. Just as philosophers have false beliefs about the role of intuitions in philosophy they have false beliefs about the role of conceptual analysis in philosophy.
- It is an open question whether it is an activity that it is possible to engage in. Proponents of the activity find it extremely challenging to defend even the claim that 'If p and if p then q are true, then q is true' is a conceptual/analytic truth.
- Even if someone can defend the view that 'If p and if p then q are true, then q is true' is some kind of conceptual/analytic truth, it is unlikely that this kind of defense can be extended more broadly to philosophically interesting claims (and the kind of arguments used by e.g. Boghossian positively counts against the possibility of Expansion).

- Finally, the most important point in the context of this book is this: Suppose you have convinced yourself that conceptual analysis is possible and that it is relevant to the particular philosophical topic you happen to be interested in. It is still an enormous leap to the conclusion that you will have to rely on something properly labeled 'intuition' in order to engage in that activity.

Centrality$_{(CA)}$ is a view of philosophy that will be endorsed only by someone who holds some very peculiar minority views about what concepts are, how to study them and the value of studying them. It goes beyond the scope of this book to evaluate fully all the possible views one might hold of concepts, their structure, their relation to philosophy and the ways in which they can be studied. But one thing can be established with certainty: the only way to defend Centrality$_{(CA)}$ is to base it on some extremely controversial views—views that are rejected by the large majority of philosophers. So construed, Centrality might still have some sectarian value, but it has lost its status as a common core of our self-conception as analytic philosophers.[9]

---

[9] I don't mean here to rule out that philosophers of different stripes can end up justifying Centrality in different ways—each full-scale justification of Centrality might end up depending on controversial assumptions. That's to be expected. What I think would detract from the interest of Centrality is if it can *only* be endorsed in combination with a range of views V that most of us don't endorse. We then have a choice, give up Centrality or buy into V in order to preserve Centrality.

11

A Big Mistake:
Experimental Philosophy

11.1 Experimental philosophy: Positive and negative

Experimental philosophers advocate the use of questionnaires to check on non-philosophers' intuitions about philosophical cases/thought experiments.[1] A central goal of experimental philosophy is to criticize the philosophical practice of appealing to intuitions about cases. The entire project of experimental philosophy only gets off the ground by assuming Centrality. To see how deeply engrained Centrality is in experimental philosophy consider the following passage in which Swain *et al.* present the aim and motivation for their research project:

> According to standard practice, a philosophical claim is *prima facie* good to the extent that it accords with our intuitions, *prima facie* bad to the extent that it does not. Given that intuitions about thought-experiments are standardly taken as reasons to accept or reject philosophical theories, then we should be interested in finding out what the relevant intuitions are. (2008, p. 140)

Practically any experimental philosophy paper will make the reliance on Centrality explicit, and I'll here restrict myself to one more illustration:

> The practice of treating intuitions as evidence has a long history in philosophy, arguably going as far back as Socrates. Philosophers engaged in this practice consult intuitions generated in response to hypothetical cases as evidence for the truth or falsity of a wide variety of philosophical claims. In contemporary philosophy,

---

[1] Early proponents of experimental philosophy include Naess (1938) and Stich (1988).

hypothetical case intuitions are appealed to in order to support, or contest, philosophical claims about the nature of knowledge, justification, meaning, moral responsibility, and morally right action—to name just a few. In fact, the practice of treating hypothetical case intuitions as evidence is so widespread in philosophy that at least one philosopher has called it "our standard justificatory procedure." (Weinberg, Alexander and Gonnerman ms., p. 1)

The goal of this chapter is to argue that experimental philosophy is a fundamentally flawed research project, but nonetheless based on a correct insight:

The Conditional Insight of Experimental Philosophy: *If Centrality is true, we should find out whether the intuitions philosophers appeal to are representative and reliable.*

Experimental philosophers endorse the antecedent of this conditional, then off they go checking. The results are depressing, at least from the point of view of the so-called standard justificatory procedure:

A growing body of empirical literature challenges philosophers' reliance on intuitions as evidence based on the fact that intuitions vary according to factors such as cultural and educational background, and socio-economic status. Our research extends this challenge. (Swain *et al.* 2008, pp. 138–9)

These results, according to Swain *et al.,* are not encouraging for us philosophers:

Experimental philosophers have begun conducting empirical research to find out what intuitions are generated in response to certain cases. But rather than supporting and explaining the practice of appealing to intuitions as evidence, the results of this research challenge the legitimacy of appealing to intuitions. Weinberg, Nichols, and Stich revealed that epistemological intuitions vary according to factors such as cultural and educational background; Machery *et al.* document a similar cultural variation in semantic intuitions; and Nichols and Knobe have discovered that the affective content of a thought-experiment can influence whether subjects have compatabilist or incompatabilist intuitions. (p. 140)

The Conditional Insight, combined with the experimental results are used to draw very general and negative conclusions about contemporary philosophy:

To the extent that intuitions are sensitive to these sorts of variables, they are ill-suited to do the work philosophers ask of them. Intuitions track more than just the philosophically-relevant content of the thought-experiments; they track factors that are irrelevant to the issues the thought-experiments attempt to address. The particular socio-economic status and cultural background of a person who considers a thought experiment should be irrelevant to whether or not that thought-experiment presents a case of knowledge. Such sensitivity to irrelevant factors undermines intuitions' status as evidence. (pp. 140–1)

The x-phi movement is sometimes described as divided into a negative and a positive or constructive camp. For the constructive experimental philosophers, the study of intuitions can *help* us do philosophy. Here is Alexander and Weinberg on the transition from negativity to positivity:[2]

> The view can be summarized as follows. Standard philosophical practice involves an appeal to intuitions as evidence for or against particular philosophical claims. Unfortunately, practitioners of standard philosophical practice too often rest content with the assumption that their own intuitions are representative of those of the broader class of philosophers and/or the folk. But, resting content with such an assumption obscures the fact that claims about the distribution of intuitions are straightforwardly empirical claims—testable predictions about how people will respond when presented with the thought-experiments. As such, we should be concerned with conducting empirical research in order to determine precisely what *are* the intuitions that are held by philosophers and non-philosophers alike. Only the results of such research can deliver the intuitions that can serve as evidential basis for or against philosophical claims. In this way, the proper foundation view conceives experimental philosophy as providing a necessary supplement to standard philosophical practice. (2007, p. 61)

Note that the positive version of the program is equally committed to Centrality: it endorses the Conditional Insight and then tries to make a positive contribution by discovering interesting facts about the patterns of intuitive reactions.

11.2 The Big Objection to experimental philosophy: It attacks a practice that doesn't exist

The Big Objection to experimental philosophy is easy to state and should be obvious: philosophers don't rely on intuitions about thought experiments, so studies of intuitions people have about thought experiments

---

[2] Rather than endorse this view, Alexander and Weinberg attribute it to Knobe and others.

have no direct relevance for philosophical arguments or theorizing. I have no quarrel with the Conditional Insight. The Big Mistake was to endorse the antecedent. Negative experimental philosophy attacks a practice that doesn't exist. Positive experimental philosophers attempt to support a practice that doesn't exist. In short: If philosophers don't rely on intuitions, then the project of checking people's intuitions is philosophically pointless.

Despite the emphasis on empirical and experimental work, the failure of experimental philosophy is the result of a lack of close empirical study of what philosophers actually do. The research program is based on an aprioristic approach to philosophical practice (in part I suspect taken over uncritically from methodological rationalists)—it suffers from a lack of careful and detailed study of how philosophers go about doing philosophy.

11.2.1 A case study in experimental philosophy

In an influential paper, Stacey Swain, Joshua Alexander, and Jonathan M. Weinberg (2008) apply experimental-philosophical methods to Keith Lehrer's Truetemp case. This paper will serve as an illustration of the kind of mistake that I claim underlies the entire movement. Recall that Lehrer's case has already been discussed in Section 8.5.2. My charge will be that they misrepresent Lehrer's case, so it will be important to pay close attention to how Swain *et al.* present the case. First they describe reliabilism as a view that incorporates the following thesis:

> [I]f a person's true belief that *p* is caused by a reliable cognitive process, then that belief qualifies as knowledge. (p. 140)

Here is what Swain *et al.* say about the case:

> Mr. Truetemp's temperature beliefs are caused by a reliable cognitive process. Therefore, according to reliabilism, Mr. Truetemp does know it is 104 degrees. But Lehrer claims that there is something lacking in Mr. Truetemp's epistemic position, such that his temperature beliefs do not count as knowledge. Purportedly, if we consider this case, we will have the intuition that Mr. Truetemp does not know that it is 104 degrees. Reliabilism's inability to account for this intuition is supposed to be reason to reject reliabilism. (p. 140)

This, however, is *not* what happens in Lehrer's paper. Swain *et al.* make two false assumptions about Lehrer's paper:

FA1: Lehrer's judgment that Mr. Truetemp does not know is based on an intuition.

FA2: The failure to account for that intuition is used as an argument against reliabilism.

Chapters 8 and 9 showed that both these assumptions are false. Chapter 8 showed that the claim *that Mr. Truetemp doesn't know* is not presented as an intuition. Chapter 9 argued more generally that conflicting judgments about a case are evaluated by evaluating the arguments given for them. Philosophical practice treats unjustified judgments about philosophical cases as worthless. As we saw in Section 8.5.2, after presenting the case, Lehrer immediately goes on to give a series of arguments for his description of it. If someone wants to challenge his judgment, she would need to evaluate and engage with those arguments. Non-justified replies to questionnaires are irrelevant to this game.[3] As a consequence, the conclusions they draw from the replies to the questionnaires are misguided. They note:

[I]ntuitions in response to this case vary according to whether, and which, other thought experiments are considered first. Our results show that compared to subjects who receive the Truetemp Case first, subjects first presented with a clear case of knowledge are less willing to attribute knowledge in the Truetemp Case, and subjects first presented with a clear case of non-knowledge are more willing to attribute knowledge in the Truetemp Case. (p. 138)

They conclude:

We contend that this instability undermines the supposed evidential status of these intuitions, such that philosophers who deal in intuitions can no longer rest comfortably in their armchairs. (p. 138)

I contend that since intuitions were not appealed to as evidence in the first place, these results should not move (or even interest) Lehrer or anyone else working on these issues.

---

[3] Of course, philosophical practice is dynamic and insofar as there now are members of the profession whose careers are based on the importance and relevance of replies to questionnaires about intuitions, there will inevitably be professional and institutional pressures towards counting such replies as an important component of philosophical practice. Giving into such pressures would have the paradoxical result of making experimental philosophy the one subfield of philosophy where appeal to intuitions really is essential.

11.3 Experimental philosophy without intuitions?

Some experimental philosophers are sensitive to the Big Objection and claim that they are using 'intuition'-talk in describing their project because they just "follow standard philosophical usage" (Alexander and Weinberg 2007, p. 72). Their points can be made, they claim, without reliance on Centrality and without 'intuition'-talk:

> Although the results are often glossed in terms of intuitions to follow standard philosophical usage, inspection of the experimental materials reveals little talk of intuitions and mostly the direct evaluation of claims. (Alexander and Weinberg 2007, p. 72)

How are we to interpret the expression, "the direct evaluation of claims", in this passage? Recall the kind of claim that e.g. Lehrer makes about the Truetemp case: *More than possession of correct information is required for knowledge—one must have some way of knowing that the information is correct. As a result, we should deny attributing knowledge to Mr. Truetemp.* Experimental-philosophical methods cannot help us evaluate that argument. The way to evaluate Lehrer's claim is to engage in standard philosophical procedure: the construction and evaluation of arguments. Jonathan Weinberg's reply to Williamson (2009a) provides a further illustration of this point. Weinberg in that paper tries to articulate the experimentalist challenge without assuming Centrality and without talk of intuitions. Here are some examples of how Weinberg presents the challenge from experimental philosophy in that paper:

> Let's call it *the experimentalist's challenge*, and those who are making the challenge *experimentalists*, as it is based on a growing body of experimental work that suggests that *judgments of the sort that philosophers rely upon so centrally in this practice* display a range of inappropriate sensitivities. (p. 456, my emphases)

> These sort of empirical findings indicate that *armchair practice with thought-experiments* may be inappropriately sensitive to a range of factors that are psychologically powerful but philosophically irrelevant. Unwanted variation in any source of evidence presents a *prima facie* challenge to any practice that would deploy it. Once they recognize that *a practice* faces such a challenge, practitioners have the intellectual obligation to see whether their practice can meet that challenge. (p. 457, my emphases)

First and most crucially, note that Weinberg owes us an account of what he means by "judgments of the sort philosophers rely upon so centrally". As we have seen, in standard presentations of experimental philosophy the relevant class was described as those that rely on intuitions. The challenge for Weinberg is to identify the class of judgments in some other way. It cannot be *all* judgments made by philosophers since philosophers make all kinds of judgments about all kinds of topics. If the goal is to undermine our confidence in *all* such judgments, that would amount to an attempt to undermine our confidence in *all* judgments and this is emphatically *not* what experimental philosophers have as their goal. Weinberg also describes the target as *armchair practice with thought experiments*. But this description is not illuminating. Recall from Chapter 9 that what are called 'thought experiments' in philosophy is in effect just philosophers drawing our attention to interesting features of the world. The judgments we make about cases are as varied as can be.

Weinberg is sensitive to all these concerns. The goal of Weinberg (2007) is to show how the experimental challenge can be limited so as to avoid general skepticism about judgments. He wants the target of experimental philosophy to be restricted to a certain subset of activities that philosophers engage in.[4] Here is another passage in which Weinberg (2007) tries to limit the target—this passage is tied up in 'intuition'-talk, but as we'll see, there's a way to purge it of that:

Intuitions may be fine as a class, taken on the whole, and the opponent has neither the need nor the desire to attack that whole class. But philosophers do not invoke a vast undifferentiated mass of intuitions in defense of their claims—rather, we cite particular intuitions about particular hypothetical cases. And the opponent is concerned that some significant number of these cases may be far less than ideal

---

[4] Here is one of the ways in which he articulates the importance of restricting the target (this is while describing the kind of premise the experimental philosopher should use in an argument against philosophical practice): "An overly-strong added premise here risks being not merely implausible, but indeed epistemically disastrous. For the stronger the premise, the greater the proportion of our cognition that will be ruled as untrustworthy. Consider a version of the premise that asserted that any fallible putative source of evidence should not be trusted. Since pretty much all of our sources of evidence, like perception and testimony, are fallible, *this version of the argument would force us to give up nigh-well all of our justification about the world*. So, even though the opponents' argument is meant to be skeptical of only a much more limited target, proposing too ambitious a candidate premise would result *in a painfully unlimited version of skepticism*. So, since pretty much all of our sources of evidence about the world are sometimes wrong, the antecedent of the missing premise had better appeal to something more than mere fallibility itself" (p. 322, emphases mine).

for this sort of appeal. For the practice appears to set no constraints on how *esoteric, unusual, farfetched*, or *generally outlandish* any given case may be. Everyone is familiar with the likes of Davidson's Swampman and Searle's Chinese room, but one can look at the very recent literature and find the likes of double-lesioned testifiers, new evil demons, and fissioning/fusioning/teleporting pairs (or are they?) of persons. So this anything-goes aspect of the practice is what makes it particularly ripe for the opponents' challenge. It does not of itself comprise the challenge, of course—that's for the rest of this paper to articulate. But I hope it makes clear that it may turn out to be a practice of appeal to a particular sort of intuition that gets challenged, and not a broad swipe at all of intuitionkind. I will refer to this practice as the "philosophers' appeals to intuitions," or just PAI for short. (p. 321, my italics)

Purged of 'intuition'-talk something like the following claim remains:

JW1: *Philosophers' practice of making judgments about* **esoteric, unusual** *and* *farfetched cases is particularly unreliable and dubious. They are the judgments that are vulnerable to the experimentalist's challenge.*

I find the appeal to the *esoteric, unusual* and *farfetched* puzzling since these features are not in any way correlated with the degree of difficulty of a judgment. Lots of strange and unusual cases are *very easy* to judge in a reliable way. Here is a very esoteric, unusual and farfetched case:

Easy Esoteric and Farfetched Case: Suppose there are two pink elephants in my office. Then yet another pink elephant comes into my office (and the first two pink elephants stay in the room). Question: How many pink elephants are in my office?

Presumably, Weinberg does not think that if a philosopher reflects on this case, she is engaged in the dubious and suspicious part of our philosophical practice. The experimental challenge better not target this 'thought experiment'. The flipside of this is that many of the *normal* (not farfetched, not unusual, not esoteric) cases are very hard. We don't need to look any further than the case studies in Chapter 9. Perry starts out with a perfectly ordinary case—a kind of event that happens all the time. One of the main points emphasized by Burge is the *ordinariness* of his cases—how they are ubiquitous. But, as the last thirty years of philosophy have proved, these are extremely hard cases to make judgments about. I suspect the charitable interpretation of Weinberg is that he is focusing on esoteric, unusual and farfetched cases that are *difficult* and that it is the great degree of difficulty that distinguishes his target, not that they are esoteric, unusual or farfetched. So, let's consider JW2:

JW2: *Philosophers' practice of making judgments about very difficult cases is particularly unreliable. It is such judgments that are vulnerable to the experimentalist's challenge.*

JW2 moves dangerously close to triviality. Of course we are less reliable when we make very difficult judgments. That's true in general—it is not a surprising feature of philosophical practice. When we try to answer very hard questions, we are not as reliable as we are when we try to answer easy questions. That's why they are difficult. Philosophy is, as we all know, very hard.

Here is where we are at: I suspect when push comes to shove, the only way to restrict the experimentalist's challenge so that it doesn't become a form of very general skepticism about human judgments, is to focus specifically on the very hard cases that philosophers often reflect on. However, it is unsurprising that our judgments about difficult issues are less reliable than our judgments about the simpler ones. We certainly don't need questionnaires to find that out. There is no universal procedure for answering deep and hard philosophical questions, but we know that it does not involve questionnaires and it does involve the construction of complex theories that draw on data and considerations from a wide and unpredictable range of intellectual domains. Perry's case is the best illustration of this unpredictable process: it starts out with seemingly simple questions about a few cases and thirty years of inconclusive investigation of those cases have drawn on facts about the linguistics of attitude constructions and indexicals, theories of human agency, motivation and self-location, and the metaphysics of propositions and properties. Answers to Perry's questions require taking a stand on all these and other questions. At no point in this process has or will answers to questionnaires be of any help.

11.4 Experimental philosophy and the expertise defense of traditional philosophy

It is sometimes suggested that the way to reply to experimental philosophy is to shift the focus from folk-intuitions to expert-intuitions. Here is how Weinberg *et al.* (2010) describe the so-called expertise defense:

> [T]he practice of appealing to *philosophical* intuitions about hypothetical cases, properly construed, should be the practice of appealing to *philosophers'* intuitions about hypothetical cases. And so studies conducted on the intuitions of untutored folk can provide no evidence against the practice of appealing to philosophical intuitions as evidence. (p. 333)

This is a point on which I agree with proponents of experimental philosophy: the expertise defense is not a good reply to their challenge. The expertise defense is just as wedded to Centrality as experimental philosophy itself. The reply assumes that philosophers do rely on intuitions—the intuitions of a subset of people. The arguments in this book show not only that we don't rely on folk-intuitions, but also show that it is a mistake to assume that we base any of our arguments on the intuitive more generally.

Concluding Remarks

Many books conclude with a section that neatly summarizes what comes before. I don't know how to do that, so instead I'll briefly remind the reader of a number of things I have *not* done in this book and why I don't think they are relevant to the questions under discussion here:

- I have said nothing about the epistemology of logic and mathematics. Is something like Gödel's view of how we access mathematical truths correct? Is a form of structuralism correct? Are mathematicians engaged in a form of conceptual analysis? Are all mathematical truths false because there are no numbers? What's the correct solution to the Benacerraf problem? These are but a few of a number of important questions that are relevant to the role of intuitions in the epistemology of mathematics and logic. I don't rule out that something some philosophical tradition could label 'intuitions' could play a role in the answers. What I have shown is that if so, then mathematics and logic differ in this respect from philosophy.
- I have said nothing about the appeal to intuitions about well-formedness in syntactic theory. I briefly discussed Hintikka's view that Kripke and others were influenced by Chomsky's views of the role of intuitions in syntax, but I didn't say anything substantive about intuitions in syntax. The point that is worth emphasizing here is that even if something some philosophical tradition would label 'intuition' plays a role in syntax, it would just show that syntax and philosophy differ in this respect. That said, I'm skeptical of the appeal to intuitions even in syntax and think the most plausible description of its methodology is given by Peter Ludlow (2011, Chapter 3). Ludlow describes the data for syntax without any mention of intuitions. An adequate discussion of Ludlow's view and the issues it raises would take us too far afield.

- There's at least a pre-theoretically useful distinction between the context of discovery and the context of justification. This book has focused solely on the role of intuitions in the latter. I have said nothing about whether something that some philosophers would label 'intuition' could play a significant role in the context of discovery. It is not implausible that something reasonably labeled 'intuitive' can serve as a creative starting point for many cognitive activities, including philosophizing. Even if this is true, it provides no support for Centrality.

Bibliography

Albrechtsen, Justin, Meissner, Christian, and Susa, Kyle, (2009), "Can Intuition Improve Deception Detection Performance?," *Journal of Experimental Social Psychology* 45, pp. 1052–5.
Alexander, Joshua, and Weinberg, Jonathan, (2007), "Analytic Epistemology and Experimental Philosophy," *Philosophy Compass* 2, pp. 56–80.
Anand, Pranav, (2006), *De De Se*, PhD Thesis, MIT.
Bealer, George, (1992), "The Incoherence of Empiricism," *Proceedings of the Aristotelian Society Supplementary Volumes* 66, pp. 99–143.
—— (1996), "On the Possibility of Philosophical Knowledge," *Philosophical Perspectives* 10, *Metaphysics*, pp. 1–34.
—— (1998), "Intuition and the Autonomy of Philosophy," in DePaul and Ramsey, cit., pp. 201–39.
—— (2000), "A Theory of the A Priori," *Pacific Philosophical Quarterly* 81, pp. 1–30.
—— (2004), "The Origins of Modal Error," *Dialectica* 58, pp. 11–42.
Boghossian, Paul, (1996), "Analyticity Reconsidered," *Nous* 30, pp. 360–91.
—— (2003), "Blind Reasoning," *Proceedings of the Aristotelian Society Supplementary Volumes* 77, pp. 225–48.
—— (2011), "Williamson on the *A Priori* and the Analytic," *Philosophy and Phenomenological Research* 82, pp. 488–97.
Boghossian, Paul, and Peacocke, Christopher (eds.), (2000), *New Essays on the A Priori*, Clarendon Press, Oxford.
BonJour, Laurence, (1998), *In Defense of Pure Reason*, Cambridge University Press, Cambridge, UK.
Brown, Jessica, and Cappelen, Herman (eds.), (2011), *Assertion: New Philosophical Essays*, Oxford University Press.
Burge, Tyler, (1979), "Individualism and the Mental," *Midwest Studies in Philosophy* 4, pp. 73–122.
—— (2009), "Five Theses on De Re States and Attitudes," in J. Almog and P. Leonardi (eds.), *The Philosophy of David Kaplan*, Oxford University Press.
Cappelen, Herman, and Hawthorne, John, (2007), "Location and Binding," *Analysis* 67, pp. 95–105.
—— (2009), *Relativism and Monadic Truth*, Oxford University Press.
Cappelen, Herman, and Lepore, Ernest, (2004), *Insensitive Semantics: A Defense of Semantic Minimalism and Speech Act Pluralism*, Blackwell Publishing.
Chalmers, David J., (1996), *The Conscious Mind*, Oxford University Press.
—— (2002), "Does Conceivability Entail Possibility?," in T. S. Gendler and J. Hawthorne (eds.), *Conceivability and Possibility*, Oxford University Press.

Chomsky, Noam, (1975) [1955], *The Logical Structure of Linguistic Theory*, Plenum Press.
Chudnoff, Elijah, (2011), "The Nature of Intuitive Justification," *Philosophical Studies* 153, pp. 313–33.
Clark, Michael, (1963), "Knowledge and Grounds: A Comment on Mr. Gettier's Paper," *Analysis* 24, pp. 46–8.
Cohen, Stewart, (1988), "How to Be a Fallibilist," *Philosophical Perspectives* 2, pp. 91–123.
Cummins, Robert, (1998), "Reflection on Reflective Equilibrium," in DePaul and Ramsey (eds.), cit., pp. 113–27.
Davidson, Donald, (1996), "The Folly of Trying to Define Truth," *Journal of Philosophy* 93, pp. 263–78.
—— (1967), "The Logical Form of Action Sentences," in N. Rescher (ed.), *The Logic of Decision and Action*, reprinted in Davidson 2001, Pittsburgh, University of Pittsburgh Press.
—— (2001), *Essays on Actions and Events*, Oxford University Press, pp. 105–21.
DePaul, Michael, and Ramsey, William (eds.), (1998), *Rethinking Intuition: The Psychology of Intuition and its Role in Philosophical Inquiry*, Rowman and Littlefield.
DeRose, Keith, (2009), *The Case for Contextualism: Knowledge, Skepticism and Context, Volume 1*, Oxford University Press.
Descartes, René [1985], *The Philosophical Writings of Descartes, Volume 2*, transl. by J. Cottingham, R. Stoothoff, D. Murdoch, Cambridge University Press.
Deutsch, Max, (2009), "Experimental Philosophy and the Theory of Reference," *Mind and Language* 24, pp. 445–66.
—— (2010), "Intuitions, Counter-Examples, and Experimental Philosophy," *Review of Philosophy and Psychology* 1, pp. 447–60.
Dorr, Cian, (2010), "Review of *Every Thing Must Go: Metaphysics Naturalized*, by James Ladyman and Don Ross." *Notre Dame Philosophical Reviews* 6. Available online at http://ndpr.nd.edu/news/24377/?id=19947.
Earlenbaugh, Joshua, and Molyneux, Bernard, (2009), "Intuitions are Inclinations to Believe," *Philosophical Studies* 145, pp. 89–109.
Evans, Jonathan, (2007), *Hypothetical Thinking: Dual Processes in Reasoning and Judgement*, Psychology Press.
Foot, Philippa, (1967), "The Problem of Abortion and the Doctrine of Double Effect," *Oxford Review* 5, pp. 5–15.
Gendler, Tamar Szabó, (2007), "Philosophical Thought Experiments, Intuitions, and Cognitive Equilibrium," *Midwest Studies in Philosophy* 31, pp. 68–89.
—— (2011), *Intuition, Imagination, and Philosophical Methodology*, Oxford University Press.
Gettier, Edmund, (1963), "Is Justified True Belief Knowledge?," *Analysis* 23, pp. 121–3.
Gilovich, T., Griffin, D., and Kahneman, D. (eds.), (2002), *Heuristics and Biases: The Psychology of Intuitive Judgement*, Cambridge University Press.
Goldman, Alvin, (1976), "Discrimination and Perceptual Knowledge," *Journal of Philosophy* 73, pp. 771–91.

—— (2007), "Philosophical Intuitions: Their Target, Their Source and Their Epistemic Status," in *Grazer Philosophische Studien* 4, pp. 1–26.
Goldman, Alvin, and Pust, Joel, (1998), "Philosophical Theory and Intuitional Evidence," in DePaul and Ramsey, cit., pp. 179–200.
Goodman, Nelson, (1955), *Fact, Fiction, and Forecast*, Cambridge, MA, Harvard University Press.
Hawthorne, John, (2004), *Knowledge and Lotteries*, Oxford, Oxford University Press.
Hintikka, Jaakko, (1999), "The Emperor's New Intuitions," *Journal of Philosophy* 96(3), pp. 127–47.
Ichikawa, Jonathan, (2009), "Knowing the Intuition and Knowing the Counterfactual," *Philosophical Studies* 145, pp. 435–43.
—— (2009), "Explaining Away Intuitions," in *Studia Philosophica Estonica* 2, Special Issue, *The Role of Intuitions in Philosophical Methodology*, ed. by D. Cohnitz and S. Haggqvist, pp. 94–116.
Ichikawa, Jonathan, and Jarvis, Benjamin, (2009), "Thought-Experiment Intuitions and Truth in Fiction," *Philosophical Studies* 142, 221–46.
Jackson, Frank, (1982), "Epiphenomenal Qualia," *Philosophical Quarterly* 32, 127–36.
—— (1998), *From Metaphysics to Ethics: A Defense of Conceptual Analysis*, Oxford University Press.
—— (2009), "Thought Experiments and Possibilities," Book Symposium on *The Philosophy of Philosophy*, *Analysis* 69, pp. 100–9.
Kamm, Frances, (1998), "Moral Intuitions, Cognitive Psychology, and the Harming-Versus-Not-Aiding Distinction," *Ethics* 108, pp. 463–88.
—— (2007), *Intricate Ethics: Rights, Responsibilities and Permissible Harm*, Oxford University Press.
Kaplan, David, (1989), "Demonstratives," in J. Almog, J. Perry, and H. Wettstein (eds.), *Themes from Kaplan*, Oxford University Press, pp. 481–563.
Kim, Jaegwon, (1997), "Moral Kinds and Natural Kinds: What's the Difference for a Naturalist?," *Philosophical Issues* 8, *Truth*, pp. 293–301.
King, Jeffrey, (2007), *The Nature and Structure of Content*, Oxford University Press.
Kornblith, Hilary, (1998), "The Role of Intuitions in Philosophical Enquiry: An Account with No Unnatural Ingredients," in DePaul and Ramsey, cit., pp. 129–41.
—— (2007), "Naturalism and Intuitions," *Grazer Philosophische Studien* 74, pp. 27–49.
Koslicki, Kathrin, (2008), *The Structure of Objects*, Oxford University Press.
Kripke, Saul, (1975), "Outline of a Theory of Truth," *Journal of Philosophy* 72, pp. 690–716.

Kripke, Saul, (1980), *Naming and Necessity*, Cambridge, MA, Harvard University Press.
Lasersohn, Peter, (2005), "Context Dependence, Disagreement, and Predicates of Personal Taste," *Linguistics and Philosophy* 28, pp. 643–86.
Lehrer, Keith, (1965), "Knowledge, Truth and Evidence," *Analysis* 25, pp. 168–75.
—— (2000), *Theory of Knowledge*, 2nd ed., Westview Press.
Lewis, David K., (1979), "Attitudes De Dicto and De Se," *Philosophical Review* 88, pp. 513–43. Reprinted in Lewis 1983, pp. 133–59.
—— (1983), *Philosophical Papers, Volume 1*, Oxford University Press.
—— (1986), *On the Plurality of Worlds*, Blackwell Publishers.
—— (1996) "Elusive Knowledge," *Australasian Journal of Philosophy* 74, pp. 549–67.
Lepore, Ernest, and Ludwig, Kirk, (2007), *Donald Davidson's Truth-Theoretic Semantics*, Oxford University Press.
Ludlow, Peter, (2011), *The Philosophy of Generative Linguistics*, Oxford University Press.
Ludwig, Kirk, (2007), "The Epistemology of Thought Experiments: First Person versus Third Person Approaches," *Midwest Studies in Philosophy* 31, pp. 128–59.
—— (2010), "Intuitions and Relativity," *Philosophical Psychology* 23, pp. 427–45.
Machery, Edouard, Mallon, Ron, Nichols, Shaun, and Stich, Stephen, (2004), "Semantics, Cross-Cultural Style," *Cognition* 92, pp. B1–B12.
MacFarlane, John, (2007), "Relativism and Disagreement," *Philosophical Studies* 132, pp. 17–31.
—— (2009), "Nonindexical Contextualism," *Synthese* 166, pp. 231–50.
Malmgren, Anna-Sara, (2011), "Rationalism and the Content of Intuitive Judgments," *Mind* 120, pp. 263–327.
Martí, Luisa, (2006), "Unarticulated Constituents Revisited," *Linguistics and Philosophy* 29, pp. 135–66.
Mercier, Hugo, and Sperber, Dan, (2009), "Intuitive and Reflective Inferences," in Evans, J. and Frankish, K. (eds.), *In Two Minds: Dual Processes and Beyond*, Oxford University Press.
Naess, Arne, (1938), "'Truth' as Conceived by those who are not Professional Philosophers," *Skrifter Norske Videnskaps-Akademi* n. 4, Oslo, II. Hist.-Filos. Klass, Jacob Dybwad, Oslo.
Nagel, Jennifer, (2011), "The Psychological Basis of the Harman-Vogel Paradox," *Philosophers' Imprint* 11, pp. 1–28.
—— (forthcoming), "Intuitions and Experiments: A Defense of the Case Method in Epistemology," forthcoming in *Philosophical and Phenomenological Research*.
Nichols, Shaun, Stich, Stephen, and Weinberg, Jonathan M., (2003). "Metaskepticism: Meditations in Ethno-Epistemology," in *The Skeptics*, ed. S. Luper. Ashgate.
Ninan, Dilip, (2010), "De Se Attitudes: Ascription and Communication," *Philosophy Compass* 7, pp. 551–67.
Parsons, Charles, (1993), "On Some Difficulties Concerning Intuitions and Intuitive Knowledge," *Mind* 102, pp. 233–46.

—— (1995), "Platonism and Mathematical Intuition in Kurt Gödel's Thought," *The Bulletin of Symbolic Logic* 1, pp. 44–74.
—— (2000), "Reason and Intuition," *Synthese* 125, pp. 299–315.
Perry, John, (1979), "The Problem of the Essential Indexical," *Nous* 13, pp. 3–21.
Plantinga, Alvin, (1979), *The Nature of Necessity*, Oxford University Press.
—— (1993), *Warrant and Proper Function*, Oxford University Press.
Plessner, Henning, Betsch, Cornelia, and Betsch, Tilmann (eds.), (2008), *Intuition in Judgment and Decision Making*, Lawrence Erlbaum.
Pollock, John, (1974), *Knowledge and Justification*, Princeton University Press.
Pryor, James, (2005), "There is Immediate Justification," in M. Steup and E. Sosa (eds.) *Contemporary Debates in Epistemology*, Blackwell.
Pust, Joel, (2000), *Intuitions as Evidence*, Garland Publishing.
—— (forthcoming), "Intuitions," forthcoming in *Stanford Encyclopedia of Philosophy*.
Rawls, John, (1971), *A Theory of Justice*, Revised Edition 1999, Harvard University Press.
Recanati, François, (2004), *Literal Meaning*, Cambridge University Press.
Schiffer, Stephen, (2003), *The Things We Mean*, Oxford University Press.
Schroeder, Mark, (2008), *Being For: Evaluating the Semantic Program of Expressivism*, Oxford University Press.
Shah, Anuj, and Oppenheimer, Daniel, (2008), "Heuristics Made Easy: An Effort-Reduction Framework," *Psychological Bulletin* 134, pp. 207–22.
Sider, Theodore, (2002), "Time Travel, Coincidences and Counterfactuals," *Philosophical Studies* 110, pp. 115–38.
—— (2007), "Against Monism," *Analysis* 67, pp. 1–7.
—— (forthcoming), "The Evil of Death: What Can Metaphysics Contribute?," B. Bradley, B., Feldman, F., and Johansson, J. (eds.), *The Oxford Handbook of Philosophy and Death*, Draft accessed online at http://tedsider.org/papers/death.pdf June 27, 2011.
Simons, Mandy, (2007), "Observations on Embedding Verbs, Evidentiality, and Presupposition," in *Lingua* 117, pp. 1034–56.
Sinnott-Armstrong, Walter, (2008), "Abstract + Concrete = Paradox," in J. Knobe and S. Nichols (eds.) *Experimental Philosophy*, Oxford University Press, pp. 209–30.
Sosa, Ernest, (1965), "The Analysis of 'Knowledge That p'" *Analysis* 25, pp. 1–8.
—— (2007a), "Intuitions: Their Nature and Epistemic Efficacy," in *Grazer Philosophische Studien*, Special issue: *Philosophical Knowledge—Its Possibility and Scope*, Christian Beyer and Alex Burri (eds.).
—— (2007b), *A Virtue Epistemology. Apt Belief and Reflective Knowledge, Volume 1*, Oxford University Press.
Stalnaker, Robert, (2008), *Our Knowledge of the Internal World*, Oxford University Press.

Stalnaker, Robert, (2011), "The Essential Contextual," in Brown and Cappelen (eds.), *Assertion*, pp. 137–50.

Stanley, Jason, and Szabó, Zoltan Gendler, (2000), "On Quantifier Domain Restriction," *Mind and Language* 15, 219–61.

Stanovich, Keith, and West, Richard, (2000), "Individual Differences in Reasoning: Implications for the Rationality Debate?," *Behavioral and Brain Sciences* 23, pp. 645–65.

—— (2008), "On the Relative Independence of Thinking Biases and Cognitive Ability," *Journal of Personality and Social Psychology* 94, pp. 672–95.

Stephenson, Tamina, (2007), "Judge Dependence, Epistemic Modals and Predicates of Personal Taste," *Linguistics and Philosophy* 30, pp. 487–525.

Stich, Stephen, (1988), "Reflective Equilibrium, Analytic Epistemology and the Problem of Cognitive Diversity," *Synthese* 74, pp. 391–413.

Swain, Stacey, Alexander, Joshua, and Weinberg, Jonathan, (2008), "The Instability of Philosophical Intuitions: Running Hot and Cold on Truetemp," *Philosophical and Phenomenological Research* 76, pp. 138–65.

Thomson, Judith Jarvis, (1971), "A Defense of Abortion," *Philosophy and Public Affairs* 1, pp. 47–66.

—— (1985) "The Trolley Problem", *The Yale Law Journal* 94, 1395–415.

Urmson, James O., (1952), "Parenthetical Verbs," *Mind* 61, pp. 480–96.

van Inwagen, Peter, (1997), "Materialism and the Psychological-Continuity Account of Personal Identity," in J. Tomberlin (ed.), *Philosophical Perspectives* 11, *Mind, Causation and World*, pp. 305–19.

Weinberg, Jonathan M., (2007) "How to Challenge Intuitions Empirically Without Risking Skepticism," *Midwest Studies in Philosophy* 31, pp. 318–43.

—— (2009), "On Doing Better, Experimental Style," Symposium on Timothy Williamson's *Philosophy of Philosophy*, *Philosophical Studies* 145, pp. 455–64.

Weinberg, Jonathan M., Gonnerman, Chad, Buckner, Cameron, and Alexander, Joshua, (2010), "Are Philosophers Expert Intuiters," Special Issue: Experimental Philosophy and Its Critics, Part I, *Philosophical Psychology* 23 (3), pp. 331–55.

Weinberg, Jonathan M., Alexander, Joshua, and Gonnerman, Chad, (manuscript), "Unstable Intuitions and Need for Cognition: How Being Thoughtful Sometimes Just Means Being Wrong in a Different Way."

Weinberg, Jonathan M., Crowley, Stephen J., Gonnermann, Chad, Swain, Stacey, and Vandewalker, Ian (manuscript), "Intuition and Calibration."

Weinberg, Jonathan M., Nichols, Shaun, and Stich, Stephen, (2001), "Normativity and Epistemic Intuitions," *Philosophical Topics*.

Williams, Bernard, (1970), "The Self and the Future," *Philosophical Review* 79, pp. 161–80.

Williams, Bernard, (1979), "Internal and External Reasons," reprinted in *Moral Luck*, Cambridge University Press, 1981, pp. 101–13.

Williamson, Timothy, (2000), *Knowledge and Its Limits*, Oxford University Press.
—— (2003), "Blind Reasoning," *Proceedings of the Aristotelian Society Supplementary Volumes* 77, pp. 249–93.
—— (2005), "Précis of Knowledge and Its Limits," *Philosophy and Phenomenological Research* 70, pp. 431–35.
—— (2007), *The Philosophy of Philosophy*, Blackwell Publishing.
—— (2009a), "Replies to Ichikawa, Martin and Weinberg," *Philosophical Studies* 145, pp. 465–76.
—— (2009b), "Replies to Kornblith, Jackson and Moore," *Analysis* 69, pp. 125–35.
—— (2011), "Reply to Boghossian," *Philosophy and Phenomenological Research* 82, pp. 498–506.

Index

a posteriori methods 109–10, 214–16
a priori methods 6, 7, 9, 16, 57, 60n10, 99, 102, 104, 124, 127n13, 136, 146, 157–8, 192, 197, 200–2, 215
a priori/a posteriori distinction 109–10
abduction, abductive inference 122–4, 169–71
Albrechtsen, J. 35n16
Alexander, J. 3–4n2, 19n18, 220–4
analysis see conceptual analysis
analytic philosohers/philosophy 1–4, 17, 21–2, 28, 49, 58, 85, 163, 203–4, 207, 218
analyticity 113, 126, 169n20, 200–1, 210–13, 217
Anand, P. 135n4
appearances 91–2, 157
armchair methods 6, 16n15, 109–10, 178, 179n26, 197, 202n7, 208, 223–5
arthritis case 54, 70, 101, 139–48

Ball, D. 194n3
Bealer, G. 2, 3–4n2, 4, 6, 8–10, 13–15, 17, 19, 42, 45–7, 52, 57, 63n4, 99–104, 112n2, 113n7, 117, 142n8, 192, 208
Betsch, C. 35n16
Betsch, T. 35n16
Block, N. 212
Boghossian, P. 99n3, 210n4, 211n5, 212–14, 217
BonJour, L. 3–4n2, 6, 9–10, 19, 52, 57, 61n1, 99, 104
Burge, T. 5, 32, 54, 59n8, 70, 101, 116, 139–48, 151, 180, 189–90, 198, 204, 215, 226

Cappelen, H. 20n19, 30n2, 39n18, 58, 75, 85n26, 175–9, 182, 191n2, 198
Chalmers, D. 182–7
charitable reinterpretation see 'intuition', charitable reinterpretation of
Centrality 2–8, 11–23, 25–9, 41–2, 47–8, 50, 60–3, 71n2, 81–3, 86–8, 91, 93, 95–8, 105–7, 111, 113–14, 116–31, 139, 157, 160, 163, 168, 170–5, 182–9, 192–5, 198–203, 205–7, 216–21, 224, 228, 230
Chisholm, R. 2, 101
Chomsky, N. 17, 22–3, 56–7, 229
Chudnoff, E. 54–5
Clark, M. 194n3
Cohen, S. 54, 163–7
concepts 3, 10, 32, 69, 103, 105–10, 113, 118, 124–6, 138, 146, 153–4, 166, 168, 173, 178, 183–4, 201, 206–11, 216–18
conceptual analysis 6–7, 30, 79, 97, 107–8, 138, 169n20, 173n23, 179, 184, 186, 195n4, 202, 205–18, 229
conceptual competence 9, 52, 57, 78–9, 103, 107, 113–15, 124–6, 130, 137, 146, 148, 154–5, 161, 168, 173, 178–9, 182, 186, 192, 197, 201–2
conceptual justification 99n3, 103, 113, 124–5, 126n11, 136, 138, 145, 168, 211
conceptual truth see analyticity
conceivability 183–7
context sensitivity 20, 35–6, 39, 63 fn.3, fn.4, 143
conditionals 58, 169n20, 177
Cummins, R. 17n16

Davidson, D. 81n20, 206, 226
defective theoretical terms see theoretical terms, as constructive or defective
definitions 51–3, 58–9, 208–10, 214
DePaul, M. 3–4n2
DeRose, K. 67
Dorr, C. 83n24
Descartes, R. 53, 66, 99
Deutsch, M. 19, 73n16, 104n3
Dever, J. 91n6
disposition, dispositional 39, 102n6, 108, 120, 174, 176, 208–9

Earlenbaugh, J. 19n17
Ekman, P. 11
empiricism 15n13, 209

epistemology 13, 22, 100, 108, 163, 167, 171, 173n23, 200, 212, 216, 229
of philosophy 201
Evans, J. 35n16
evidence
    as knowledge 13–14
    as propositional 14n12
    psychologization of 114, 193, 202–4
evidence neutrality 202–4
experimental philosophy 1, 3–4, 17, 19, 53, 91n5, 97–8, 106–7, 128, 131n1, 167, 219–28
    as negative vs. positive 91n3, 219–22
experiments 1, 6, 97 see also thought experiments
expertise defense see philosophical expertise
explaining away intuitions see intuitions, explaining away

fake barn cases 171–5
Fodor, J. 66, 69–70
Foot, P. 158–60
Friesen, W. V. 11

Gendler, T. S. 191
generics 15, 96, 110, 188
Gettier, E. 54–5, 110, 117, 123, 136, 193–4, 197–8, 203, 212, 216–17
Gettier cases see Gettier, E.
Gilovich, T. 35n16
Gödel, K. 10, 17, 41n21, 53, 56–7, 102–3, 229
Goldman, A. 2, 3–4n2, 6n6, 9, 17, 52, 98, 107–9, 163, 171–5, 184, 205, 207–10
Gonnerman, C. 219–20
Goodman, N. 23
Griffin, D. 35n16

Hawthorne, J. 5, 20n19, 75, 175–9, 182, 198
hedge terms, hedging 36–8, 39n18, 41–2, 45–7, 62, 64n5, 65–9, 76–7, 81, 88n1, 90, 134, 162, 164–5, 171, 174
Hintikka, J. 3–4n2, 21–3, 56, 72n13, 229
Husserl, E. 53

Ichikawa, J. 54, 92n7, 157n14, 169n20, 197n5
inference to the best explanation see abduction

'intuition' 1–12, 17–18, 23–30, 39–42, 50–88, 95–6, 111, 114, 144n9, 167n19, 175, 184n29, 187, 192–3, 204, 207, 209–10, 218, 224, 226, 229–30
    as a technical term 50–60
    charitable reinterpretation of 61–81, 167n19
    disagreement over theoretical role of 55–7
    in English 28–9, 39–42
    verbal virus theory of see verbal virus theory
intuitions 1–30, 35n19, 40–2, 48, 53–6, 76–131, 135, 137–8, 142, 144, 146–8, 154–5, 160–73, 177, 181–7, 192, 194–7, 199–200, 205–8, 217, 219–30
    explaining away 88–93
'intuitive' 4–5, 7–8, 11–12, 18, 23–93, 95, 106n8, 167n19, 183, 199, 230
'intuitively' 11–12, 29–31, 35–8, 41, 46–8, 62, 64–9, 71, 76–7, 79, 86, 90

justification 7, 9–10, 60n5, 102–5, 112–13, 119–20, 124–5, 126n11, 135–6, 138, 143, 145, 155, 160–2, 166, 168, 186, 188–9, 192, 196, 211, 214, 220, 230
Jackson, F. 3–4n2, 76–7, 211–12
James, W. 206
Jarvis, B. 54, 157n14, 169n20, 197n5

Kahneman, D. 35n16
Kamm, F. 162
Kant, I. 53, 56n5
Kaplan, D. 5
Kim, J. 63, 78, 79n19
King, J. 68–9
knowledge 5–6, 8, 11, 13, 17n15, 27–8, 53, 55n3, 61n1, 63n3, 69, 76–7, 99, 103, 106–7, 109–10, 146, 166, 167n19, 168, 172, 177, 184, 192, 194n3, 198, 202n7, 203, 211n4, 213–4, 216–17, 220–4
Kornblith, H. 98, 109, 207–9
Koslicki, K. 64
Kripke, S. 22–3, 67, 71–5, 229

Ladyman, J. 83n24
Lasersohn, P. 175n25
Lehrer, K. 163, 167–71, 194n3, 222–4

Lepore, E. 20n19, 30n2, 39n18, 58, 85n26, 191n1
Lewis, D. K. 9, 27, 52, 64, 83–4, 114, 138n6
linguistics 20, 22–3, 56–7, 132, 135–6, 196, 227
linguistic competence 113, 145
logical form 35, 156, 197–9
lottery cases 64, 163–6
Ludwig, K. 6n6, 9, 12n11, 17, 28, 52–3
Ludlow, P. 229

MacFarlane, J. 75, 175n25
Machery, E. 4n2, 19n18, 220
Malmgren, A.-S. 53–4, 169n20, 197n5
Martí, L. 20n19
Meissner, C. 35n16
Mercier, H. 10, 35n16
method of cases 6, 10, 95–6, 105–6, 132, 190
modal *see* modality
modality 10, 20, 39–40, 52, 68–9, 74, 96, 100, 102, 104, 107–8, 113, 115, 119, 127, 138, 146–7, 158, 177, 182–7, 190, 192, 196, 212n6, 215
Molyneux, B. 19n17
Moore, G. E. 23, 56–7
Müller-Lyer illusion 92

Naess, A. 219n1
Nagel, J. 10–1, 34
natural kinds 21, 34–5, 63, 78, 209
naturalism 201, 208
necessary, necessity *see* modality
Nichols, S. 220
Ninan, D. 135n4, 181n27

Oppenheimer, D. 35n16

Parsons, C. 10–1, 41n21, 53, 56, 61, 68, 102–3
Peacocke, C. 99n3
Perry, J. 54, 116, 123, 132–39, 142, 149, 151–2, 160, 180, 187–90, 194, 198, 204, 226–7
Plantinga, A. 9–10, 54, 67, 99, 101–2, 117
phenomenology (of intuitions) 9, 52, 78, 80, 101, 105, 112, 113n7, 116–18, 120, 124, 128n14, 136, 138, 144, 153, 155, 161, 166, 168, 173, 178, 181, 186, 192
philosophical analysis *see* conceptual analysis
philosophical exceptionalism 16, 19

philosophical expertise 20, 52, 55, 59, 68, 128, 227–8
philosophical progress 195, 199, 214, 216
Plessner, H. 35n16
Pollock, J. 117
possibility, possible *see* modality
pragmatic, pragmatics 44, 60n10
predicates of personal taste 175–6, 196
Pryor, J. 112n3
psychological 3, 8, 11, 38, 65n6, 84n24, 107–8, 112–13n5, 194n3, 203–4
psychology 18, 28, 34, 35n16, 93, 120, 135–6, 157, 166, 173, 174, 177–8, 196–7
Pust, J. 3–4n2, 6n6, 8–10, 17, 19, 28, 49, 52, 98, 102n6, 107–8, 113n7, 205, 207–10, 216, 224
Putnam, H. 54, 101

Quine, W. V. O. 15n13, 125, 146, 210, 215

Ramsey, W. 3n2
Ramseyfication 50, 55
rationalism 102
  methodological 19, 96, 98–100, 103, 105–6, 109, 116, 131n1, 169n20, 222
  moderate 99, 103
Rawls, J. 17, 23, 53, 57, 59
Recanati, F. 20n19
reflective equilibrium 83, 101
relativism about truth 175–8
reliabilism 169–70, 222–3
reliability (of intuitions) 17, 91, 107–8, 167, 207, 220, 226–7
Ross, D. 83n24

Schiffer, S. 32, 67, 78, 86
Schroeder, M. 32
science, philosophy of 13
Searle, J. 226
'seem' 24, 28–9, 41–8, 64n5, 101, 164
seemings 8, 42, 47n33, 101, 108
semantic, semantics 12, 20–1, 30, 37–9, 50, 58–61, 85, 133, 176–7, 197–8, 220
Shah, A. 35n16
Sider, T. 66–7, 70–1, 79
Simons, M. 36–7, 39n18
Sinnott-Armstrong, W. 52
Sgaravatti, D. 204n9
skepticism 72n14, 81–2n21, 85–7, 123, 165, 203, 225, 227

Sober, E. 66, 69–70
Sosa, E. 3–4n2, 9, 17, 52, 98, 102n6, 108–9, 194n3
Sperber, D. 10, 35n16
Spinoza, B. 99
Stalnaker, R. 132, 135n4
Stanley, J. 20n19
Stanovich, K. 35n16
Stephenson, T. 175n25
Stich, S. 17, 19, 98, 219n1, 220
Strohminger, M. 169n20
Susa, K. 35n16
Swain, S. 3–4n2, 19n18, 167, 219–20, 222
Szabó, Z. G. 20n19

Tappenden, J. 210n4
theoretical terms 27, 47n33, 48–9, 143, 190
 as constructive or defective 50–60
thought experiments 5–6, 18, 21, 70, 96, 98, 109–10, 116, 122–3, 127–8, 130, 132–3, 140–2, 144–5, 147–8, 152, 154, 156–8, 160, 167, 169, 179–80, 182n28, 189–94, 196–9, 211–12, 219–21, 223–6

Thomson, J. J. 116, 148–54, 156–61, 165, 191, 198
Thomson's violinist 148–58, 191
trolley cases 148, 158–63
Truetemp 163, 167–71, 222–4

understanding *see* conceptual competence; linguistic competence
Urmson, J. O. 36

van Inwagen, P. 9, 27, 52, 83–4, 114
verbal virus theory 22, 49–50

Weinberg, J. M. 3–4, 17, 19, 52, 98, 106–8, 118, 121, 157, 207, 220–2, 224–7
West, R. 35n16
Williams, B. 179–82, 198
Williamson, T. 2, 5–6, 9, 13–14, 16, 19, 27, 54, 64, 80, 83–5, 98, 103, 109–10, 114–15, 125, 157n14, 169n20, 184, 188, 193, 194n3, 197–9, 200–4, 210–13, 216–17, 224
Wittgenstein, L. 23

zombies 182–7